CONSTRUCTION MARKETING AND STRATEGIC PLANNING

Warren Friedman

President
Tecton Media Inc.

McGraw-Hill Book Company

New York / St. Louis / San Francisco / Auckland / Bogotá / Hamburg
Johannesburg / London / Madrid / Mexico / Montreal / New Delhi
Panama / Paris / São Paulo / Singapore / Sydney / Tokyo / Toronto

Library of Congress Cataloging in Publication Data
Friedman, Warren.
   Construction marketing and strategic planning.

      1.Construction industry—United States
2.Contractors—United States. 3.Contractors'
operations—United States—Marketing. I.Title.
HD9715.U52F7 1984   624'.068'8   83-24884
ISBN 0-07-022437-4

 2 3 4 5 6 7 8 9 0   DOC/DOC   8 9 8 7 6 5 4

ISBN 0-07-022437-4

The editors for this book were Joan Zseleczky and Olive H. Collen, the
designer was Mark E. Safran, and the production supervisor was Thomas
G. Kowalczyk. It was set in Caledonia by University Graphics, Inc.

Printed and bound by R. R. Donnelley & Sons Company.

FOR SUSAN, MELISSA, AND ALEXANDRA

ABOUT THE AUTHOR

Warren Friedman, a graduate civil engineer, is president and founder of Tecton Media, Inc., one of this country's leading construction marketing firms. Tecton's clients include construction companies of virtually all types and sizes, ranging in annual volume from several million dollars to over a billion dollars.

Mr. Friedman is a popular speaker at seminars around the country, including those co-sponsored by Tecton Media and *Engineering News-Record*, and at local chapters of AGC and ABC. He has also published dozens of articles in such respected journals as *Constructor* and *Builder and Contractor*.

Contents

Foreword:
A Message From the
President of the AGC

This book, *Construction Marketing and Strategic Planning,* was commissioned by The Associated General Contractors of America (AGC) with the objective of ensuring that AGC members have access to the best possible resources for marketing their construction services. We realize that *Construction Marketing and Strategic Planning* will have wide use throughout the construction industry and that all who avail themselves of this carefully researched material are sure to benefit.

The author, Warren Friedman, was chosen to undertake this project based on his experience in and concentration on construction marketing and strategic business planning. His approach is based on practical day-to-day construction company operations. We are grateful to him for a job well done.

I would also like to take this opportunity to thank and to express AGC's appreciation to James W. Lail, chairman of the AGC Construction Marketing Committee and president of Raines Brothers, Inc., Chattanooga, Tennessee, and his predecessors as chairman, Peter G. Doyle, president and chief operating officer of Linbeck Construction Corporation, Houston, Texas, and Alex J. Etkin, chairman of A. J. Etkin Construction Co., Oak Park, Michigan. The dedication of all the AGC members who served on the Construction Marketing Committee and who worked so diligently on this project during the past few years make it possible for you to benefit from this latest AGC endeavor.

The construction industry has been and always will be a highly competitive industry. In the future, as in the past, those who succeed in it will be successful because they have taken advantage of all their resources.

I hope you will benefit from using this resource.

RICHARD S. PEPPER
President, Associated General Contractors of America

Preface:
To Those Who Manage
Construction Companies

The objective of this book is to help you make your construction business more profitable through long-range planning and effective marketing. If your company already practices formal planning or marketing, this book will provide you with ideas for improving that effort. If you have never formally planned or marketed your services, it will show you where to begin and how to follow through for ultimate success.

In the increasingly competitive decade of the 1980s, a construction company—no matter what its size—cannot afford to depend on a single project type, client, or market sector for its future work. The world and the construction industry are changing rapidly, and that change is accelerating. Every day new markets emerge, older markets shrink, opportunities arise, funding shifts, government regulations multiply, business cycles alter, competition tightens, and inflation exacts its relentless and invisible tax on a company's capital. It is clearly becoming increasingly difficult to manage a construction business in today's environment.

The effective construction executive needs all the management tools he or she can obtain to successfully steer the company through a sea of change. This book provides some of the management techniques required to control the destiny of the individual company. It will show you the specific actions you can take to help control the amount and type of work your company obtains and to build your organization to any size and shape you desire. It is not the intent of this book to show you how to become a giant in the construction industry—that may not be your objective at all—

but rather to show you how you can achieve your desires and goals and make your company more profitable, no matter what size it is today.

No construction company began life with an annual volume of $100 million. Every construction company started small. The differences in size and profitabliity of contractors are directly related to each company's ability to market and to manage. Simply, a construction company has the same needs as any other business—to obtain work and to perform it profitably. Today, more and more contractors of all sizes are finding that modern business management techniques, including marketing, are vital both to winning a sufficient volume of new work and to making an adequate return on investment.

Whether your goals for your construction business are increasing volume, showing higher profits, building a more dynamic organization, attracting better people, eliminating peaks and valleys in year-to-year revenue, entering new markets, or just improving your presentation techniques, or any combination of the above, effective planning and marketing can play a key role in making those goals a reality.

MARKETING AND STRATEGIC PLANNING DEFINED

Marketing is a corporate function comprising a number of activities that involve the exchange of the construction company's services for economic gain. Under the modern marketing concept, the focus of those activities is the customer and his or her needs. Many management experts go further and contend that it is the purpose of a business to serve customers. Once this concept is adopted by a contractor, he or she can begin to plan the business around the construction and related needs of present and future customers. Starting with the customer's (or client's or owner's) needs, construction company management can plan for its own needs to serve those customers.

Marketing, therefore, begins with satisfying client needs and flows back to the individual contractor, who can then plan for ways to meet those needs. This planning process will involve the contractor's resources, experience, capabilities, desires, and financial and other requirements.

Any construction company that is in business and has obtained substantial work in the public or private sector has been performing marketing—that is, performing activities relating to the exchange of its services for economic gain, however unorganized or informal. For the contractor serving the public-sector owner, "marketing" consists of having the capabilities to serve that customer. Selling is minimal, in that the public owner advertises needs, is required to allow any contractor to submit a bid, and then buys on the basis of the lowest price. The contractor serving the public customer has made a marketing decision by selecting the markets or customers to be served.

To serve the private-sector owner, the contractor needs a more formal approach to marketing. Not only must the decision be made to serve the particular private-sector market or markets, but the owners' needs must be discovered, business relationships built, purchasers persuaded, new markets penetrated, market presence established, and planning performed. Accomplishing that will require that the construction company perform a number of interrelated activities, which constitutes a marketing function. It can be performed by one person or can require an entire department, depending on the company's size and objectives.

Marketing provides the contractor with a more dynamic, more aggressive approach to the marketplace. Rather than being in a reactive posture, dependent on one or two customers or markets, construction company management will be in a better position to determine the company's destiny. The result will be a stronger, more profitable construction organization, ready to meet the challenges of the 1980s and beyond.

WHOM THIS BOOK IS FOR

This book presents a systems approach to marketing in a simple, straightforward way, based largely on the experience of companies in the construction business that have become more successful through marketing. It will show you how your company can be more successful too. The book addresses the day-to-day tasks of sales and marketing executives, as well as the fundamental issues faced by company presidents whose firms must market themselves to survive. Designed to help both company presidents and sales and marketing executives do a better marketing job, it will help presidents gain a greater understanding of their role in strategic planning and marketing and the importance of these in helping the company achieve its objectives. For the sales and marketing executive, the book contains a number of ideas, conveys successful experiences of other construction companies, and defines the nature and extent of sales and marketing responsibilities.

Since marketing involves almost every aspect of the construction company, marketing will be responsible for selling the company's capabilities and services. In some cases, since it is marketing's job to analyze customer needs, the company may have to alter its capabilities and services to satisfy client needs. Marketing generates the customers who produce the revenues that affect income, and thus it has an impact on the contractor's bottom line.

Every organization needs a direction and a purpose, defined by goals and objectives. Otherwise, a construction company, like any other business enterprise, will drift and react to the pressures of the moment, allowing others to decide its course. But with a clear sense of direction, any construction company can achieve considerable control over its future.

Marketing—or the business of obtaining business—is a catalyst energizing and galvanizing many other aspects of a construction company's operations. Marketing, to be effective, requires planning, so that the company has a stated purpose, a direction, and specific objectives and goals. It is the setting of those goals and the commitment to a companywide effort to achieve them that has resulted, for many construction companies, in improved growth and profitability, increased return on investment, a more dynamic organization where good people are attracted and remain, and increased value or worth.

Results like these are not achieved overnight, but they can be realized. Marketing—rooted in long-range planning—can be the driving force for attaining them.

CONCLUSION

The construction marketplace, reflecting the world around it, will encounter difficult times ahead. Contractors will be the most affected group in the industry. For them, trends that emerged in the 1970s that will gather force and continue through the 1980s include these:

1. It will become increasingly difficult to manage the individual construction company.
2. Competition will tighten as the construction marketplace remains level in real terms of construction put in place.
3. Competition in the private sector will intensify as owners select contractors more and more on the basis of professional qualifications and performance, rather than that of lowest hard-dollar bid.
4. Contractors who can provide cost and schedule input from the earliest phases, and sophisticated management during construction, will be more in demand.
5. The successful contractor will have a greater decision-making role in the design process, as costs continue to escalate and schedules lengthen.
6. To survive, contractors will need to upgrade the sophistication of their management of projects and their own organizations.
7. A major part of that effort will have to include sophisticated communication, marketing, and business planning.
8. The bigger contractors will continue to expand and diversify, and the smaller local or specialty contractor may prosper, if well managed, or will be acquired by larger firms.
9. The days of the medium-sized contractors may be numbered, unless these companies take quick and affirmative steps to plan, operate, and market their operations effectively.

According to an ancient Chinese proverb, "A journey of a thousand miles begins with a single step." That step on the road to effective marketing and a successful future for the individual construction company is strategic planning.

Acknowledgments

Many individuals in many parts of the nation deserve credit for their assistance, support, and, in some instances hard work, in making this book possible.

First, I am indebted to Thomas Dailey, former AGC president, who had the confidence in me to produce a book on this subject. It is my pleasure to thank Robert Sundt for his early thoughts on the book and for providing a wealth of information on his company that kindled much of the initial inspiration.

I owe a major debt to James Lail, chairman of the AGC Marketing Committee, for his considerable and unyielding efforts and cooperation. In no small part, this book was completed in response to his determination, encouragement, and dedication.

Michael Youngblut, of AGC staff, provided vital assistance in completing tasks that kept the project moving. Frank Schneller, through his final reading of the manuscript, gave me many suggestions for improvement.

Jeremy Robinson of McGraw-Hill deserves my gratitude for his encouragement to write the book and for believing in the need for it. Joan Zseleczky helped with constant advice and reassurance during the many months of preparation.

I am grateful to those who are owed the most for this book—my firm's clients. Through them and through their taking my associates and me into their confidence and allowing us to work with them on their marketing and management needs, they made this book possible. Through our relationships with them I gained invaluable experience and insight into the needs of construction companies.

Many of the basic management and marketing ideas for this book that are adapted to the special needs of contractors came from Peter Drucker, Philip Kotler, and George Steiner. In addition, there are many management and marketing authors, as well as numerous construction executives, who have contributed ideas and case history information. My thanks to them.

My colleagues at Tecton all helped in different ways: Mark Frantz, Michael Sexton, William Linton, Elizabeth Blair, Kenneth Smith, Lindsay Diehl, and Karen Grossman. I am obliged to Barbara Harkins for many nights and weekends of word processing and editorial assistance in the preparation of the manuscript.

I am especially indebted to my wife, Susan, for providing me the time, encouragement, and support needed to complete this book.

Warren Friedman

Mankind is then divided into those who are still what they were, and those who have changed: into the men of the present age and the men of the past.

—*John Stuart Mill*

Part 1

PLANNING THE FUTURE OF YOUR CONSTRUCTION BUSINESS

1

The Strategic Planning Process: What It Is

Effective marketing begins with planning, and proper planning begins with a long-range view of the entire business.

Engineering News-Record (ENR) and Tecton Media, Inc., conducted a survey late in 1980 to determine the extent of formal marketing practices among the top 400 contractors (as rated annually by *ENR*). As the survey has shown, formal business or market planning emerged as a vital management function in 1970, as a median year, for construction companies with annual volumes of over $500 million. For companies in the $40-million-to-$500-million category, 1978 was the median year that they began a planning function.

As change in the world and in the construction industry accelerates, planning will become increasingly necessary for growth, profit, and survival. This will hold as true for the small construction company (under $5 million) as for the largest. Because smaller companies are most vulnerable to failure during difficult economic times, business and market planning is as crucial to them as to the larger contractors.

There are other important advantages in planning. Banks and surety companies are much more likely to finance a contractor's needs if he or she has a well-prepared long-range plan. USF&G, Baltimore, the nation's largest surety writer, and the Bank of America, which has hundreds of construction customers, are just two financial institutions that encourage construction companies to develop long-range business and marketing plans.

Peter Drucker sums up the importance of planning to the success of small and medium-sized business:

Diseases of the small or medium-sized successful business: our tax system; the lack of managers to succeed the founder; and the dependence on one product or on a small number of customers. These diseases often occur together. But each of them by itself is enough to force out of existence a successful small business. And once these diseases have set in they are usually incurable.

But they can be prevented—if tackled early enough. . . .

Financial and tax planning, planning of executive age-balance, planning of markets and products may appear to be heavy additional burdens to ask small business management to undertake. But everyone who is at all familiar with the problems of the small and medium-sized business believes that the majority of these companies could continue to live and prosper if the men at their heads would only spend on preventive planning a fraction of the imagination, care and work they spent on building up the business in the first place.

What the experts think was best summed up by a leading banker in an Ohio industrial city—a man who has been friend, father-confessor and adviser to countless small businesses and their owners:

"I know," he said, "how the surgeons in the accident ward down at the hospital must feel when the highway casualties are brought in Saturday nights: frustration at being unable to do much more than make the patient's last hours a bit more comfortable; rage at the needless waste and destruction of so much that could live constructively and productively; and sadness when I ponder what might have been had these friends of mine only started to think about the future of their business a few years sooner."[1]

CORPORATE PLANS AND MARKETING PLANS: THE DIFFERENCE

While all plans are concerned with the future, planning is conducted in businesses in many different ways, and many different terms are used to describe it, including market planning, corporate planning, and strategic planning. Even among companies using the same term, the planning process varies widely.

This book will focus on a process that can be described as market-oriented business planning. The premise is that the marketing plan and the business plan are entirely interrelated: the scope of a company's marketing plan is proportional to the scope of its overall business plan, and, in turn, its business plan must be based on realistic market input. The following defines the differences between corporate, or business, plans and marketing plans.

Corporate Plan.   The corporate plan describes the overall business plan for the corporation. It might be an annual, intermediate, or long-range plan. The corporate plan deals with company missions, growth strategies, portfolio decisions, investment decisions, and current objectives and goals. It usually does not contain details on the activities of individual business units. The medium-sized to larger company will have those details contained in divisional plans. In some cases, the corporate plan will be the sum total of divisional plans. In the smaller company, however, the corporate plan *will* describe those details, including marketing, financial, construction, and personnel strategies.

Marketing Plan.   The marketing plan describes the various marketing objectives, strategies, and tactics the company will use to meet its overall corporate objectives. It should contain an executive summary, situation analysis, objectives and goals, strategy, mission statement, action programs, budgets, and controls.

Before developing a marketing plan, the managers of a construction company must examine the total enterprise and its place in the construction industry and agree on a direction for the future. The marketing portion of the plan will provide the detailed program for the company to achieve its objectives.

EXPANDED TABLE OF CONTENTS OF A CORPORATE PLAN

There is little uniformity in the way written plans are prepared for businesses. A complete plan would include a statement of basic purposes and missions as well as detailed studies of the future outlook in areas of interest to the company. A major section would be devoted to strategic plans, followed by medium-range programs, short-range budgets and plans, and operational instructions.

Table 1-1 briefly outlines the contents of a corporate plan, which is broader in scope than the marketing plan. It incorporates the more detailed marketing plan, shown in Table 1-2, and serves as a foundation for it. Combined, they form a marketing-oriented business plan.

Actual plans will most likely not fit this pattern but will be prepared with the particular needs and interest of the company in mind. Table 1-3 is an expanded table of contents for a hypothetical medium-sized construction company.

For larger construction companies, the documentation of the corporate plan will cover many more categories than noted above and will be much more voluminous. For smaller companies, the outline will be scantier. But the basic headings will remain the same for all.

A major problem of each company is to determine which areas should be covered in a plan, how deeply they will be studied, and how detailed the plan will be. No company can afford to study in great depth every facet of its business every year.

TABLE 1-1 Contents of Corporate Plan

I. Corporate purposes
II. Basic corporate five- and ten-year sales and profit objectives
III. Basic premises
IV. Basic objectives, policies, and strategies
V. Detailed medium-range plans
VI. One-year plans (including marketing)

TABLE 1-2 Contents of Marketing Plan

1. Table of contents	Subjects covered in plan and where to find them
2. Introduction	Purpose and uses of plan
3. Executive digest	Summary of major provisions of plan
4. Company mission, scope, and goals	Nature of business (markets), services, and project types; contribution to corporate purpose; company profile; capabilities; where company wants to go
5. Situation analysis	Facts and assumptions on which plan is based
a. Assumptions	Report on economy, environment, politics, social, technological, and competitive factors
b. Company resources	Key personnel, talents, resources, capabilities, and techniques; an analysis of strengths and weaknesses
c. Market potentials, forecasts, facts	Quantitative and qualitative information about size (dollars and units) of each market, growth rates, customer profiles, and customer wants, needs, and attitudes
d. Market share	Company share of total markets served
e. Revenue history	Revenue over past three to five years in each market; current position versus previous year's objectives
f. Sales expenses and profit forecasts	Project type or market-volume-profit-investment forecast
g. Current and new opportunities	High-potential markets and services
6. Current marketing organization	Structure and purpose; lines of authority; responsibilities
7. Marketing objectives	Results to be produced and where the company wants to be next year (and in future years)
8. Marketing strategies, policies, procedures	General courses of action to reach objectives
9. Action programs	Specific courses of action (tactics) with respect to sales, service, promotion, advertising, pricing, marketing research, new services and markets, product planning and development
10. Schedules/assignments	Who does what, where, how, and when (milestones)
11. Personnel plan	Availability and needs
12. Budgets	Required resources, costs, and risks
13. Pro forma P & L and balance sheet	Accounting statements from controller
14. Controls	Procedures for measuring and controlling progress of planned actions
15. Continuity	Procedures for keeping plans updated

TABLE 1-3 Expansion of Table of Contents of a Corporate Plan: Corporate Long-Range Plan for American Construction Company (ACC)

I. Corporate purposes: The fundamental purposes of ACC. Two basic purposes are given, which is standard.

    a. Two prime objectives of ACC are: To improve earnings through productive effort primarily applied (but not limited) to construction of commercial and industrial facilities. To conduct the business in a manner that is constructive, honorable, and mutually profitable for stockholders, employees, customers, suppliers, and the general community.

    b. These objectives are amplified further: To earn a reasonable return on investment with due regard to the interest of customers, employees, subcontractors, and suppliers.
To expand revenues while increasing profits.
To produce top-quality construction.
To grow at a steady rate.

II. Basic corporate five- and ten-year revenue and profit objectives:

    a. The five-year annual revenues and profit objectives are:

	Revenues	Pretax profits	Pretax (%) profit	Federal tax	Aftertax (%) profit
		(Specified in dollars and percentages)			
First year					
Second year					
Third year					
Fourth year					
Fifth year					

    b. The ten-year revenues and profit objectives are: Revenues will be $50,000,000 and earnings, after taxes, will be $1,000,000.

III. Basic premises: Forecasts of future markets, technology, and competition and evaluations of internal strengths and weaknesses. A framework of premises follows:

    a. External projections and forecasts:
- Survey of general business conditions, including total construction industry forecast
- Survey of the markets for company services, based upon general economic conditions for commercial and industrial construction in ACC's current geographic markets
- Forecast of company revenues based on the above two forecasts (ACC made forecasts for each of the next five years. Since the company is in the Midwest, construction spending for its services in the Midwest were estimated.)

    b. Competition:
Because competition is keen for most ACC services, objective estimates of its strengths are important. After looking at what its major competition was likely to do, the firm looked at itself. Several advantages have placed ACC in advance of competition in certain project-type markets, one of which is an ability to deliver light industrial projects on or ahead of schedule. However, in order to fully realize the growth commensurate with that advantage, the company must overcome several weaknesses and develop a marketing function.

    c. Internal examination of the past and projections
Analysis of various parts of the enterprise, e.g., market and project type analysis:
1. Project type(s), performance (i.e., sales volume, profit margin)
2. Customer class served

TABLE 1-3 Expansion of Table of Contents of a Corporate Plan: Corporate Long-Range Plan for American Construction Company (ACC) (*continued*)

    3. Comparison with major competitors
    4. Possibilities for improvement
    5. Suggestions with regard to new project markets
  Financial analysis:
    1. Profit position
    2. Working capital
    3. Cash position
    4. Impact of financial policy on pricing
    5. Prospects for future financing
  Construction capability analysis:
    1. Plant and equipment (maintenance and depreciation)
    2. Productive capacity and productivity
    3. Percent of capacity utilized
    4. Suggestions for improving productivity, reducing costs, utilizing excess capacity, and planning expansion
  Technical analysis:
    1. Construction capabilities and techniques
    2. Suggestions for improving effectiveness
  Employees:
    1. Employment and future needs
    2. Technical personnel deficiencies
    3. Appraisal of employee attitudes
  Facilities:
    1. Evaluation of current facilities to meet new business
    2. Replacement policy and needs

IV. Basic objectives, policies, and strategies: This covers every important area of the business.

a. Profit	*f.* Production
b. Sales	*g.* Personnel
c. Finance	*h.* Acquisitions
d. Marketing	*i.* Organization
e. Capital Additions	*j.* Long-range planning

The more concrete the specifications here can be, the easier it usually is to implement the plans. It is especially important for a business manager to know precisely what he or she is seeking and the method to be employed to achieve it. For example, ACC marketing objectives were set forth as follows:

- To increase sales of light industrial manufacturing plant construction 100 percent in the next five years.

- To increase sales of warehouse and distribution facility construction 200 percent during the next five years.

- To penetrate the western market to the point where the company will be a significant factor in it at the end of five years.

- To enter the southeastern market within five years by establishing a branch office or a joint venture, or by acquiring another contractor.

TABLE 1-3 Expansion of Table of Contents of a Corporate Plan: Corporate Long-Range Plan for American Construction Company (ACC) (*continued*)

For each of these objectives the company prepared a detailed series of plans, ranging from a strategy to sell design/build services to owners in geographic regions where its main plants are located to details such as marketing special services to selected specified clients, training employees, and arranging top management meetings with clients.

Further strategies that might be included in this section of the plan, with special regard to marketing, are organization, possibility of joint ventures, salespeople's compensation plans, and estimating policies.

Drawing a proper line of demarcation between the strategic plans and the detailed marketing and operational plans is difficult. Ideally, the two blend together in a continuous line.

V. Detailed medium-range plans: More detailed plans growing out of the above. For ACC these plans were developed for each of the succeeding five years:

    a. Pro forma balance sheet, yearly
    b. Income statement, yearly
    c. Capital expenditure schedule, yearly
    d. Schedule for major markets and services, yearly
    e. Employment schedule, yearly
    f. Detailed schedule to acquire within three years a company with design capability in industrial facilities

THE PLANNING PROCESS

Planning is thinking systematically about the future and making current decisions on that basis. It must be an integral part of management. The planning process begins with objectives; defines strategies, policies, and detailed plans to achieve them; establishes an organization to implement decisions; and includes review of performance and feedback to introduce a new planning cycle. Planning is a continuous process, because changes in the construction industry and in the general business environment are continuous.

Dravo Corporation, Pittsburgh, a diversified engineering and construction company, describes its planning process in its 1979 annual report.

At Dravo Corporation strategic planning is an annual, formalized process by which management determines corporate business directions for the five-year period following a given planning year. A more immediate result of effective planning is the creation of an environment in which current business alternatives may be reviewed in proper relationship to long-range objectives of the corporation.

Planning at Dravo involves every member of the management team. It includes an extensive annual examination of both external conditions and internal resources, and results in the allocation of those resources in accordance with cor-

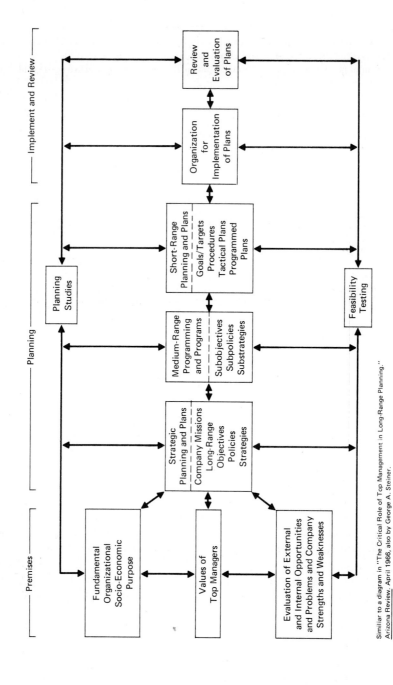

Similiar to a diagram in "The Critical Role of Top Management in Long-Range Planning."
Arizona Review, April 1966, also by George A. Steiner.

FIG. 1-1 Structure and process of business planning. *(From George A. Steiner, Top Management Planning, The Macmillan Company, New York, 1969, p. 33.)*

porate goals. The planning process, then, is viewed as a primary responsibility of management.

The business and market perspective provided in previous planning cycles have shaped the character and operating philosophy of our company today. Similarly, corporate performance during the first half of the 1980s will reflect plans already formulated. Key elements of our strategy for the new decade are presented in this section.[2]

A caption on the same page provides an insight into the form of Dravo's planning process:

Each autumn, members of the Corporate Policy Committee schedule time away from their routine duties to conduct an in-depth review and evaluation of the plans of each operating and staff unit in the context of overall Dravo plans and objectives.[3]

When a company embarks on planning, statistics and specific tactical actions are emphasized. More advanced planning systems also contain sections on strategy. As companies gain experience, they tend to standardize the plan formats so that top management can compare plans among divisions or project types.

As planning advances still further, managers use financial analysis to justify recommendations in terms of profit margin, cash flow, and return on investment or assets. In some companies, computer programs are developed to help managers evaluate alternatives and to formulate contingency plans.

A graphic illustration of the planning process is shown in Figure 1-1. Many companies performing long-range planning have systems that fit this model, which is very "flexible and adaptable to almost any size or type of business, style of management, or stage in the development of organized formal planning."[4]

PLANNING FOR SMALL AND MEDIUM-SIZED CONSTRUCTION COMPANIES

The majority of small and medium-sized construction companies do little, if any, long-range planning. But a number of contractors in that size range have applied planning techniques for their companies and have obtained positive results.

Utley-James Inc., Detroit, is a medium-sized $70 to $80 million general construction company performing industrial, commercial, and institutional building work, with 90 percent of it in the private sector. Richard Linington, president, reports:

Our planning looks one year ahead accurately and looks five years ahead generally. In the late 1960s we elected to get out of the Michigan business cycle. By the mid-1970s, 90 percent of our work was outside the state. In planning we look at high profit and loss areas, to see whether we have a problem to avoid or opportunities to aim at. We set volume and profit objectives for geographic expansion and each market. We get overall direction with our planning. We establish specific strategies with individual clients and targets.

Charles Cunningham Construction Corporation, Santa Clara, California, grew from $2 million a year in 1975 to over $18 million in 1979. Charles L. Cunningham, president of the commercial and industrial building firm, started the company with a five-year plan and describes the company's planning process as involving four major steps:

1. Establish corporate goals for both gross volume and net profit.
2. Target specific markets to obtain the mix of work needed both to achieve the goals and to fit the capabilities of each project superintendent. For example, some of the company's supers can build a warehouse project with extraordinary speed; others have good administrative talents for longer, slower, and more complex projects.

   We figure out what mix of work will keep each man busy, challenged, and operating at the peak of his talents. Being able to find the right work to fit your supers is the secret of success.

3. Account for all other nonmarketing resources required for growth (e.g., equipment, headquarters office support).
4. Plan for alternative situations based on economic conditions.

   When recession and high interest rates strike, we switch from a 50%–50% or better split of private to public work to a mix as heavy as 75% public.

Cunningham Construction Corporation's plan also reflects the company's expansion and diversification program. The company opened a branch office in Reno. The Reno office specializes in tilt-up warehouse and industrial facilities, while the Santa Clara headquarters performs more commercial work, especially banks, and public buildings of all types.

FORECASTING AND PREDICTING VERSUS PLANNING

Many contractors confuse forecasting and predicting with planning. Although the future cannot be predicted, plans are based on forecasts, which are judgments about the future based on present information. To be sure, the more accurate the forecasts, the better the plan will be, although planning can be effective even if a forecast is not too accurate at first.

Planning is determining what a company wants in the future and developing methods to achieve it. Forecasting may describe the type of external environment that can be expected. Planning will determine how to take advantage of it or how to protect the company from danger if the environment is hostile.

BARRIERS TO PLANNING

The above examples are not typical of most contractors. Average contractors, especially the smaller ones, face many barriers to long-range planning. They are pressed for time. They solve most company problems themselves. They are constantly fighting "brush fires." Typically, they keep ideas, plans, and intentions secret, so that if any do not materialize they will not be embarrassed.

When asked why they do little or no long-range planning, typical small to medium-sized construction contractors respond:

- That's for big companies, not me.
- Why should I? I'm doing O.K.
- You can't forecast the future, so how can you do long-range planning?
- I am in a cash squeeze, and that's all I can think about now.
- It's too complicated.
- My business is simple, and I know what the problems are.
- I can do all the planning I need in my head. Anyway, I don't want to discuss my plans with anyone. Why give someone a chance to find out and lose my competitive advantage?

None of the above justifies the avoidance of planning. The contractor who avoids planning for the future because he or she is doing well today is being shortsighted. Prosperity today is not assurance of profits tomorrow.

NOTES

[1]Peter F. Drucker, "Success Won't Save Your Business," in *Successful Management*, the editors of *Nation's Business*, Doubleday, New York, 1964, pp. 318, 332–333.

[2]Annual Report, Dravo Corporation, Pittsburgh, 1979.

[3]Ibid.

[4]George A. Steiner, *Top Management Planning*, The Macmillan Company, New York, 1969, p. 31.

2

Developing the Company's Strategic Planning Process

Corporate planning—planning for the company as a whole—is simple, not complex. This does not mean it is easy. The difficulties arise because the decisions are so huge and pivotal for the company, because they are often judgmental, and because the future is so uncertain.

The corporate overview portion of a marketing-oriented business plan is a statement concerning the long-term destiny of a company. Many management experts believe that the destiny of any company, whatever its size, will depend upon two, three, or four absolutely huge decisions. If management gets these right, the company will be well positioned to take advantage of whatever opportunities come along. Getting them wrong may not mean just getting caught with the wrong foot in the wrong court; it could mean not being in the right ball game. Corporate planning consists of identifying what those few decisions are for any construction company and getting them right.[1]

For example, several years ago the top executives of a medium-size heavy contractor in the Northeast—call it CBA Construction—met to review the company and its operations. What they concluded was that they essentially served one client, the State Department of Transportation, and largely for highway and bridge work. They made several key decisions. They decided to diversify and expand into a neighboring state, primarily through joint ventures. They recognized the need to enter the private sector, and they expanded their capabilities and markets through the purchase of a mechanical contractor. Two years later when their former single client, the State Department of Transportation, stopped letting contracts for a year and a half, three of the company's former competitors filed for bankruptcy. CBA Construction by that time was well positioned in new markets and continued to prosper.

TOP EXECUTIVE INVOLVEMENT

The penalties for getting answers wrong are so high today because the world is a very uncertain place and competition is razor sharp. Corporate planning is the one exercise that cannot be delegated to anyone. It must be done by the chief executive, plus two or three top managers—people in whose hands the reins of power actually rest. They should meet together to discuss the destiny of their company in the same systematic and professional way they would meet to discuss any other major problem. They will probably have to meet at least a half-day a month over a six- to twelve-month period. Each meeting should focus on a sequence of questions designed to search out and identify those three or four decisions on which the company's destiny depends.

According to Thomas F. Faught, President, Dravo Corporation, "The planning environment, or climate, is the most important factor in the entire process. If the Chief Executive Officer does not dedicate a significant portion of his time to the planning process, and hold his senior managers directly responsible for the soundness of their plans (including relating some of their incentive compensation awards to future benefits) the planning process will evolve into nothing more than a mechanical exercise—a time-consuming one at that."

TIME AND PLACE

In the small to medium-sized construction company, top management time for planning is at a premium. The day-to-day struggle for survival saps the amount of attention that can be devoted to planning. The lack of planning itself can precipitate an ever-continuing series of brush fires that might otherwise have been avoided.

The top executives in most construction companies not only have little time for planning; they have had little or no training in it. The top managers of a construction company are frequently the founders. The skills needed to start the company usually do not include planning ability. Often the key characteristics of the construction company founder are field or office management ability, or certain engineering skills, together with a flair for sales. The top managers of large companies are often chosen because of their planning abilities. In the larger construction companies layers of management keep most of the brush fires from consuming top management time.

One of the main barriers to planning in the smaller construction company is lack of time and place. With the premium on management time and the importance of day-to-day crises, there are simply no periods of peace and quiet. Finding the proper time to plan takes care of the space problem. One construction company president set aside every other Wednesday night as a planning evening when everything was quiet in the office. Sometimes he used Sunday afternoon for the same purpose. Other construction companies take their top executives to a hotel or resort for planning weekends every few months.

A series of meetings with top company executives can be planned around the tasks to be performed in the development of a marketing-oriented business plan (Figure 2-1). Each meeting can be used to review material prepared for the topic and to assign subtasks for the next meeting.

AIDS TO PLANNING

Two basic aids to planning are pencil and paper. The decision to write down ideas requires a great deal of conscious effort. Very often the exercise of writing ideas down is a step toward a useful formality, to which managers of the smaller construction companies may not be accustomed.

Another planning aid is the use of printed forms. Table 2-1 presents such a form, along with instructions for using it. Completion of this form should not be considered to be the entire planning process. It is simply useful in starting the planning wheels turning. Since no numerical estimates are required, executives who have not engaged in planning previously should not feel uncomfortable in thinking about the future. Exact numbers are not needed to start planning.

This planning form is designed to fit on one page, so that top executives may keep all of their thinking about the future of the company in full view. They can also ponder the various interrelationships among the parts of the company now and in the future. While the form shows space for thinking two years ahead, it is easy to extend it for any number of years. If it is desired to plan five to ten years ahead, different techniques may be required.

Using the planning form leads to other aspects of planning, such as:

1. Obtaining more specific information.

2. Raising questions.

3. Encouraging the start of goal and policy formulation.

An effective way to begin the planning process is to ask some basic questions and set objectives. This is not as easy as it sounds. It

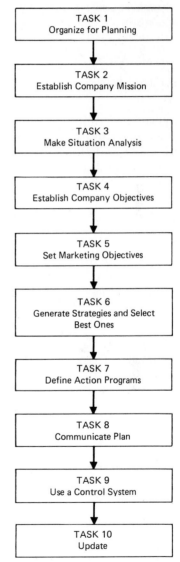

FIG. 2-1 Tasks of marketing planning. *(Adapted from Cochrane Chase and Kenneth L. Barusch,* Marketing Problem Solver, *Chilton Book Company, Radnor, Pa., 1977, p. 72.)*

TABLE 2-1 Master Planning Form°

Item	Change		Comment
	Next year	Year after next	
Construction capabilities			
Project-type market mix			
Services			
Subcontractors			
Suppliers			
Inventory			
Storage			
Quality control			
Office space			
Leasehold improvements			
Equipment			
Employees			
Fringe benefits			
Customers			
Terms of contracts			
Pricing			
Marketing			
Advertising and promotion			
Market research			
Financing			
Insurance			
Investments			
Management reports			
Management procedures			
Management organization			
Government environment			
Economic environment			
Industrial environment			
Competition			
Community environment			

Instructions: If a quantitative change is anticipated—i.e., a change in size or amount—use the following symbols: L = large, M = medium, and S = small. Quantitative changes are assumed to be increases unless preceded by a minus sign. If a qualitative change is anticipated, use the following symbols: l = large, m = medium, s = small.

Note that the notions of small, medium, and large changes are obviously subjective and will vary with the person using the form. In general, a small change denotes some sort of minimum level of change that is thought important enough to make note of. Most of the expected changes will probably fall in the medium category, indicating significant change of some magnitude. The large category will usually be reserved for unusual changes of striking impact.

The notion of qualitative changes may need some clarification. This category of change would cover such items as a change in customer mix (which might or might not result in an increased number of customers). Using new subcontractors and changing the experience requirements of new personnel would also be examples of qualitative changes.

°Adapted from Roger A. Golde, "Practical Planning for Small Business," *Harvard Business Review*, September–October 1964, p. 151.

is naive to say, "Our objective is to make a profit—period." Of course that is what it is, but maximizing profits involves answering such questions as:

- What business are we in?
- What is our place in the industry?
- What customers are we serving? Where is our market?
- What is our company image among our major customers?
- What business do we want to be in five years from now?
- What are our specific goals for profit improvement?
- Need we have plans for "product" improvement? If so, what?
- What is our greatest strength? Are we using it well?
- What is our greatest problem? How are we to solve it?
- What share of the market do we want? Next month? Next year?
- Are our personnel policies acceptable to employees?
- How can we finance growth?

Preparing a list of answers to such questions is an excellent way to start along the road to systematic and useful long-range business planning.

A decision about any of these questions can have a significant impact on most of the others. What is most important is to get at the major issues, think about them continuously, and set up specific action plans.

Following are additional questions that will stimulate further thinking about major issues:

- How do operating figures compare historically?
- What new ratios should be looked at (e.g., revenues per employee, return on investment, profits by project type)?
- What companies compete with our company?
- What services compete with our services?
- What element of the economic environment affects our company the most?
- What piece of information would I most like to have about the industry or the competition? What would I do with this information once I had it?
- Who does not buy our services? Why not?
- What should the company stop offering?
- What am I doing that should be done by others or perhaps not at all?
- How could estimating help marketing?
- How could marketing help production?
- How could personnel policies help finances?
- Suppose a key employee has a serious accident today? Suppose I do?
- What if we modified our services? Would it appeal to new customers?

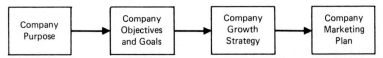

FIG. 2-2   The strategic management process. *(Adapted from Philip Kotler, Marketing Management: Analysis, Planning, and Control, 4th ed., Prentice-Hall, Inc., Englewood Cliffs, N.J., 1980, p. 65.)*

STRATEGIC MANAGEMENT PROCESS

The answers to the above questions will fall into distinct categories. These categories sequentially form major steps in the strategic management process, as shown in Figure 2-2.

Early planning systems were based on projecting current sales and economic trends five or ten years out, using those numbers as the basis for investment and other corporate decisions. Within the last decade, however, the notion of a continuously growing economy gave way to the actuality of a highly discontinuous one. Double-digit inflation, raw materials shortages, new technologies, government regulations, high interest costs, and more aggressive competition have led managers to believe that the only certainty is surprise, followed by more surprises. How can a construction company plan for an "age of discontinuity" and "future shock?"

The answer is that more companies are switching from extrapolative planning to strategic planning. Strategic planning is based on the fact that all markets undergo evolutionary changes, including changing client needs, technologies, competitors, and laws. The company should be looking out a "strategic window," watching these changes and assessing the requirements for continued success in each market.[2]

COMPANY PURPOSE

A business organization exists to accomplish something in the larger environment. The primary reason for developing a statement of purpose is to supply clear guidelines when management faces tough business decisions. The statement of purpose should be as specific as possible and couched in terms of accomplishing something outside the company. Statements of purpose such as "to make money" or "to become the leading contractor in this area" fail to express accomplishments that will result in profits and leadership.

A well thought out statement of purpose gives employees a sense of direction, opportunity, significance, and achievement. Top executives can solicit ideas from managers and other employees, but responsibility for the statement of purpose rests with the highest levels of management. The statement of purpose will evolve largely from the answers to two questions: "What is our business," and "What should it be?"[3]

When a construction company starts up, its purpose or mission is clear. In time, however, one or more of the following things will happen:

1. The purpose becomes unclear as the company grows and develops new services and capabilities, and as it enters new markets.

2. The original purpose remains clear but some managers lose interest in it.

3. The original purpose loses its appropriateness to the company as the company evolves.

When any or all the above occur, the company begins to drift, and management needs to search for a new or updated purpose.

The company's statement of purpose (sometimes referred to as its mission or statement of identity) should take into account the following key elements:

1. *Company history* must be honored, including past areas, achievements, and policies. For example, it would not make sense for a local highway contractor to try to become a national building contractor.

2. *Current desires* of management and owners must be considered and consensus reached on the various personal goals and preferences. Older managers near retirement tend to be conservative about growth and expansion, whereas younger managers often have more ambitious goals. A compromise must be achieved to allow the company to move forward with support from all managers and owners.

3. The *external environment* influences the purpose of the company. External factors—such as markets, the national economy, the economy of the company's geographic area, competition, government funding and regulations, inflation, interest rates, and customer preferences—define the major threats and opportunities. A contractor whose purpose is to be a growth company in a declining market would have a difficult time fulfilling that purpose.

4. *Company resources* place limitations on the purpose or mission by containing growth, expansion, and new market entry. Resources encompass financial strength, including working capital, surety or bonding limit, and line of credit; personnel resources, in administrative, supervisory, and management staff; and equipment.

5. *Distinct capabilities* are what a company does best, and it should base its purpose on them. Bechtel could aim to be the leading multifamily residential builder in the country, but that would not be taking advantage of its main capability—engineering and construction of major industrial and civil works projects.

Developing a statement of purpose will be a new and valuable exercise for the construction company beginning to perform long-range planning. The publicly held construction company must define its purpose (or mission or business) every year in its annual report. Some examples of companies defining their business in terms of specific business domains are:

> Dravo Corporation's worldwide activities encompass a broad range of process, technological, engineering, construction, facility operation and other services to the mining, minerals and metals, electric power, petroleum, chemical, pulp and paper, food processing and transportation industries and to the public sector. The company

is also involved in natural resources development, barge transportation, manufacturing and equipment sales and rental.[4]

> Raymond International Builders, Inc. is a New York Stock Exchange listed company engaged worldwide in engineering and construction. The company's activities include design engineering and construction services, the installation of foundations, marine heavy construction, and the fabrication and installation of permanent offshore drilling and production platforms. The company carries out these activities through its principal subsidiaries, Raymond International Builders, Inc., Kaiser Engineers, Inc., Raymond Offshore Constructors, Inc., and their affiliates.[5]

Despite its size, Turner Construction Company states its business simply as follows:

> Turner Construction Company is a leading international builder of commercial, institutional, industrial, environmental, government and multi-unit housing projects. Founded in 1902, the company operates as general contractors, construction managers and construction consultants.[6]

For some construction companies, the corporate statement of purpose changes significantly if the company diversifies. For instance, Blount Inc.'s 1980 acquisition of Washington Steel Corporation caused the company to define its business as follows:

> Blount Inc., operating through its subsidiaries, is an international company with significant positions in three basic industries: construction, agribusiness and specialty steel.[7]

As a result of acquisitions, Blount has substantially changed the character of its business.

> More than 40 percent of 1980 revenues and 54 percent of 1980 operating income was generated by operating units new to Blount in the past five years.[8]

In recent years, many companies, within and outside of construction, have been moving toward broader and more client-oriented definitions of their business, such as, "We assist industrial corporations with the construction, renovation, or expansion of their facilities." Another client-oriented approach to corporate purpose is to address clients' needs for total facilities development. The CRS Group, Inc., a Houston-based architecture, engineering, and construction management firm, defines its business this way:

> The CRS Group, Inc. is a Design/Construct company providing comprehensive services in project management, architecture, engineering, and construction. We work for clients throughout the world.
>
> Our clients are both public and private, with projects ranging from a single building to an entire new city. We have pioneered the development of advanced management systems for projects, computer-aided design techniques, and energy conservation for buildings.
>
> The CRS Group, Inc. provides services in a variety of ways. We can perform

a design/build contract, we can operate as a consultant, or we can provide architecture, engineering, or construction management services separately.[9]

Another approach to developing a statement of purpose is to make it broad and market based. Theodore Levitt, professor of marketing at the Harvard Graduate School of Business, argues that products and technologies are transient, while basic market needs endure forever.[10] Levitt's classic example of a business that defined itself too narrowly and then fell upon troubled times is the railroads. Had railroad companies, which viewed their business as one with future success virtually guaranteed, defined their businesses more broadly as serving the transportation market, they could have become involved with other modes of transportation, such as air and sea, and been highly profitable, diversified enterprises today. Blount and the CRS Group have successfully broadened the definition of their business (see Figure 2-3).

Management must steer a course between being too narrow and being too broad. The statement of purpose can be a business definition combined with an objective or mission, but the company still must evolve. For Blount to have stated its purpose 10 or 15 years ago, when it was a regional contractor, as that of being a "multi-industry, multi-national corporation" would have been stating its mission too broadly. Similarly, when the CRS Group was essentially a regional architectural firm called Caudill, Rowlett & Scott, for it to have stated its purpose as being an "international design/ construct company" would have been misleading. Both Blount and the CRS Group evolved through successive broadening of their businesses and their stated purposes.

Another useful characteristic of a company's statement of purpose is that it be elevating and motivating. Computer Sciences Corporation, a major computer services and communications systems company, sees its mission as follows:

Computer Sciences' basic business objective is to be the preeminent company worldwide in the solution of client problems in information systems technology,

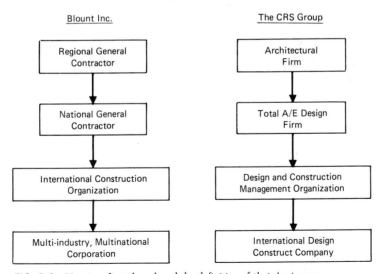

FIG. 2-3 How two firms broadened the definition of their businesses.

while earning a profit return sufficient to enable us to achieve our other objectives in our responsibilities to clients, shareholders and employees.[11]

A company's objective or purpose should become the focus of its efforts for five to twenty years. Purposes should not change every couple of years in response to external factors or unrelated opportunities. However, a company should restate its objective whenever it no longer works or when it becomes too limiting for new opportunities that would be beneficial to the company. As the pace of change quickens, construction companies will have to reconsider their basic statement of purpose more often.

HOW TO SET CONCRETE OBJECTIVES

The construction company's statement of purpose or mission defines in general or descriptive terms how management views the company's place in the business world and its direction. Management's next task is to translate that purpose into specific objectives and goals that will support the realization of that purpose.

In long-range planning for marketing, objectives fall into two main categories: (1) corporate objectives, relating to the overall construction company's performance; and (2) marketing objectives, relating to specific areas of marketplace achievement that will help the company meet its corporate objectives. The most common corporate objectives concern profitability, return on investment (or equity or net assets), growth, and risk diversification. Marketing objectives relate to:

- Share of market
- Geographic expansion
- Project-type markets
- Market presence or visibility
- Public- or private-sector mix
- Mergers or acquisition

GOALS AND OBJECTIVES

Setting objectives is one of the most important tasks that management performs. Effective leaders in construction and other businesses are those who work with their associates to establish mutual and meaningful objectives toward which the organization moves. Setting specific goals and objectives helps to avoid developments that occur solely as a result of random forces.

Statements of objectives are often too vague to be of help in solving difficult company problems. To be useful for planning, objectives must be translated into specific goals, such as "Increase gross revenue by 20 percent per year for the next five years." Merely to state an objective of "growth" is not useful. For goals to be meaningful for planning, they must be significant, reasonable, challenging, specific and measurable, connected to a reward system, and consistent with each other.

Every construction business, large or small, will succeed or fail depending on a few strategic factors. One of the aims of the long-range planning process is to discover those strategic factors that will be responsible for future success. Since finance is one of the most critical factors for success, it is a good first area to analyze for the purpose of setting specific objectives and goals.

In setting objectives it must be recognized that a construction company will face certain trade-offs. Robert Weinberg has identified eight basic strategic trade-offs facing any firm:[12]

1. Short-term profits versus long-term growth
2. Profit margin versus competitive position
3. Direct sales effort versus market development effort
4. Penetration of existing markets versus development of new markets
5. Related versus nonrelated new opportunities as a souce of long-term growth
6. Profit versus nonprofit goals (that is, social responsibilities)
7. Growth versus stability
8. "Riskless" environment versus high-risk environment

Once management has agreed on the key strategic factors that will determine the concept of the business and its course for the future, the more specific financial and growth objectives can be established.

NOTES

[1] John Argenti, "Corporate Planning," *Director*, April 1979.

[2] Derck F. Abell, "Strategic Windows," *Journal of Marketing*, July 1978, pp. 21–26.

[3] See Peter F. Drucker, *Management: Tasks, Responsibilities, Practices*, Harper & Row, New York, 1974, p. 75.

[4] Annual Report, Dravo Corporation, Pittsburgh, 1979.

[5] Annual Report, Raymond International, Inc., Houston, 1980.

[6] Annual Report, Turner Construction Company, New York, 1979, inside front cover.

[7] Annual Report, Blount Inc., Montgomery, 1980, inside front cover.

[8] Ibid, p. 2.

[9] Annual Report, The CRS Group, Inc., Houston, 1980, p. 1.

[10] Theodore Levitt, "Marketing Myopia," *Harvard Business Review*, September–October, 1975, pp. 26 ff.

[11] Annual Report, Computer Sciences Corporation, El Segundo, CA, 1980.

[12] Presented in a seminar, "Developing Management Strategies for Short-Term Profits and Long-Term Growth," New York, September 30–October 1, 1969. Sponsored by AMR International, Inc.

3

Setting Financial and Growth Objectives

Since financial performance is the ultimate test of business success, it is a good area to analyze first for the purpose of setting specific objectives and goals.

RETURN ON INVESTMENT

In recent years, managers have increasingly recognized that return on investment (ROI) is the most valid measurement of the performance of a business over time. In a *Harvard Business Review* article, Lambrix and Singhvi stated:

> Managers working to achieve realistic ROI targets are likely to manage their businesses more effectively than those who strive to achieve results that are an unrealistic expectation in a given economic scenario.[1]

Following World War II and until the early 1970s, the economy was characterized by real growth, low-cost energy, low interest rates, and manageable inflation. Established contractors of most sizes were generally profitable, with the exception of a bad year now and then. Most never paused to calculate rates of growth or return on investment. If the company turned a profit, it was proof of effective management. In many cases, that profit was considerable—in percentage and in total dollar amount.

By the late 1970s, many of these same contractors found their profits evaporating and losses appearing. Analysis revealed that the return on investment of these con-

TABLE 3-1 Sales Objectives°

Area	First year	Second year	Third year	Fourth year	Fifth year
Sales					
Pretax profits					
Pretax profits, %					
Federal tax					
Aftertax profits, %					
ROI, %					

°Adapted from George A. Steiner, *Top Management Planning*, The Macmillan Company, New York, 1969, p. 110.

struction companies was slowly declining, at a time when interest rates and inflation were rising.

One of the first specific goals that a contractor should establish is the setting of a realistic ROI. One method is to use return on net assets (RONA), where return equals aftertax operating profit divided by net assets less current liabilities, excluding any current portion of long-term debt. In brief, RONA measures the productivity of assets.

The question a company must ask is, "What percentage ROI or RONA do we want each year?" When that question is answered, it naturally raises a great many more. One immediate question is, "Given our present profit margins, what sales revenues will be required to achieve that ROI goal?" (Table 3-1) Another question is, "Will present construction capabilities and markets permit the company to achieve that objective?" If not, a number of other questions arise. Can the target be met by new services or capabilities? If so, which ones? If not, should an acquisition or joint venture be considered?

Dealing with these questions opens a "decision tree" with many branches. What personnel will be needed? What financing will be required? What effects will there be on profit margins (recalling the strategic trade-offs)?

TABLE 3-2 ABC Construction Company Pro Forma Financial Statement—Real Growth in Volume Required to Achieve Net Worth Goal in Current Dollars (in millions)

	1980	1981	1982	1983	1984	1985
Volume/% increase	$17/–	$17/0	$20/18	$25/25	$30/20	$35/17
10% gross margin	1.7	1.7	2.0	2.5	3.0	3.5
Overhead	0.75	0.9	1.0	1.1	1.2	1.3
Profit before taxes	0.9	0.8	1.0	1.4	1.8	2.2
Retained earnings	0.45	0.4	0.5	0.7	0.9	1.1
Net worth	1.5	1.9	2.4	3.1	4.0	5.1
% ROI	—	28	28	28	28	28

Assumptions: a. Gross margin remains 10% of volume.
b. Overhead assumed to rise 20% in 1981 for expanded marketing and other departments, such as data processing/financial. Thereafter assumed increase is 10% per annum.
c. Retained earnings are assumed to be 100%.

A reasonable ROI target for construction companies—considering the risks inherent in this business, as well as expected returns from alternate forms of investment—would be in the range of 15 to 20 percent. M. M. Sundt Construction Co., Tucson, targets a 15 percent return and evolves its planning backward from that goal.

An example of the way one company approached the setting of objectives is shown in Table 3-2. The company is real; only the name is disguised. ABC Construction Company, as we will call it, is a general contractor performing building, industrial, and wastewater treatment projects. The family-held company has been in business since 1942 and has grown in stages to a volume of about $17 million.

In 1981 top management, consisting essentially of a chairman and a president, father and son, set a target for the net worth of the company to be $5 million by 1985. To achieve the $5 million net worth, ABC Construction needs to increase its net worth by 28 percent per year. To do that, the company must grow, after the first year, by an average of 20 percent per year in revenues. The projection is based on certain assumptions:

1. That the company will do what is necessary in sales and marketing to double its volume in five years.

2. That overhead will increase at a rate of about 10 percent per year, after a 20 percent increase in the first year for marketing and data processing start-up costs.

3. That the company will be able to maintain a gross profit margin of 10 percent per year, even while growing.

4. That earnings will be 100 percent retained.

The pro forma financial statement shown in Table 3-2 is a relatively simple one. For companies with a profit-sharing plan, a portion of income before taxes can be retained for the plan, reducing taxes and increasing net worth faster. Other factors not taken into account are depreciation and appreciation. A company's investments in buildings and equipment may increase in value and qualify for depreciation allowances, which will reduce taxes and increase net worth faster.

Table 3-3 shows the company's program, by market segment, for achieving its growth goals.

EFFECTS OF INFLATION

To obtain a truer value for future net worth, an inflation factor must be considered. ABC Construction Company's net worth goal could have been stated in constant (1980) dollars. That would have resulted in the need for higher growth rates, which could show that the $5 million figure was unrealistic. If inflation can be assumed to continue at 10 percent per year, then ABC's net worth in 1985 would be about $2.5 million in 1980 dollars.

Let us look at another example (see Table 3-4). The XYZ Construction Corporation took inflation into account in setting its objectives. XYZ's objectives are based

TABLE 3-3 ABC Construction Company Sales Volume by Market Projection in Current Dollars (in millions)

Market	1976–1979 average	1980*	1981	1982	1983	1984	1985
Private							
Office and commercial	$3.1/20%	$1/5%	$3/20%	$4/20%	$6/25%	$9/30%	$11/30%
Industrial	0.4/3%	1/5%	2/10%	3/15%	3/10%	3/10%	1/10%
Industrial maintenance and small projects†	N.A.	0	1/5%	1/5%	1/5%	1/5%	2/5%
Institutional	2.3/15%	6/35%	3/20%	2/10%	3/10%	1/5%	2/5%
Residential	1.7/11%	4/25%	1/5%	1/5%	1/5%	1/5%	1/5%
Metal building	N.A.	1/5%	2/10%	3/15%	3/10%	3/10%	3/10%
Public							
Waste and water	6.1/39%	4/25%	4/25%	5/25%	7/30%	9/30%	11/30%
Other public works	1.8/12%	0	1/5%	1/5%	1/5%	1/5%	2/5%
Total	15.4/100%	17/100%	17/100%	20/100%	25/100%	30/100%	35/100%

*Estimated

†Under $250,000, 1976–1981; under $1,000,000, 1981–1985

TABLE 3-4 XYZ Construction Corporation Pro Forma—Gradual Real Growth, Construction Operations (in millions)

	1979	1980	1981	1982	1983	1984	1985
Real growth rate	—	5	5	5	10	10	15
Volume	66	76	87	100	120	145	181
Gross margin	3.3	3.8	4.4	5.0	6.0	7.3	9.1
Overhead	1.1	1.3	1.5	1.7	1.9	2.1	2.3
Profit (pretax)	2.2	2.5	2.9	3.3	4.1	5.2	6.8
Profit (aftertax)	1.1	1.3	1.4	1.7	2.0	2.6	3.4
Equity	2.2	3.5	4.9	6.6	8.6	11.2	14.6

Assumptions: a. Real growth is over a 10% inflation rate.
 b. Year-end volume in 1980 totals $76 million.
 c. Gross margins remain 5% of volume.
 d. Overhead grows even with inflation; an additional 1981 expense was for data processing and marketing.
 e. Return on equity based on $3.3 million investment in 1980; 100% of earnings reinvested.

on growth, since a historical analysis showed that the company's overhead had doubled in 10 years, while volume was static and competitors were gaining an increasing share of the market.

XYZ Construction assumed that inflation would continue at 10 percent per year, and management wanted growth to be at a reasonably slow rate for two to three years, then begin to rise to faster rates in the longer term. For XYZ to achieve a reasonable real growth rate of 5 percent over inflation for three years, 10 percent for two years, and 15 percent for one year, the company would need almost to triple its volume (in future dollars). As a consequence, the owners' equity would increase sixfold, without inflation, and triple, if discounted for inflation. It is easy to see that even a modest growth rate requires a sizable increase in volume when inflation is added.

Representations of XYZ's shrinking real volume are shown in Figure 3-1. The company's volume in 1970 was $40.3 million. By 1979 its volume rose to $66.3 million in apparent growth for the company. But the value of the dollar had fallen due to

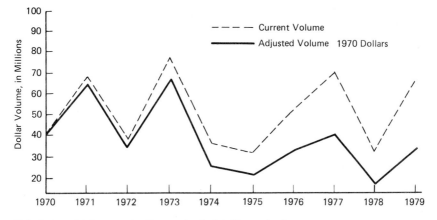

FIG. 3-1 XYZ Construction Corporations's shrinking real volume.

inflation, from $1.95 relative to 1970 to $1.00 in 1979, or a 50 percent drop. XYZ's real 1979 volume, adjusted for inflation, was $34 million, or 15 percent less work in place than the company did in 1970.

Any business today that does not discount its income and return on investment for inflation is obtaining a false sense of its performance. The return on equity that must be achieved by a corporation to produce any real return for its owners has increased dramatically in recent years. To outrun inflation, a company must produce a return on equity that will offset the implicit tax on capital exacted by inflation and the explicit taxes exacted on both dividends and gains in value produced by retained earnings.

It is true that net worth or equity has been presented here in a stripped-down version, without accounting for depreciation, inflating assets, interest, and other income through a cash management program. Fundamentally, however, there is a strong relationship in an inflationary world between the need for growth and the key financial performance areas of a construction business: profitability and return on investment.

Growth in volume, then, is not growth for its own sake, but for the sake of a company that performs well.

TO GROW OR NOT TO GROW, AND HOW MUCH

The concept of growth for a construction company is a complex one. When first confronted with the idea of growth, the typical construction executive will probably respond, "I'm not interested in volume. I'm interested in profits."

Profits are essential to the survival of a business. But a steady flow of profits at a constant level would mean a declining return on investment. That is true for two reasons: simple arithmetic and inflation.

Without growth, a construction company that has an annual volume of $60 million, aftertax profits of $1 million, and a net worth of $3 million faces a diminishing return, as shown below (dollar amounts are in millions):

	Year 1	Year 2	Year 3	Year 4
Revenue	$60	$60	$60	$60
Net income°	1	.9	.8	.7
Equity	3	3.9	4.7	5.4
Net worth	4	4.8	5.5	6.1
Return	33%	23%	17%	13%

°Net income will decline by 10% a year because of inflation and increasing overhead.

Important aspects of the business that must be included in the overall growth strategy include personnel recruitment, equipment planning, computerized cost and schedule control systems, and office space requirements.

Bonding capacity and bank lines of credit also play a role in limiting or supporting growth, and they determine to what extent growth can occur. Bonding companies and banks are becoming more interested in reviewing marketing or business plans of construction contractors. Their cooperation and support can play a crucial role in the success of a growth strategy.

Most importantly, the company has to be managed in such a way that all people—down to the lower-ranking employees—are willing to shoulder new and bigger responsibilities. A company can grow only as fast as its people can grow. The key to growth is the people in the organization and their desire and capability for growth.

GROWTH: THE PEOPLE NEED

Aside from the dollars and cents needs for growth, there is the people need. Larry G. Gerwig, vice president (formerly vice president of marketing and estimating) of Enterprise Building Corporation, Dunedin, Florida, views growth this way:

> There is no way to keep a good team together, and pay inflationary and merit salary increases, and provide opportunities for good people without growing. Good people today are just going to go elsewhere, if you can attract them in the first place, without growth. If you want the company to be maintained, growth has to be permanent. You have to be on a growth path forever.

A construction company that cannot attract, motivate, and retain talented and competent people will not survive. Increasingly, the educated person with management potential looks for more than a job. He or she looks for a career and for opportunity. This upward pressure for career opportunities will not be satisfied by the retirement of older people alone. The expectations of young, educated people are a factor requiring internal growth.

GROWTH FOR SURVIVAL

When the construction market is expanding, there is ample room for the growth of most construction companies. Buoyed by the swelling marketplace, companies that are not planning for growth or taking steps in that direction decline slowly. More aggressive contractors grow rapidly. Many companies grow by accident rather than by managed decisions. But when the construction marketplace as a whole is not expanding, when there are protracted economic slumps in many geographic areas, and when changes in the ways of doing business are accelerating, then the construction company managed by reaction can decline fast. Management needs to develop a strategy for planning and managing growth.

With the rapidly changing methods of doing business in the private sector, with the turnabout from 95 percent bid to 90 percent negotiated work among some owners, not even an expanding marketplace will mean automatic growth for all contractors. For example, one family-held construction company in the Southwest grew to

$50 million in volume by bidding for most of its work. Then the owners began seeking contractors with more sophisticated management systems for negotiated work. The company stopped growing and began to lose its share of the market quickly. It was losing out not only to other local contractors, but to those moving in from the Northeast and Midwest.

At the opposite end of the spectrum from the construction executive who has no interest in growth is the one who "wants the company to become a $100 million company" or a "$1 billion company" when it is a $10 million or a $50 million company. Somewhere between lies a rational approach to growth based on economic performance or necessity. Growth requires a total company strategy. The company has to prepare for growth.

SENSIBLE GROWTH OBJECTIVES

To summarize, some of the economic reasons for growth are:

1. To maintain adequate return on investment.
2. To ensure profits required to provide an adequate return.
3. To maintain market standing.
4. To provide opportunities for talented and competent people.
5. To outstrip inflation.

To satisfy the above needs, management must determine the minimum rate of growth needed to remain a strong, viable, forward-moving construction company.

The most logical point to begin for setting a minimum rate of growth is with one of the fundamental measures of economic performance: return on investment. As noted earlier in this chapter, working backward from a desired rate of return will determine profits and revenue needed to meet the objective.

An ROI slightly above the projected inflation rate should be considered a minimum desired return, requiring the minimum necessary volume growth. Higher rates of return can be targeted, but they will require higher risk. Management must determine the point beyond which a greater return (requiring greater volume and profitability) can be obtained only by a sharp increase in risk.

That point represents the optimal growth rate, rather than a maximum rate. A construction company should target its growth objectives between the minimal and the optimal rates. Beyond the optimum, the price of growth will be too high and the company could risk its soundness due to "buying in" at lower prices, lower productivity, overextension, and unexpected problems in new project or geographic markets.

GROWTH AND THE GENERATION GAP

There are only two ways for a construction company to implement new growth strategies: either top management must decide to grow and be able to change, or it must step aside. The matter of future growth is the single management issue that most often splits older and younger construction company managers into two opposing camps. The issue divides parents and children, entrepreneurial founders and younger managers, and first-generation construction owners and second-generation heirs apparent.

Younger managers who are looking forward to 10 to 30 years more with the company, and who are in tune with today's economic and social realities, will be a force for growth. Senior managers and principals may often be a force for maintaining the status quo.

Most top managers know what the company needs to make it grow but can lack the desire or will to change. Many first-generation top construction executives are bound by certain habits and constraints, such as geography, inability to delegate responsibility, comfort level with personal contacts, and lack of desire for increased risk. Their opposition is rooted in:

1. *Tradition.* The company never needed growth objectives before and has done quite well without them.

2. *Growth without Goals.* The company has in fact grown in previous years by tackling bigger and bigger projects.

3. *Project-by-Project Orientation.* Many construction company founders believe—and with some validity—that if management pays attention to cost and schedule on each project, the company's growth will take care of itself.

4. *Nest-Egg Protection.* After a number of years in the construction business— most of them profitable—the founder, older partner, or principal has accumulated a sizable net worth and is fairly wealthy. He or she views a growth policy as a threat to that nest-egg.

5. *Growth Means Risk.* Many construction company founders consider planned growth a needless risk, without sufficient return. They view it as a venturing out into the world of the unknown, to more distant places, to new types of construction, to dependence on unfamiliar people and suppliers and untried subcontractors and labor forces. Growth, to them, means unnecessary headaches and surprises.

6. *Loss of Control.* It is typical for an entrepreneur in any business who has started with meager means and built a substantial company to want to keep everything under his or her thumb. The degree to which any construction company grows, even by accident, depends on the degree to which the founder can delegate responsibility. With a growth policy, the founder usually perceives a loss of direct control over every aspect of the business, or at least over those he or she still controls.

    Externally, a growth policy is seen as a departure from senior management's comfortable world of personal contacts among owners, design firms, subcontractors, suppliers, government agencies, bankers, and bonding agents. Starting new and potentially troublesome business relationships is not a welcome prospect for a senior principal.

7. *Time Demands.* As senior managers move closer to retirement, they spend an increasing percentage of their time outside the business in community, civic, cultural, and charitable activities, professional associations, other busi-

nesses, hobbies, and sports. Often, business growth demands more of the manager's time, creating a conflict with personal pursuits.

All the above factors are real and may be difficult to change. It is often only after senior managers are convinced by younger managers of the greater risk of unplanned or accidental growth that they will agree to a growth policy. Younger managers must be sensitive to the factors causing resistance on the part of senior principals, since under their leadership the company has been successful. Their desires for their personal lives, activities, and impending retirement are valid considerations that must be taken into account.

In some cases the discussion of growth may broaden into such topics as management succession, stock purchase or redemption, or other areas such as the principal stockholders' time devoted to the business and investment recapture.

Many construction companies have grown to major size under one founder or early manager, such as Peter Kiewit Sons' Co., while others have never grown beyond a volume of $1 million or $2 million. Another example is Huber, Hunt & Nichols, Inc. of Indianapolis, which in one generation became a $400- to $500-million-a-year national firm. It was the desire of the firm to develop a major nationwide construction organization. Through an aggressive growth policy, the company has succeeded in fulfilling its primary objective.

In some construction companies the second generation of management—family or not—has sparked tremendous growth. Examples are Perini, Gilbane Building Co., and the Bechtel Group, Inc. In others, significant growth has not occurred until the third generation, as at M. M. Sundt and Fluor Corp. It is not which generation of management that matters; it is the change in management attitudes, habits, and outlook that achieves growth.

Most of the major construction companies that have grown in excess of $100 million in annual revenue have done so after the departure of the founder, usually after two or three generations of management.

HOW TO PREPARE FOR GROWTH

A construction company that wants to grow must prepare for it. To prepare for growth, top management must:

1. Be aware of the need for growth for financial, market, or organizational reasons.
2. Honestly decide whether it wants to change.
3. Define the key business activities and groom a top management team to be responsible for them.

In his book *Fast-Growth Management*, Mack Hanan sees the role of the chief executive officer as that of "Mr. Return on Investment." In Hanan's view, one of the ways to safeguard that role is to manage people, not functions. "Growth is hastened when management style favors people. . . . Growth managers manage their managers

. . . not the function itself. . . . You must manage directively, according to policy, instead of participatively. . . . You must manage by standards of performance instead of by motivation. . . . You must manage on the basis of shared rewards instead of on salary-based compensation arrangements."[2]

When top management has determined its desire for growth and its willingness to change lifelong successful approaches to managing, the construction company can develop an overall growth strategy.

AN ALTERNATIVE TO GROWTH

Of course, not every construction company will want to grow. And many that want to grow may not be able to because they face a local, regional, or national construction economy that is declining. A shrinking construction market fosters increased competition and lower prices, causing many projects to be bid at cost or less. Contractors in a sound financial position tend to be selective during such times, preferring reduced volume to unprofitable projects.

If a contractor determines that its markets are in a temporary decline, as in a slow year or two as part of the construction business cycle, then a planned no-growth approach may likewise be a temporary detour on a long-term growth path.

If, however, the contractor's analysis of its markets reveals that they are on a long-term downward trend, or are not projected to grow, and the company cannot profitably increase its market share and does not want to penetrate new projects or geographic markets, the company may want to plan for a trimmed-down operation. Some contractors have done this successfully, when downsizing was well planned. After all, a well-managed company can be profitable at any size.

The advantages of downsizing are:

1. Greater control over a small operation.
2. Potential increase in profitability (through reduction in overhead) and return on investment, if investment is reduced through sale of certain assets.
3. Lower risk.
4. Fewer personnel and organizational problems.

The disadvantages of downsizing are:

1. A necessary reduction in office and field personnel, potentially resulting in a morale problem.
2. Possible loss of talented, upwardly mobile managers, because of lack of advancement opportunities.
3. Possible reduction of return on investment.
4. Greater dependence on one or two markets.
5. Reversal of business momentum that may be difficult to control.

Downsizing can be a viable—or necessary—alternative to growth, if the contractor recognizes the disadvantages and carefully plans the action.

COMPANY GROWTH STRATEGY

After top management has established the company's purpose, defined its return and profit objectives, and accepted the need for growth, it knows where it wants to go. What the company then needs is an overall strategy for achieving its objectives: the company's concept of how it is going to win the war. Major choices of direction must be made and resources allocated in support of these choices. The tactics for winning the battles are the specific daily, weekly, and monthly tasks needed to achieve the company's objectives. Whether it is a local earth-moving company or a worldwide engineering and construction giant, every construction company needs a growth strategy.

A realistic strategy is founded on need and desire and limited by the company's resources.

NOTES

[1]Robert J. Lambrix and Surendra S. Singhvi, "How to Set Volume-Sensitive ROI Targets," *Harvard Business Review,* March–April 1981, p. 174.

[2]Mack Hanan, *Fast-Growth Management,* AMACOM, Division of American Management Associations, New York, 1979, p. 51.

4

Charting the Company's Resources for Marketing

To develop a strong, coherent strategy for growth and profitability, management must assess both internal and external factors. When a construction company is not performing as well as its competitors, the cause may be in either the company's internal situation or its external environment. Both change constantly and need to be reviewed periodically.

In the past, construction executives have been primarily concerned with the company's internal activities. Today, however, the concept of their role is changing. Effective managers know that the increasingly complex external environment affects their internal organization.

A profitable construction company possesses a number of internal tangible and intangible assets that can be formally listed and charted. When these are analyzed in relation to the external environment, a picture of the best course for the company to follow emerges. Decisions directing the process that matches the organization's resources and capabilities with the threats and opportunities it faces in the external environment are what should concern management.

In developing an effective strategy, managers must determine whether proposed endeavors are compatible with current capacities. According to Rowe, Mason, and Dickel:

> The first task is to *identify a distinctive competence* for the organization. A distinctive competence is something the organization does particularly well. It refers to the organization's unique resources and capabilities for conducting its business.

It also describes the strengths of the organization and its ability to overcome its weaknesses.[1]

The first step in making this determination involves taking stock of company resources, looking at what the company has to offer construction buyers. This is a company's marketing inventory. A marketing inventory examines both tangible and intangible resources, including organizational factors. Internal factors include:

- Company characteristics—history, profitability, and performance
- Financial resources—cash, other assets, bonding capacity, and credit line
- Human resources—management, office, and field supervisory and labor personnel
- Equipment
- Special capabilities in certain construction markets
- Special capabilities in project management
- Organizational structure, leadership, and morale

The marketing inventory relates the company to its external environment with respect to:

- Competition and marketing position
- Current client relationships
- Reputation
- Current marketing functions
- Government regulations and funding projections
- Overall economic climate
- Outlook for the company's markets

Since some of these factors affect the company's future positively and others negatively, it is possible to set up a marketing balance sheet listing the company's marketing assets (strengths) and liabilities (weaknesses).

MARKETING ASSETS: STRENGTHS

Any construction company that has operated successfully and profitably for most of its corporate life has a number of positive characteristics or strengths. On balance, these have outweighed the shortcomings, so that the company continues to exist. If the company is managed in an informal or not highly organized way, some people, both inside and outside, might attribute its success to luck. Still, whether or not the company is involved in formal planning, and whether or not it is methodical in its management approach, the strengths outweigh its weaknesses.

By listing and analyzing the company's strengths, management can clearly see:

- What has made the company successful in the past.

- What assets the company has in its arsenal to wage a campaign against its competition.

Construction companies successfully operating in the public sector or in the competitive low-bid market have assets or strengths that are transferable for marketing purposes to the private sector.

The major strengths found in medium-sized construction companies are fairly typical and can be used as a guide in identifying success factors. In the following example the company's name has been changed.

1. *Performance, Longevity.* Miller Construction Company is a ficticious full-service contractor offering clients responsive, on-schedule, within-budget performance. Performance is its major strength—the key element in marketing the company to owners and developers. In a survey of clients, architects, specialty contractors, and suppliers, Miller Construction rated as high as or higher than almost all competitors in the categories of schedule and budget performance.

2. *Client Relations.* The company's philosophy of responsive service to its clients remains a key to maintaining repeat business. Miller works especially hard communicating honestly and objectively with clients to avoid disputes, delays, and extras on their projects. (A company operating in the public sector may have a similar record, which would be a strength in planned entrance into the private sector.)

3. *Organization: Talented and Experienced People.* Miller Construction's ability to build projects faster and within budget stems directly from the caliber of the people it attracts and employs in the field and in the office. It is an organization of talented, experienced, and motivated individuals. Several employees have past experience in different areas, such as mechanical work, which may allow the company to penetrate new and diversified markets.

4. *Subcontractor Relationships.* Miller's record of efficient scheduling of trades and on-time payments to subcontractors and suppliers gives the company strong "buying power." Miller receives prompt delivery, good service, and competitive prices, which allow the company to provide better scheduling, quality, and economy to owners.

5. *Equipment, Field Forces.* Throughout its operating area, Miller maintains an extensive fleet of equipment to service project sites at competitive rates—and to earn additional profits from each project. Miller's in-house force is capable of constructing 15 to 20 percent of any project plus doing all site development. This capability enables the company to exercise more control over each project.

6. *Diversity of Markets.* Miller's diverse experience enables the company to respond to changing market conditions. Miller has constructed offices, high-rise and low-rise housing, industrial plants, warehouses, hospitals, and waste-water treatment plants. The company builds in both the private and the

public sectors. Added to this is the company's ability to develop its own properties.

7. *Position in Commercial Markets.* Miller enjoys an outstanding reputation within and a solid share of the retail and office markets in two states. The company's on-schedule performance record and ability to adapt to change have resulted in many successfully completed projects for a core of repeat clients.

8. *Position in Business Community.* Miller is a large, well-known, and respected general contractor in its home state. Owners, civic leaders, architects, specialty contractors, and suppliers acknowledge this fact. This position should help the company secure negotiated projects for years to come.

9. *Location within Growing Region.* The company's offices are located near economically expanding regions, presenting a full spectrum of opportunities within all Miller's existing markets.

10. *Financial Strength.* Miller is in a financially strong and stable position. The company has completed every project since 1943, establishing the company's stability. With a high bonding capacity and substantial net worth, the company currently sustains an annual volume of business exceeding $100 million.

11. *Other Special Competences: Development Capability.* Having developed rental residential properties and having had in-house real estate development experience, Miller has an advantage in marketing. The company can provide turnkey services to private companies that either develop their own properties or search for contractors to develop properties for them.

MARKETING LIABILITIES: WEAKNESSES

Every construction company faces obstacles to its continued growth. Some exist in the form of internal company problems; others relate to the company not keeping pace with a changing marketplace. As noted above, in the profitable construction company strengths outweigh weaknesses. However these weaknesses, or marketing liabilities, must be addressed and corrected if the company is to meet the challenges of the future and continue to prosper. The following examples of weaknesses are drawn from actual companies and are typical of small, medium, and large contractors. (Note: The following weaknesses are given as examples only; they do not relate to the above strengths and in some instances could contradict them if they were derived from a single company.)

1. *Lack of Corporate Goals and Direction.* Miller Construction Company operates largely on a project-by-project basis without established volume and profit goals, overall direction, or a program for achieving corporate objectives. While the company has been successful for many years without formal business planning, the complexity of today's business environment requires objectives and planning for continuing opportunities and profits.

2. *Lack of Marketing Function, Tools, and Understanding.* Miller lacks the marketing function to achieve a growing corporate volume and profit. The modern marketing concept is not clearly understood or implemented. Those involved with finding new business spend a relatively small portion of their time in it, mostly geared toward entertaining existing clients or prospects. These efforts are important, but they are only a small part of a successful marketing function. In addition, the company has relatively weak marketing tools, such as brochures, newsletters, reprints, presentation materials, and proposals.

3. *Dependence on Weakening Market.* Feedback from developers and others, plus review of current projections, indicates that the commercial office and retail markets will soften. Regional retail centers could be significantly affected. This type of construction represented approximately 65 percent of Miller's volume of business in the previous fiscal year. Thus, a substantial downturn in the type of new construction Miller performs most is expected.

4. *Lack of Sophisticated Management Tools.* Miller has achieved an outstanding performance reputation even without the sophisticated management tools used by companies of similar size. More sophisticated project control, cost, and scheduling techniques, such as CPM, are sought by clients today, instead of bar charts and the other traditional methods normally presented by Miller.

5. *Management Transition.* Miller people are concerned about the future leadership of the company. Staff members perceive a significant generation gap between top-level management and two much younger vice presidents in line to assume control. There is some doubt as to whether existing client contacts established by older executives will remain strong in the future.

6. *Morale: Lack of Opportunity, Recognition, and Discipline.* Miller Construction Company lacks adequate channels for advancement and the opportunity for additional assumption of responsibilities. The company has lost good people to competitors as a result. A lack of discipline has encouraged some loss of control, toleration of mediocrity, lack of cooperation in sharing equipment, and unnecessary sloppiness on projects.

7. *Division between Field and Office.* Communication problems exist between the field and office forces during construction. Cost control reports are often not valid or up to date for use in the field as a result of delays between estimating and accounting regarding change orders during construction.

8. *Shorthanded Staff.* Miller is not implementing a sophisticated project cost control system because the office and field staff is inadequate. The current estimating staff is usually under pressure to develop costs, estimate new work, and keep current projects moving, as well as to provide answers to the field. Furthermore, fully qualified and experienced replacement personnel will be needed as people advance, retire, or become unavailable.

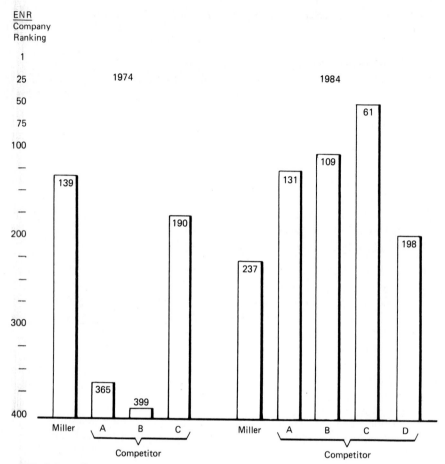

FIG. 4-1   Miller Construction Company versus local competitors (based on national rankings).

9. *Loss of Market Standing to Competition.* As indicated in Figure 4-1 and Table 4-1, Miller is undergoing a gradual decline compared to its strongest locally based competitors. While the other companies shown appear to have continued upward after the 1973–1974 recession, Miller, after a brief recovery, returned to a downward trend. Within Miller's market area, other contractors are gaining at its expense.

10. *Fluctuating Volume.* Table 4-1 also indicates the wide fluctuations of Miller's volume. Although the construction industry is subject to fluctuations, it appears that Miller has experienced far wider fluctuations year to year than the industry and its market area contractors. This is a result of a lack of planning and marketing.

11. *Restricted Local Market.* Miller's home state has enjoyed recent growth, but being tied to one market, Miller can react only to the conditions of a

TABLE 4-1 Miller Construction Company and Local Building Contractors' National Ranking

		1984	1983	1982	1981	1980	1979	1978	1977	1976	1975	1974
Competitor A	Rank	131	225	203	245	290	305	183	339	—	314	365
	$ Volume	114.0	60.5	54.5	38.4	33.4	35.8	50.1	28.2	—	24.7	20.8
Competitor B	Rank	109	150	176	147	—	278	275	—	—	—	399
	$ Volume	132.3	85.9	62.1	67.3	—	39.3	35.1	—	—	—	19.1
Competitor C	Rank	61	71	72	121	213	93	143	175	152	125	190
	$ Volume	228.6	175.4	167.6	78.1	42.5	114.0	64.5	48.5	48.8	51.1	36.5
Competitor D	Rank	198	237	—	—	—	—	—	—	—	—	—
	$ Volume	83.0	57.2	—	—	—	—	—	—	—	—	—
Miller	Rank	237	—	170	191	320	313	113	239	103	175	139
	$ Volume	66.3	29.8	64.6	50.3	30.8	34.4	75.8	38.6	67.9	40.3	47.3
Competitor E	Rank	286	379	345	—	228	280	325	—	—	—	—
	$ Volume	54.2	34.4	32.9	—	40.4	39.0	32.0	—	—	—	—
Competitor F	Rank	291	196	279	246	—	283	288	293	242	198	267
	$ Volume	53.5	70.4	41.4	38.4	—	38.7	36.0	32.0	33.5	36.6	27.6
Competitor G	Rank	292	253	—	322	378	—	—	—	—	—	—
	$ Volume	53.3	53.6	—	30.2	25.1	—	—	—	—	—	—
Competitor H	Rank	319	238	310	—	349	—	222	298	278	—	234
	$ Volume	48.5	57.0	37.0	—	28.0	—	43.2	31.5	30.1	—	31.0
Competitor I	Rank	—	400	388	272	—	—	267	337	—	324	—
	$ Volume	—	32.0	28.7	35.8	—	—	38.6	28.4	—	24.2	—
Miller's position		5	10	2	3	4	6	1	2	1	2	1

single area. Additionally, the area is not immune to overbuilding followed by collapse of construction demand—a cycle to which the construction industry is prone.

12. *Dependence on Government-Funded Projects.* Miller's volume is composed of more than 30 percent government-funded public construction. Although this should be a portion of Miller's market mix, dependence on it places the company at the mercy of fluctuations in government spending. When government spending declines, competition increases and contracts are won at prices that allow no profit—and often guarantee losses.

Several of the weaknesses of Miller Construction Company relate to operations. They affect the company's marketing efforts in four ways:

1. They could be perceived by owners as shortcomings of the organization, preventing Miller from presenting a strong sales story.

2. They affect the quality of the "product"—the Miller Construction Company and its services—that is being sold to owners.

3. A smoothly operating construction company is more likely to sustain an effective marketing effort.

4. Marketing and sales will magnify operational problems, not solve them.

Organizational weaknesses should be identified and steps taken to correct them before the company undertakes a major marketing program.

THREATS AND OPPORTUNITIES

Strengths and weaknesses are largely internally created and controlled. A contractor must also consider threats and opportunities, which are externally created and controlled.

> An opportunity is *any favorable situation in the organization's environment,* often a trend or change of some kind or an overlooked need, that supports the demand for a product or service and permits the firm to enhance its position. . . . A threat is *any unfavorable situation in the organization's environment* that is potentially damaging to the organization and its strategy. It may be a barrier, a constraint, or anything that might inflict problems, damages, or injury to the organization.[2]

Construction company executives must determine which threats and opportunities could have substantial impact on the future of their organization. This evaluation requires continued observation, so the company can react immediately to reduce the impact of threats and take advantage of the opportunities. A company can assign one executive to monitor each issue and recommend the actions that would best serve the contractor's interests.

Threats.   Each construction company faces its own set of threats and opportunities. They may be similar to the ones shown below or they may be more extensive.

Executives of Miller Construction Company identified five primary threats to the company's future. To calculate the level of importance of each, they averaged the degree of impact and probability estimated by various individuals. Some issues in this category were evaluated by only one or two executives but were still judged to be

TABLE 4-2 Threats to Miller's Future

	Degree of impact	Probability	Threat index°
Primary threats			
Inflation	6.5	7	45
Interest rate increase	8	5	40
Recession	6	6	36
Poor management transition	9	4	36
Retail construction decline	6	5	30
Secondary threats			
Government funding change	6	5	30
Less competitive prices	7	4	28
Loss of repeat clients	9	3	27
Loss of key employees	6	4	24
Opening of local office by major competition	6	4	24
Labor strikes	4	4	16

°The threat index is found by multiplying the average of managers' intuitive estimates, on a scale of 1 to 10, of the degree of impact by the probability of each threat.

TABLE 4-3 Opportunities Identified by Miller

	Payoff	Ease of entry	Opportunity
Major opportunities			
Develop own property	7	7.5	52
Perform work now done by subs	7	7	49
Expand geographic market radius	6	6	36
Lesser opportunities			
Construct metal buildings	7	3	21
Develop national accounts	3	7	21
Enjoy a boom in renovation	5	4	20
Be acquired by another company	3.5	5	17
Acquire another company	4	4	16
Do more public bidding	5	3	15
Undertake a joint venture on large project	4	2.5	10

major threats. Six other threats were identified by Miller executives as of lesser consequence to the company's future (Table 4-2).

Opportunities.   Miller Construction Company identified three areas of major opportunities for the company. Seven additional opportunities were considered to be of lesser importance by Miller's executives (Table 4-3).

Threat Analysis.   What are the major threats faced by your company? On a scale of 1 to 10, what is the importance of each to your company? (Note: 1 is the lowest impact and not likely to occur; 10 is the highest and very likely to occur.)

What other trends are affecting your business now or might affect it in the future? Examples include population change, legislation, new competition, lawsuits, loss of an important client, energy rationing, growth of open shop, political changes, and specific government funding or program changes.

Opportunity Analysis.   What are your company's major opportunities? On a scale of 1 to 10, what is the possibility of your taking advantage of each and the likely payoff in total profits? (Note: 1 is very difficult and a low payoff; 10 is easily done and a very high payoff.)

What trends are affecting your business now or might affect it in the future? Examples are a joint venture on a large project, a new CM division, acquisition of or by another firm, the purchase of an operating company, a drop in interest rates, international work, new types of work done in-house, new services, financial arrangements, political change, and starting an open shop or union operation.

THE COMPANY CAPABILITY PROFILE

After you list your company's corporate resources and the services the company is capable of providing, a good way to begin your assessment is to chart the company's

Managerial

	Weakness	Normal	Strength	
1. Corporate Image, Longevity				
2. Use of Strategic Plans and Strategic Analysis				
3. Environmental Assessment and Forecasting				
4. Speed of Response to Changing Conditions				
5. Flexibility of Organizational Structure				
6. Management Communication and Control				
7. Entrepreneurial Orientation				
8. Ability to Attract and Retain Effective and Professional People				
9. Ability to Meet Changing Technology				
10. Ability to Handle Inflation				
11. Aggressiveness in Meeting Competition				
12. Other				

Case _____

Name _____

FIG. 4-2 Company capability profile. *(Adapted from Alan J. Rowe, Richard O. Mason, and Karl E. Dickel, Strategic Management and Business Policy: A Methodological Approach, Addison-Wesley Publishing Co., Reading, Mass., 1982, pp. 20–21.)*

strengths and weaknesses. This has many important advantages. It allows management to see quickly and clearly where its strengths lie and how important these strengths are. It helps the company to determine whether its current resources are

Competitive

	Weakness	Normal		Strength
1. Service, Strength, Quality, Uniqueness				
2. Customer Loyalty and Satisfaction				
3. Market Share				
4. Tight Cost Control				
5. Estimating Ability				
6. R&D Investment in New-Product/New – Service Development				
7. High Barriers to Entry into the Company's Market				
8. Multiple Markets				
9. Advantage Taken of Market Growth Potential				
10. Subs, Strength and Material Availability				
11. Relationships with Other Construction Professionals				
12. Customer Concentration				
13. Other Marketing Capacity				

Fig. 4-2   (*continued*)

being used in the best possible way and whether its "market mix" is sufficient to achieve the greatest return on investment. It also reveals gaps between planned targets and projected performance.

One method of charting strengths and weaknesses is to draw up a Company Capability Profile (Figure 4-2). This depiction of the company's capabilities in dealing with both the internal and the external environment makes it possible to examine relative strengths and weaknesses, determine gaps in performance, and see where opportunities exist for further utilizing current resources. In developing the company profile, the following features of the organization should be identified:

Financial

	Weakness	Normal	Strength	
1. Access to Capital when Required				
2. Access to Bonding when Required				
3. Degree of Capacity Utilization				
4. Ease of Exit from the Market				
5. Profitability, Return on Investment				
6. Liquidity, Available Internal Funds				
7. Degree of Leverage, Financial Stability				
8. Ability to Compete on Prices				
9. Capital Investment, Capacity to Meet Demand				
10. Stability of Costs				
11. Ability to Sustain Effort in Cyclic Demand				
12. Other				

Fig. 4-2 (*continued*)

1. The underpinnings upon which the firm depends for its continued existence.
2. The forces that can destroy the basic underpinnings.
3. The factors that pose a threat and the level of their impact.
4. The seriousness of any gap that may exist in each factor.
5. The company's overall ability to compete effectively in its chosen industry.
6. The vulnerability analysis based on the information obtained.[3]

Company capability charts should be filled out individually by a variety of people, so that results can be compared before the information is tabulated. The fact that

Technical

	Weakness	Normal	Strength	
1. Technical Skills				
2. Quality Superintendents/ Project Managers				
3. Resource and Personnel Utilization				
4. Level of Technology Used in Construction				
5. Scheduling Ability				
6. Value Added to Service				
7. Availability of Labor				
8. Intensity of Labor in the Service				
9. Economies of Scale				
10. Newness of Equipment				
11. Application of Computer Technology				
12. Level of Coordination and Integration				
13. Other: Design/Build Capability or Other Preconstruction Services				
14. Government Regulation and Restraints				

Analysis: _____
_____
_____
_____

Fig. 4-2 (*continued*)

the ratings obtained from the profile are highly subjective may be one of the chart's greatest strengths. Valuable insights can be provided by asking personnel at many levels of the organization to chart and rate the company and its performance. This allows management to see whether employees understand company objectives, and it reassures employees that management realizes their opinions are worthwhile. Most important, it gives managers valuable information about whether or not their own opinions (particularly those about the quality of management) are accurate.

UNDERSTANDING THE OUTSIDE ENVIRONMENT

In developing an effective strategy for understanding a company's outside environment, a primary task is to find a niche in that environment.

> A niche is a social and economic situation for which the organization is well suited. An effective niche is one that positions the organization in such a way that it can take advantage of the opportunities that present themselves and avert threats from the environment.[4]

Assessing the company's environment, or environmental scanning (Figure 4-3), is the first step in determining and analyzing threats and opportunities. Management should try to identify those events and trends that currently have an impact on the organization and also those that may affect the company's performance in the future.
Environmental factors fall into seven major categories:.

- Economic factors
- Political factors
- Social factors
- Technological factors
- Competitive factors
- Geographical factors
- Natural resources

In addition to events and trends, management must also examine the demands made upon the company by persons or groups who can affect the company's future or who depend upon the company for achievement of their goals. These include employees, owners, and managers; groups of individuals, such as public interest groups; departments of local, state, and federal government; and entire organizations such as creditors, suppliers, competitors, and, most important, potential buyers. The determination of their various needs and preferences (particularly the preferences of potential buyers of construction services) will be discussed in other chapters. An environmental scan should at least consider external influences in a general way.
Experience shows that the environmental assessment process is often best accomplished in group sessions. According to Neubauer and Solomon, such brainstorming should be done with the following objectives:

Case _____

Name _____

Economic Factors
(Eg. Business Cycle, Inflationary Trends, Consumption, Employment, Investment, Monetary and Fiscal Policies)

_____

_____

_____

_____

_____

Political Factors
(Eg. Political Power, Different Ideologies, Interest Groups, Social Stability, Legislation, and Regulation)

_____

_____

_____

_____

_____

Social Factors
(Eg. Age Distribution, Geographic Distribution, Income Distribution, Mobility, Education, Family Values, Work and Business Attitudes)

_____

_____

_____

_____

_____

FIG. 4-3 Environmental scanning. *(From Alan J. Rowe, Richard O. Mason, and Karl E. Dickel, Strategic Management and Business Policy: A Methodological Approach, Addison-Wesley Publishing Co., Reading, Mass., 1982, pp. 58–59.)*

Technological Factors
(Eg. Rate of Technological Change, Future Raw Material Availability, Raw Material Cost, Technological
Developments in Related Areas)

_____

_____

_____

_____

_____

Competitive Factors
(Eg. Entry and Exit of Major Competitors, Major Strategic Changes by Competitors, Competition Size,
Number, Capacity, Location, Methods, Production/Market Segments)

_____

_____

_____

_____

_____

Geographic Factors
(Eg. Branch Location, Relocation of Facilities, Headquarters, Foreign Markets)

_____

_____

_____

_____

_____

FIG. 4-3   (*continued*)

- To develop a structured way of thinking about the identification and analysis of *relevant* trends and constituent expectations in the external corporate environment.

- To stress the importance of systematic assessment of the impact of environmental change on (1) the "business we are in" (mission) as well as (2) the "action programs we have chosen to fulfill the mission" (strategies).

- To provide a forum for sharing and debating divergent views on relevant environmental changes.
- To increase the drive for identification of potential opportunities for new strategic options that could be exploited, not just recognition of threats.
- To help translate vague opinions into more explicit perceptions.[5]

THE WOTS-UP ANALYSIS

In developing strategies, a key task "is to *find the best match* between the organization's distinctive competences and its available niches."[6] A good first step in the analysis of potential is the WOTS-UP analysis. WOTS-UP is an acronym for weaknesses, opportunities, threats, and strengths. By charting the relationship between external and internal conditions, this analysis helps management to determine whether or not the organization is able to deal with the opportunities and threats in its environment. A WOTS-UP analysis should be conducted in the following way:

1. Collect a set of key facts about the organization and its environment. This data base will include facts about the organization's markets, competition, financial resources, facilities, employees, inventories, marketing and sales system, equipment, management, environmental setting (e.g., technological, political, social, and economic trends), history, and reputation.

2. Evaluate each fact to determine whether it constitutes an opportunity, threat, strength, or weakness for the organization. Record your evaluation in the proper column in the WOTS-UP form.[7]

The form (Figure 4-4) should first be filled in individually and the results compared and discussed by the management group. One reason for this is that certain facts may give rise to more than one evaluation. For example, the move toward multiple prime contracts on large construction projects might be construed as both a threat and an opportunity. An effective strategy must account for both possibilities.

The most important part of the assessment process can also be the most difficult: determining how it all fits together. A company is, after all, not merely its component parts. The way the different components interact, and the way they balance (or do not balance), make a company and its problems unique (Figure 4-5).

Remember that a company is not static. It is at all times in a temporary state of equilibrium between the internal and the external forces that operate upon it. Changes in the outside environment, in the economy, in interest rates, and in construction buying preferences all have a profound effect on companies. Managers must not only administer the internal affairs of their companies; they must also integrate into the overall functioning of the organization the demands imposed by external

Case _____

Name _____

Opportunities

_____

_____

_____

_____

_____

_____

_____

_____

_____

_____

Threats

_____

_____

_____

_____

_____

_____

_____

_____

_____

_____

Strengths

_____

_____

_____

_____

_____

_____

_____

_____

_____

_____

Weaknesses

_____

_____

_____

_____

_____

_____

_____

_____

_____

_____

(Check If Critical)

FIG. 4-4 WOTS-UP analysis. *(From Alan J. Rowe, Richard O. Mason, and Karl E. Dickel, Strategic Management and Business Policy: A Methodological Approach, Addison-Wesley Publishing Co., Reading, Mass., 1982, p. 23.)*

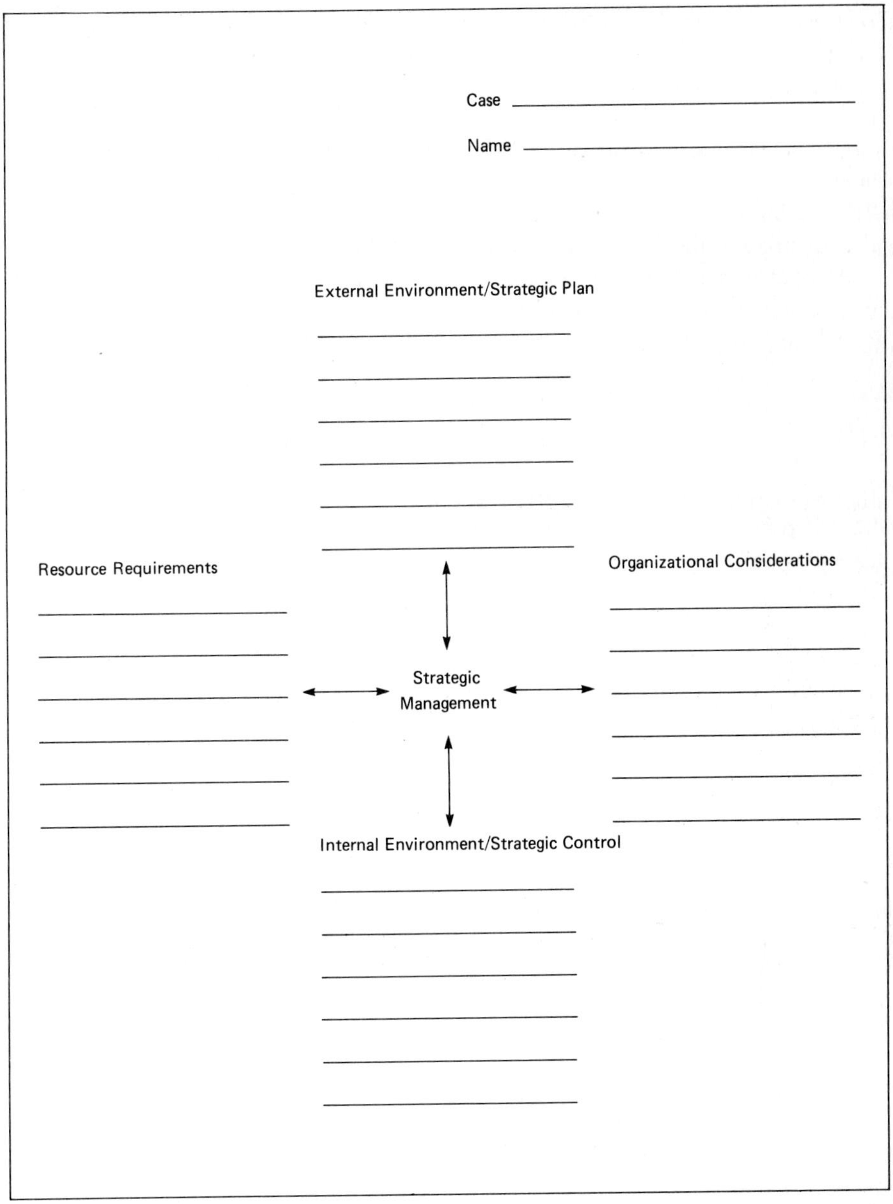

Case _____

Name _____

External Environment/Strategic Plan

_____

_____

_____

_____

_____

_____

Resource Requirements

_____

_____

_____

_____

_____

_____

Organizational Considerations

_____

_____

_____

_____

_____

Strategic
Management

Internal Environment/Strategic Control

_____

_____

_____

_____

_____

_____

FIG. 4-5 Strategic four-factor analysis. *(From Alan J. Rowe, Richard O. Mason, and Karl E. Dickel, Strategic Management and Business Policy: A Methodological Approach, Addision-Wesley Publishing Co., Reading, Mass., 1982, p. 18.)*

forces over which they have far less control. Both internal and external factors must be considered in the allocation of resources to meet company goals.

Strategic planning uses information from both internal and external environments to develop goals and the necessary strategies for their accomplishment. Resource allocation and organizational structure are the means for implementing strategies. Strategic control focuses on the internal requirement for meeting objectives by measuring performance and determining which organizational structure will use what resources to meet external (market) demands.

After analyzing the company's internal strengths and weaknesses, and the external environment and its attendant threats and opportunities, management will have the tools required to develop a strategy for future growth and profitability.

NOTES

[1]Alan J. Rowe, Richard O. Mason, and Karl E. Dickel, *Strategic Management and Business Policy: A Methodological Approach*, Addison-Wesley Publishing Co., Reading, MA, 1982, p. 19.

[2]Ibid., pp. 19, 22.

[3]Ibid., p. 19.

[4]Ibid.

[5]Friedrich Neubauer and Norman B. Solomon, "A Managerial Approach to Environmental Assessment," *Long-Range Planning*, April 1977.

[6]Rowe et al., op. cit., p. 19.

[7]Ibid., p. 22.

5

Strategic Growth Alternatives

A thorough analysis of internal and external factors, as detailed in Chapter 4, provides management with an indication of potential areas of growth that match organizational capabilities with market conditions. Management is then able to examine the alternatives for accomplishing the company's objectives.

Strategic growth alternatives can be broken down into three categories (Table 5-1):

- *Concentration or Intensive Growth.* Opportunities available to the company within its current operations. Usually a particular project type is involved.
- *Integrated Growth.* Opportunities available through integration with current activities of the company. Integration is achieved when a company stretches its capacities by moving backward, forward, horizontally, or vertically within the operating areas surrounding its current capabilities.
- *Diversification.* Adding new services or entering new fields.

The following description of the M. M. Sundt Construction Co. illustrates many of these growth strategies.

CASE HISTORY: GROWTH BASED ON DIVERSIFICATION

M. M. Sundt Construction Co. of Tucson grew dramatically from a $15 million a year local construction company in the mid-1960s to a regional and international concern with a volume of over $280 million by 1980, through a strong planning, marketing, and diversification effort.

TABLE 5-1 Growth Opportunity Areas°

Concentration or intensive growth	Integrated growth	Diversification
Market penetration	Horizontal integration	Concentric diversification
Market development	Vertical integration	Horizontal diversification
New service development	Backward integration	Conglomerate diversification
	Forward integration	

°Adapted from Philip Kotler, *Marketing Management: Analysis, Planning, and Control*, 4th ed., Prentice-Hall, Inc., Englewood Cliffs, N.J., 1980, p. 73.

When Sundt made a commitment to growth in the mid-1960s, it was performing both heavy and building construction in Arizona, primarily in the Tucson area. To diversify its project-type mix, the company began bidding for Defense Department contracts on Minuteman missile silos and space-related construction projects.

As the Phoenix market grew, the company established a major branch office there to compete for office buildings, hospitals, hotels, and other commercial, light industrial, and institutional work. Much of the company's construction management work developed in that office and is offered to clients in the area.

When the U.S. Housing and Urban Development Department's Operation Breakthrough Program promised to industrialize the housing field, Sundt developed a fiberglass panel system. The venture was not successful and the company lost money. But out of the experience emerged a fiberglass manufacturing plant in Sundt's yard that produces tanks and vessels for corrosive materials at power plants, petrochemical plants, and industrial facilities, to which the company was also offering construction services.

In the early 1970s, a long-time joint-venture partner, a pipeline contractor in northern California, was acquired by Sundt.

The outflow from the Middle East of petrodollars to finance major capital development programs caught Sundt's attention. Arizona and Saudi Arabia have one thing in common: both are desert lands, and since Sundt knows how to build in the desert, top management reasoned, why not give Saudi Arabia a try? An effort there landed a contract with ARAMCO to build 1400 units of housing, several school buildings, a wastewater treatment plant, and a number of other community facilities such as medical clinics.

In the western United States, concrete slipforming core construction methods began to be used more and more. Sundt perfected the technique and before long became a leader in that specialty.

Aggregate and ready-mix concrete plants in New Mexico were acquired by the Sundt organization in the late 1960s. The company's project types include mining facilities, power plants, flood control projects, wastewater treatment plants, high-rise office towers, hospitals, highways, government buildings, university buildings, and an array of special projects, from the building of an observatory to the reconstruction of the London Bridge.

STRATEGIC GROWTH ALTERNATIVES

Concentration. When a construction company generates more—more projects, more revenue, more profits—with its own people and resources, or with additions to its own organization, its growth is intensive or concentrated.

Some advantages of concentration are:

- Utilization of distinctive competences
- Increased efficiency from specialization
- Establishment of image and reputation

Many companies have been able to accomplish this as long as their markets continued to grow. Either instinctively or by design, they took one of the following courses of action.

Market penetration is seeking to provide increased services to current markets by stimulating major clients to provide more work. One Midwest contractor maintains an aggressive client relations effort with northern Indiana steel mills to obtain a steady and growing share of the steel producers' construction work. Sundt's renewed community facilities contracts with ARAMCO also represent market penetration.

New-market development is achieving increased sales by taking current services and project experience into new markets.

A contractor can open additional geographic markets through regional, national, and international expansion. Sundt's entry into the Nevada, California, and Colorado markets represented new-market development through regional expansion. The contracts it sought and obtained in Saudi Arabia are an example of how Sundt expanded internationally by exporting its desert construction expertise.

Sundt's entry into the Phoenix market, only 100 miles from its headquarters in Tucson, also represents geographic expansion. While relatively close geographically, Phoenix might as well have been two states away. The city had its own owners, design firms, subcontractors, suppliers, and other sources in the construction community. For Sundt, penetration of the local Phoenix market was as difficult as any major geographic expansion.

Sundt established itself in Phoenix by opening an office, by launching an active sales and marketing campaign, and by winning projects of the type the company had experience with. Sundt's first project in Phoenix was a major hospital. Using its own people and resources to construct projects it knew how to build, it became more widely known in a nearby area. Sundt began to achieve growth through market development.

To achieve new-market development, a company is not necessarily required to change or expand geographically. Becoming more widely known to owners and design firms in a company's primary geographic area, for project types the company has built, is another means of generating concentrated growth through market development.

The disadvantage of concentrating on a certain type of project as a growth technique is that every type of construction goes through cycles. A company that relies solely on concentration will have problems when the business cycle of its type of project turns down.

Internal growth through market development and geographic expansion can be achieved through existing clients. An example of this is R. E. Dailey & Co. of Detroit, which broadened geographically through repeat assignments in many states for a long-term client, a Detroit-based major retailing corporation. Since Dailey performed well on massive regional warehouse and distribution centers, the client gave Dailey the opportunity to build similar facilities in states as distant as Georgia and California.

Another example is the Gilbane Bldg. Co., based in Rhode Island. A major national beer brewer provided this contractor with significant opportunities for new-market development through geographic expansion. Gilbane performed well on a large brewery in western New York, and the client negotiated with Gilbane for five more regional installations in North Carolina, California, and other states.

New-service (or new-product) development consists of developing new or improved services (or products) for the current market. These new services might include construction management, design/build, preconstruction, project feasibility, or plant maintenance.

In the early 1970s, Sundt set up an organization to pursue construction management work, primarily in the Phoenix market. Due to the broad diversity of Sundt's markets and management desires, construction management (CM) represents only a small percentage of the company's overall volume.

About the same time similar decisions were made by other construction companies, such as Gilbane, which changed totally the type of work it performed so that upward of 80 percent was performed on a CM basis or through some type of cost-plus-negotiated-fee arrangement. A case history on the Barton-Malow Company presented later in this chapter describes how a company grew dramatically through a strategy based on delivering CM services.

As a key marketing strategy, Rauenhorst Corporation (now Opus Corporation) of Minneapolis adopted design/build as its only service offered to corporate owners and developers. The company more than quintupled its volume in five years. Making projects viable by developing creative financial solutions, or by helping to arrange financing, can provide a construction company with additional work and growth in its own area.

A union contractor may also want to consider expanding market opportunities by going "double breasted": purchasing or establishing a separate open-shop company. Other options include converting the present firm to open shop or operating open shop outside the firm's labor agreements area. In one New England city, a union contractor in business for more than thirty years started up a separate open-shop firm, and within three years the $15 million annual revenues of the new company were more than two-thirds that of the original firm. In running and marketing double-breasted construction operations, however, a firm must meet certain "separateness" standards to avoid problems under the National Labor Relations Act. For detailed information about this, see AGC's "A Practical Guide to Open-Shop Construction."

A company can develop a service to handle small construction projects. These smaller projects can be managed by a separate team or division. Turner Construction Company, for example, has divisions within its branch offices to manage jobs under $12 million or so. E & F Construction, an $80-million contractor in Connecticut, has a division to manage small industrial construction projects from $50,000 to $2 million.

Another way for a company to grow is to develop related services, such as contract maintenance. A number of contractors located near industrial plants have developed a capability to service those plants on an on-call basis. Contracts can range from several thousand dollars to $1 million or more. In some instances, the owner will sign a contract for ongoing maintenance.

Integrated Growth.   There are several ways of achieving integrated growth.

Horizontal integration takes place when a contractor purchases or gains control over one or more of its competitors. This can be a short-cut route to obtaining new management talent and to acquiring an additional client base. Its advantages include:

- Possible improvement in cost control
- Improvement in economies of scale
- Possible synergy from combinations of markets or technologies

Sundt used this method when it acquired its long-time joint-venture partner in California.

Of course, there are no guarantees that the new management talent will choose to stay with the company. And in some industries horizontal integration is prevented by antitrust legislation, but that is not likely to be a problem in the construction industry.

Vertical integration involves controlling the firm's suppliers or its channels of distribution.

Backward integration consists of purchasing supply systems. Highway and paving contractors who purchase asphalt plants are using backward integration.

Sundt, for a time, owned and operated a contractor supply company that provided it with competitive advantages on price and delivery as well as an additional source of profits. The advantages are that the contractor shares in the supplier's growth or profits, and uncertainty over availability or cost of future supplies is reduced.

Forward integration in general industry means that a company gains ownership of or greater control over its distribution systems, these being intermediaries between the company and its customers. In construction, the distribution systems for contractors could be considered design firms, and forward integration would mean purchasing an existing A/E firm or starting a design department.

The success of integration depends on the degree of the acquisition's compatibility with the overall company strategy. There is increased risk with forward integration because it extends the firm's scope of operations and requires management to develop new types of expertise. It does empower the contractor to work on the same type of project in a more complete way, however. Contractors must develop good defensive strategies to compensate for fluctuations in the business cycle.

Diversification.   If an analysis of the opportunities from growth and profits within a construction company's markets does not show much potential, then diversification should be considered. The company should identify areas where it can apply its strengths or help itself to overcome a problem. Three types of diversification are concentric diversification, horizontal diversification, and conglomerate diversification.

Concentric or related-services diversification adds new services or new fields that have technical or marketing synergies with the company's existing services. New services would be purchased by new types of clients. Harbert Corporation, Birmingham, Alabama, like many contractors with heavy earth-moving equipment, purchased or leased coal mines, representing a related-services diversification step for the company. Its equipment and management know-how was applied to serving a new type of customer, the coal purchaser, whether it was a distributor, utility, steel company, or exporter.

Horizontal or unrelated-services diversification adds new services or products that appeal to current customers even though these services or products are unrelated technologically to firm's current ones. Sundt's fiberglass manufacturing operation, which supplies vessels to mining corporations, some of which are Sundt's clients, is an example of unrelated-services diversification.

A construction company's purchase of a specialized or engineering firm would likewise represent unrelated-services diversification. Several large construction companies have diversified horizontally. Similarly, a construction company that builds hospitals could distribute hospital equipment—anything from furniture to mechanical systems to high-technology items. Major oil companies, for example, sell electronic and gift items through the mail to existing charge customers by enclosing promotional flyers with the monthly bill.

Conglomerate diversification occurs when a construction company adds new services or products that are unrelated to its current ones. The motivating factor for this type of diversification is to offset a deficiency or to seek an opportunity. Because of seasonality or the cyclical nature of certain markets, such as some publicly funded ones, a construction company can purchase a manufacturing company in another industry. One heavy contractor in the Southeast owns pipelines that supply natural gas to industrial and utility companies. Waste disposal is another diversification step that some construction companies have taken. One midwestern building and heavy contractor owns a nationwide manufacturing company that produces ties for concrete forms. Blount diversified from its construction business years ago. Today, through purchase of existing companies, Blount is also in the agricultural and steel businesses.

Bechtel Group, Inc., with $8 billion plus in annual revenues worldwide, has a strategy of separating its people-intensive engineering and construction operations from its investments in office buildings, oil and gas, real estate, and venture capital investments.

As a diversification strategy, Bechtel invests in oil services and drilling companies, oil and gas leases, and real estate. Bechtel also purchased an interest in an old-line Wall Street firm to play a role in helping to finance massive engineering and construction projects.

Bechtel's strategy is to invest in businesses that (1) do not go too far afield from its basic operations, (2) do not require it to provide management, and (3) do not distract company management from engineering and construction.

Steve White, president of Bechtel Investments, states, "While our business remains focused on engineering and construction, these investments are intended to diversify Bechtel's assets away from the engineering and construction business as a hedge against erosion of capital by inflation."

The advantages of such diversification are:

- Utilization of cash resources

- Spread of risk among several project types

- Improvement in profitability through movement into higher-growth areas

The major disadvantage of diversification is the danger that financial and human resources will be spread too thin.

Another method of gaining proficiency or increasing assets is the joint venture, a consortium agreement between two or more entities. A joint venture makes possible:

- Large-scale projects whose scope and financial requirements are beyond those of a single company

- Complementary benefits, as when company A is strong financially and company B is strong technically

- Foreign ventures

Sundt's first project in Saudi Arabia, one of many that followed, was a joint venture.

CASE HISTORY: GROWTH BASED ON CM STRATEGY

During the seven-year period from 1974 through 1981, the volume of work put in place by Barton-Malow increased nearly tenfold from $73 million to more than $700 million. Following is a summary of that success story.

History.   The company was founded in 1924 by Carl Barton. Arnold Malow joined in 1927. For a number of years the company was engaged in negotiated construction work for industrial companies in the Detroit area, primarily automobile and steel manufacturing concerns. At one steel mill the company had nearly 2000 people employed on a continuing basis.

During World War II, Barton-Malow provided construction services for plants converting from the manufacture of civilian goods to the making of material for the war effort.

By 1950 the company's volume was about $7 million, with a third coming from its industrial work. One of the company's first institutional projects came in 1952, when it was low bidder on a hospital project worth $5 million. During the 1950s the company expanded and became involved with the installation of electric plating equipment for chrome plating. Barton-Malow worked on a turnkey basis in a number of states east of the Mississippi River installing the plating equipment. This type of equipment was used mainly in the automobile and appliance industries.

By the mid-1950s the company's primary source of business, its supply of labor for a major steel mill, dwindled to zero as unions claimed more of the work for in-plant personnel. Barton-Malow then faced a loss of a major portion of its volume. The company began to diversify by bidding on hospitals, schools, and other types of projects in southeastern Michigan. In 1959 the company was the successful bidder on a $9-million research center for Parke-Davis in Ann Arbor, Michigan. The architect was Skidmore, Owings & Merrill, a major national architectural firm. The project opened doors for the company and began to change management's thinking about the company's capabilities in new project types.

Marketing. Barton-Malow's sales and marketing efforts in the 1950s and 1960s were much like the efforts of many other general contractors working in the private sector. People within the company stayed in contact with architects, engineers, and clients on a social and business basis, even though the company had no formal sales and marketing program. In the early 1970s, a company vice president, Rolland Wilkening, was selected as a member of an AGC committee to review GSA documents relating to a new service called construction management (CM). Construction management was a new delivery system for construction projects in which the general contractor or construction manager worked for the owner on a professional-fee basis, reviewing design to ensure that budgets and schedules were met.

Wilkening saw construction management as something for Barton-Malow to look into. With the rapidly escalating construction costs of the late 1960s and the early 1970s, nearly every construction project was running well over budget. Cost escalations of 1 percent a month were common. As Wilkening noted, "It was easy to get the ear of someone faced with a new construction project in 1972." Barton-Malow developed a slide presentation on the construction management concept (Figures 5-1, 5-2, and 5-3).

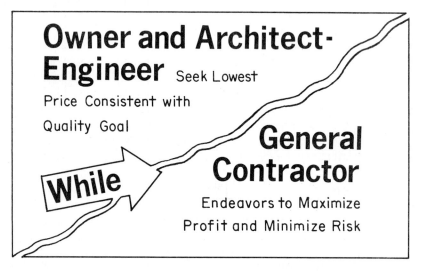

FIG. 5-1 Traditional building team relationship. *(From Barton-Malow CM slide presentation.)*

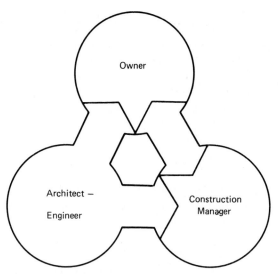

FIG. 5-2 Building team relationship under CM concept. *(From Barton-Malow CM slide presentation.)*

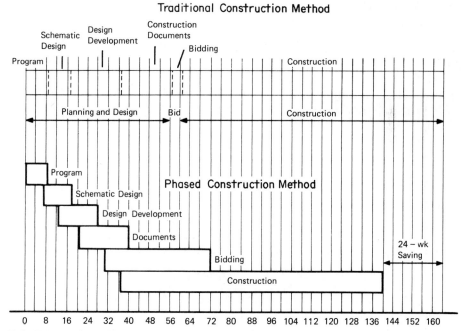

FIG. 5-3 Traditional versus phased construction methods. *(From Barton-Malow CM slide presentation.)*

Barton-Malow received invitations from hospitals, community colleges, schools, industrial companies, and developers to show the slide presentation and explain the new delivery system called construction management. Because of the attractiveness of the proposed method, which offered within-budget, on-schedule completion, Barton-Malow began to obtain numerous CM contracts. Many of these involved the building of public schools.

On one of the schools built under the CM concept, Barton-Malow developed a good working relationship with a local architectural firm. The school was a $12 million project that stayed within budget and met its occupancy date at a time when construction costs were escalating rapidly.

Single Project Launches Company to National Prominence. By coincidence, that same architect obtained a contract to design a multi-use stadium for the city of Pontiac. The project became known as the Pontiac Silverdome and was an 80,000-seat domed stadium enclosed with an air-inflated fabric roof. The architect asked Barton-Malow to present the construction management concept to the owner. Several other firms were also asked to present their qualifications as construction manager. After the interview process was completed, Barton-Malow was selected as construction manager in 1971. Due to litigation delays and the time involved for the preparation of the funding documents, ground was not broken until September 1973 for the $55.7-million project. The stadium was occupied in October 1975, about nine months ahead of schedule.

That a major, visible, public facility could be built within budget and within a shortened schedule was unusual at that time. The name Barton-Malow became widely known throughout the state of Michigan, the Midwest, and even nationally. The company received national publicity, and executives of the company were interviewed on radio and television and made presentations to numerous service clubs like Rotary and Kiwanis, and others. The company also took out a display ad at the Detroit Metro airport, which focused on Barton-Malow's achievement in building the Silverdome on time and within budget.

Barton-Malow had made a motion picture of the project showing its progress, problems, and construction details, and the points of view of company executives. The film became widely sought after. Barton-Malow made copies available for various universities for their engineering and construction management students. The film became a major sales tool on construction management and on Barton-Malow. The Pontiac Silverdome and its tide of publicity propelled Barton-Malow into the national scene, and the company began making presentations and winning projects in many states.

In the film, executives describe the construction activities, problems, and schedule and their meaning for Barton-Malow. The film even features a testimonial from the architect on the construction management method and on Barton-Malow. It ends with Ben Maibach, Jr., chairman of Barton-Malow, saying, "Our goal for every project: to finish it on time, within budget." The film gets its message across.

More Than a Sales Effort: A New Project. As Barton-Malow began to win more construction management contracts, the company began to see its future in this type of delivery system. As a major part of its role in the construction management process, the company found that it needed to work on a peer basis with architectural and engineering firms in order to gain their respect and review their designs intelligently. As a result, the company hired a number of architects and engineers to work in-house. By 1982, the company employed 60 design professionals who worked closely with their counterparts in the design firms of projects Barton-Malow worked on. This ensured effective control of budgets and schedules for the company's clients. As the company sold more construction management projects, it constantly improved the professionalism of the people it hired as well as its computerized cost and schedule control systems.

In the ten-year period from 1972 to 1982, the company reversed its mix of work from 90 percent lump-sum bid to 10 percent, with 90 percent of its work being fee-based construction management. Wilkening states, "We direct our presentation to show how we can control a budget, control time, control quality. We show how we've done it. We have 14 to 15 certified value engineers on staff. We review systems to maximize the facility for the least amount of money."

Keeping the Momentum Going with Marketing.   Wilkening believes that Barton-Malow is selling a completely different service than it did fifteen years ago: "All we're selling are services, and like any other service business, we have to go out and sell it." In 1978 Barton-Malow identified marketing as a separate function within the company, appointed a vice president of marketing, and within two years developed a separate department. A reorganization of the company followed, centered around project types or market types, with a group developed for each of them:

- Commercial/institutional projects
- Industrial projects
- Health care projects
- Special projects

A marketing plan for each group was developed. The company opened sales offices in Minnesota and Florida, areas where the company had already performed on CM projects. Each of the sales offices now has a business development person, and each of the project-type groups has a contract service manager who is responsible for sales. All the salespeople report to the vice president of marketing and planning. In addition to the salespeople, Barton-Malow has an in-house person to oversee public relations and augments that person with an outside public relations firm.

Beyond the day-to-day sales activities of its business development people, Barton-Malow personnel attend conferences and conventions to ensure further company exposure and to describe its CM approach. The company's marketing tools consist of a corporate brochure (made up of individual sheets aimed at various market segments), a company newsletter, reprints of various articles, the Silverdome film and other films, and case history flyers.

By 1982 the company had become one of the nation's largest construction managers and contractors. The overall strategy or strategies selected by management for its future were a result of the objective analyses described in Chapter 4 and of extensive internal management discussions.

No single strategy is perfect. Too many factors must be carefully weighed, not the least of which are the personal desires of current and soon-to-be management. Once a strategy has been worked out, it must still be tested in the marketplace, where its success is based on the understanding of the decision makers who purchase construction services.

6

How Owners Buy
Construction Services

Marketing is so basic that it cannot be considered a sepa-
rate function ... it is the whole business seen from the point of
view of its final result, that is, from the customer's point of
view.[1]

In developing new growth and marketing strategies, a company must discover
the most important factors in buying situations for current and prospective clients. It
is buyers, after all, who determine what will be successful in the marketplace.

> The marketing concept holds that the problem of all business firms is to
> develop client or customer loyalties and satisfaction, and that the key to doing this
> is to focus on their needs. Perhaps the short-run problem of firms is to persuade
> clients to buy existing services, but the long-run objective is clearly to create the
> services buyers need and to ensure that they are aware of them.[2]

When selling construction services, a firm must keep in mind that the buyer's
primary business is not construction. The construction buyer is making a purchase in
order to further some organizational objective: "(1) to make money, (2) to reduce
operating costs, [or] (3) to satisfy a social or legal obligation."[3] Companies that buy
construction services must adapt to a changing environment. As they do so, what they
require from contractors also changes.

THE IMPORTANCE OF THE PRICE FACTOR

Since the majority of construction has historically been bid work, contractors tend to be most prepared to talk about price. There is no question that price is still an extremely important factor in the selection of a contractor, but it is no longer necessarily the most important factor. The manufacturer of a high-technology item may consider a non-fixed-cost, fast-track approach that results in a production line's being on stream months early to be well worth the possible additional construction cost. A corporate office owner may be most interested in construction methods and materials that will result in lower operating costs and long-term savings.

One example of a company that has changed its construction buying policies to reflect changing needs is IBM. According to Arnold P. Richter, Director of Design and Construction, IBM has historically considered price as a primary criterion for contractor selection.[4] However, increasing competition and rapidly changing technology in the electronics field have necessitated changes in IBM's construction priorities. One major change is the need for more rapid development of production facilities, caused by the necessity of bringing new products to market faster. IBM is now willing to break ground on a construction project, after selecting a contractor on a fee basis, to begin fast-track construction, with the expectation of increased profits on the sale of a product. A larger share of the market can be captured if customers are reached sooner.

The emphasis on reduced schedules has caused a change in contracting strategies. During the early 1980s, IBM's contracting policy broadened from almost exclusively lump-sum contracts to also include design/build, phased, cost plus fixed fee, guaranteed maximum–share in the savings, prepurchase, or some combination of all these.

High-technology item programs have resulted in the need for special construction expertise to handle a variety of construction problems. IBM needs contractors familiar with special construction methods relating to clean rooms, interstitial space, chemical handling, waste treatment, D.I. water, process control, and automatic storage. Legislation, such as the Clean Air Act and the Clean Water Act, has necessitated construction of facilities capable of providing groundwater protection and the safe treatment of hazardous wastes. IBM is also interested in the construction of energy-efficient facilities and wants to deal with construction professionals who are knowledgeable about materials selection, energy management systems, fuel storage, stand-by generation, multifuel boilers, and the use of coal (Figure 6-1).

In the retail industry, business conditions are causing substantial reductions in new-store construction plans of such major retailers as J. C. Penney, Federated, Allied, and K mart. According to the September 1981 issue of *Executive Chain Store Age*, the pace of retail space construction slowed down in 1981 as tight money, poor market conditions, and fewer available shopping center sites put the clamps on chain store expansion. In 1981 retailers devoted about 6.9 percent less to capital expenditures. The article continued, "Where the leading chains spent more than $4.2 billion on new stores and remodeling campaigns in 1980, that figure is expected to slip $300 million to $3.9 billion by the end of 1982."[5]

To protect its market share, J. C. Penney is developing a new strategy calling for an extensive modernization program and a radical decrease in the construction of new facilities. From a high of 86 new stores constructed in 1976, Penney dropped to a low of 48 new stores in 1981. From 1982 through 1986, the number of new stores constructed by Penney will be one-half the number built in the previous six years: the gross square footage will be nearly two-thirds less. The company will spend the same amount of money as in previous years, or perhaps slightly more, but the money will be allocated to remodeling approximately 355 older stores.

According to F. J. Depkovich, vice president and director of store and facility planning for J. C. Penney, this change in focus may offer new opportunities to contractors willing to bid (all Penney's contracts are bid from a select-bidders list), to work on smaller portions of larger jobs, to travel beyond their normal operating radius, or to explore joint-venturing.

Small jobs will include partition and electrical work, ceiling modifications, floor covering, fixture installation, and painting. Most of this will be subcontracted locally. Larger jobs will be in the same trades but greater in scope and will also include HVAC, sprinkler systems, and occasionally the modification of exterior entrances.

Since regional construction managers are responsible for the development of bid lists at J. C. Penney, they were asked about the points they consider essential in making their decisions. Gordon L. Clawson, eastern regional construction manager for Penney in Pittsburgh, listed nine pertinent points:

1. History of performance for the J. C. Penney Company
2. History of successful performance in respective field of work, including on-time completions, cost within budget, and limited punch lists
3. Successful relationships and repeat business with subcontractors
4. History of on-time payments to suppliers and subcontractors
5. Adequate financial status to fund the project fully
6. Availability of experienced field personnel and adequate field organization
7. Availability of home-office backup
8. Knowledge and use of latest technologies of construction
9. Appropriate geographic area of operation

Clawson also stated that the company would analyze any specialty of the contractor. Mario A. Zambetti, Penney's southeastern regional construction manager in Atlanta, stressed four additional points. According to him, the contractor should:

1. Be sensitive to J. C. Penney Company needs.
2. Be able to stay on schedule.
3. Exercise sufficient quality control measures.
4. Be cost-conscious.

Date _____

Preliminary Information

    Present Firm Name _____

    Former Firm Name(s) _____

                           _____

    Address of Home Office _____

                           _____

                        Telephone _____

    Name(s) of Principal(s) _____   _____

                          _____   _____

Branch or Division Offices

Address	Person in Charge	Telephone

Type of Organization

    Individual _____   Established in Year of _____

    Partnership _____   Established in Year of _____

    Corporation _____   Established in Year of _____   in State of _____

FIG. 6-1 IBM "contractor" information form.

George Bridwell, regional construction manager for Penney in Chicago, indicated that the contractor should:

1. Have the reputation of using good subcontractors and for building a good-quality building.
2. Have a good record of solving problems, rather than creating problems that cause delays and excessive extra costs.

Type of Contractor

       General   _____

       Package Design-Build   _____

       Entrepreneur (Lease Back)   _____

       Pollution Control   _____

       Subcontractor in: _____

              Concrete/Masonry   _____

              HVAC   _____

              Structural Steel   _____

              Site and Foundation   _____

              Electrical   _____

              Other _____

Personnel Information

Key Personnel	Home Office	Branch Offices
Project Managers	_____	_____
Field Superintendents	_____	_____
Foremen: Labor	_____	_____
Concrete	_____	_____
Carpentry	_____	_____
Stru. Steel	_____	_____
Masonry	_____	_____
Plumbing	_____	_____
Heating	_____	_____
Electrical	_____	_____
Other	_____	_____
Designers	_____	_____
Engineers	_____	_____
Safety	_____	_____
Purchasing	_____	_____
Shop Drawings	_____	_____
Other	_____	_____

Total Key Personnel: _____

Total Number of Employees: _____

Project Information

    Geographical Area

    State specific states in which work has been done during the past 10 years:

    _____

    State specific foreign countries in which work has been done during the past 10 years:

    _____

FIG. 6-1 *(Continued)*

Project Information (cont'd)

Number and Size of Projects (completed during past (5) years):

Metropolitan Office Buildings _____
Range of Size in Approx. Sq Ft _____   to _____.

Suburban Office Buildings _____
Range of Size in Approx. Sq Ft _____   to _____.

Administration Buildings _____
Range of Size in Approx. Sq Ft _____   to _____.

Manufacturing Buildings _____
Range of Size in Approx. Sq Ft _____   to _____.

Engineering Laboratories _____
Range of Size in Approx. Sq Ft _____   to _____.

Research Laboratories _____
Range of Size in Approx. Sq Ft _____   to _____.

Warehouses _____
Range of Size in Approx. Sq Ft _____   to _____.

Work Distribution

List categorically work normally performed by own forces:

List categorically work normally subcontracted to others:

Annual Volume of Work (Averaged Over Last 3 Years):

Construction Value per Year: $ _____ .

Approximate Total Sq Footage Per Year _____ .

Size of Projects for Which Best Qualified:

Maximum $ _____ sq ft _____
Minimum $ _____ sq ft _____
Avg. or Normal $ _____ sq ft _____

Former Projects Done for IBM (Please Describe):

FIG. 6-1   (*Continued*)

3. Be flexible in regard to adapting building schedules to specific timing problems that may affect store installation.

From the Western Regional Office, Frank Zimmerman in Los Angeles had this final comment:

Please send as separate exhibits the following additional information:

A.   Organizational chart showing breakdown of officials and delegation of
     authority within the firm.

B.   A list of the major projects completed during the past 10 years.
     Include the following:
                 Name and Type of Project; Year of Construction
                 Geographical Location and Approximate Size in Sq Ft
                 Owner and Representative (Include name, title, address, and
                             phone number of Owner's representative
                             in charge of the work.)
                 Type of Contract (Lump Sum, Percentage of Cost, CPFF)
                             (General Construction, Design-Build, Subcontract)
                             (Competitive bid, Negotiated)
                 Name of Architect or Engineer
                 Final Construction Cost

C.   A list of the major projects currently being undertaken by the firm.
     Include all the same information as in (B) above.

D.   A list of any awards, citations or special recognition received.

E.   A copy of a current financial statement, bank references, and the latest
     Dun and Bradstreet Analytical Report.

F.   Your latest brochure showing representative projects recently completed.

Please return all information to: Manager
                                         Contracts Administration Department
                                         Real Estate and Construction Division
                                         International Business Machines Corporation
                                         540 White Plains Road
                                         Tarrytown, New York 10591

FIG. 6-1   *(Continued)*

Supervision must be of top quality in order to maintain a smooth-running job. Penney, therefore, tries to check on the performance of the superintendent.

Summing up these factors, Depkovich says:

Quality of job, quality of supervision, [and] integrity with Penney and the subcontractors comes through loud and clear. These regional managers want someone who understands their needs, who will work with them, who will stay flexible and exercise good management control. Companies that do this will be eligible for the J. C. Penney bidders list.[6]

All construction buyers seek high-quality personnel, a superior product, and corporate integrity. The construction buyer, however, cannot evaluate the quality of advice, efficiency of personnel, accuracy and efficiency of construction methods, or the reliability of promises until the job is well underway.

In a *Harvard Business Review* article, Warren J. Wittreich delineated what he believes to be the differences between product and service buying and marketing. He grouped these under three headings:

1. *Minimizing uncertainty.* A professional service must make a direct contribution to the *reduction of the uncertainties* involved in managing a business [and] . . . must take into account the impact of its performance on the client's business.

2. *Understanding problems.* A professional service must come directly to grips with a fundamental problem of the business purchasing that service. The successful performance of the service, far more so than the successful production of a product, depends on an understanding of the client's business.

3. *Buying the professional.* A professional service can only be purchased meaningfully from someone *who is capable of rendering the service.* Selling ability and personality by themselves are meaningless.[7]

These principles also apply to construction purchasers and contractors. A construction firm trying to sell its services must first sell itself.

Construction buyers of all types want contractors with experience on similar projects. Many believe that prior experience is the best indicator of probable future success. A company that does not have such experience may yet have certain employees with prior experience from other employment, and this can be emphasized by the contractor. Having built other projects for the same industry can also be a benefit; experience and an understanding of the concerns of people within certain types of industries are sometimes critical. For example, certain manufacturing industries would require that contractors be experienced in constructing toxic-waste facilities.

Even if a company has not performed on similar projects, under certain circumstances it may be helpful to have performed under similar working conditions. Sundt, as we have seen, was selected for work in Saudi Arabia partially by virtue of its emphasizing its experience working in the desert.

Like IBM, a construction buyer may require certain construction methods or familiarity with certain trades in order to solve the special problems of a project. Experience in high-technology mechanical work, heavy concrete or steel structures, unusual or high-precision tolerances, or special finishes may be called for. It is necessary for the contractor to demonstrate what makes his or her company technically best suited to do the work.

QUALITY OF PERSONNEL ASSIGNED
TO A PROJECT

Construction buyers want to know the personnel who will be assigned to the job. They want to work with competent people who understand the project and seem cooperative and easy to work with. Buyers also want to be assured that the personnel assigned to their project have enough clout within the contractor's organization to commit people and mobilize resources expeditiously.

Buyers are distrustful of absentee management. They want to know the project manager and the field superintendent. A survey of construction buyers was conducted by Tecton Media, Inc. for one of its clients, a large regional contractor. The purpose of the survey was to determine the specific selection criteria for construction managers. These included:

- Ability to manage a complex project better than the client
- Experience in CPM scheduling, packaging bids, and negotiating
- Ability to determine the most economical building and environmental systems and expertise in life-cycle cost analysis
- Evidence of a "team player" attitude (it should be noted, however, that some clients may want strong construction managers who can relieve them of the burden of making decisions about matters with which they do not feel they have suitable experience)
- Past record of running all crafts productively but not alienating subcontractors
- Capability to handle the heavy administrative functions and paperwork
- Past performance record and reputation

According to Richard L. Lang, senior vice president of Lockwood Greene, A/E firms want to evaluate a contractor's entire proposed project team: project executive, project manager, field superintendent, scheduler, and cost estimator.[8]

Owners want to know how construction firms plan to staff the job and whether suitable people will be available when they are needed. Edward Holland of Monsanto says, "We want to know your company's ability to perform in an open shop or union environment and what specific success you have had with project agreements—what crafts you hire on a direct basis."[9] Owners ask whether the contractor has a productivity program, what experience it has had increasing the productivity of operations, and how productivity was measured. They want to know about training programs and how well the contractor has used apprentices, helpers, and subjourneymen.

Maximizing minority participation may be an important corporate objective, since all businesses are under pressure to increase minority involvement. The client may favor a contractor who can ensure that there is minority involvement on the project among subcontractors and suppliers. Governmental agencies have quotas and require recordkeeping procedures to document minority involvement. Other construction buyers may require this as well.

Construction buyers are concerned about safety. Buyers wish to be assured that the contractor has a good safety program, not only because of governmental regulations, but also because accidents on projects cause so much bad publicity for the owner.

Most buyers prefer contractors who are familiar with the geographical area. Area familiarity will give the contractor the following advantages:

- Established contacts with code and other jurisdictional authorities
- Familiarity with local labor relationships and contracts
- Knowledge of local economic influences
- Established relationships with local contractors and suppliers
- Familiarity with local environmental requirements

For the smaller contractor, these relationships could be vital when attempting to form joint ventures with larger companies that are better qualified in other respects. Large contractors should be aware that it may be politically important to the owner to maximize local participation in the project in order to aid the company's assimilation into the community.

It is a mistake, however, to assume that the construction buyer always wants "local talent." The buyer may feel that it enhances his or her personal reputation or that of the company to bring in a noted expert. The buyer may wish to break up local groups by bringing in outside competition.[10] If several projects in different locations are in various stages of planning, the owner may be more interested in a contractor's mobility and ability to staff the job with local labor.

When making efforts to qualify bidders, both D. Burt Carmody of Union Carbide and James C. Haney of PPG Industries stress that owners need to know whether their projects are within the scope of the contractor's operation.[11] Is the company of sufficient size to be compatible with the project, or will it be seriously overextended? According to Carmody, Union Carbide has a policy that a contract should require no more than 25 percent of a contractor's capabilities. The company sometimes lets projects that exceed these requirements, but only if the project is so large that it would strain the abilities of even the largest contractor.

It is important for a contractor not to imply that the project is too small for its operation. Charles Thomsen tells this story:

> Once a vice president and I were interviewing for a project with a budget of about $300 million. We hit them with a case history for a $3 billion project and ten minutes of hyperbole about our experience with some of the world's largest construction management jobs.
>
> One of the men said, "With all of those big projects, are you interested in our little $300 million job?" They thought they had the biggest project around. We popped their balloon. They hired another firm. That popped ours.[12]

Prospective buyers want to know about the contractor's project control systems and in-house support services. Other buyers may require cost reports or some other important control document. There is some argument about the value of numerous sophisticated systems. On the other hand, it is important for contractors to realize that these features may be far more important to some clients than their actual utility on the project suggests. It could be important for a company to install sophisticated systems to establish its credibility as expert. Financial concerns often center around cost predictability and budget containment. Buyers may look for companies with a history of avoiding numerous extras and change orders.

Having gathered as much objective information as possible, the construction buyer will next look for outside opinions. One source will be references. A contractor, of course, does not have complete control over the quality and type of information that a reference will give to another prospective buyer, but references should be selected who can say the kind of things that the contractor's firm cannot say about itself. Some of the subjective areas a reference can discuss that might place the contractor in a favorable position are:

- Management's availability for discussions with the buyer company
- The company's history of satisfied repeat clients
- The firm's ability to cope with changes in scope during the course of construction
- The contractor's performance under pressure
- The firm's willingness to go beyond what the drawings call for
- Honest relationship with the owner—even when the contractor must relay bad news
- The contractor's completion of the job and expeditious resolution of the punch list

WHAT OWNERS CONSIDER MOST IMPORTANT

A survey of 95 of the largest CM firms and 220 public and private owners, conducted in mid-1980 by L. William Murray, concluded that "the most important asset to be marketed by the CM firm is the technical and operational expertise of the proposed project manager."[13]

The study points out the importance of the CM firm's proposal and its experience:

> The proposal permits the firm to discuss its expertise, its understanding of the client's problems, and its knowledge of CM processes. To the client, the proposal represents a 'product' which can be evaluated in an effort to determine the quality of services offered by the CM firm.[14]

The survey revealed many areas of disagreement between what clients want to see and the proposal actually submitted by the CM firm:

1. *Costs.* The cost of CM services is not as important to the client as the typical CM firm believes it to be. All other things being equal, the CM firm that

proposes the highest-quality services wins the bid. Even with substantial cost differences, CM quality outweighs cost considerations. In almost 90 percent of the responses to the survey there were specific client comments that even in competitively bid (CM fee) situations, superior CM quality was used to justify the contract award to other than the lowest bidder.

2. *CM Quality.* CM firms feel that the primary demonstration of the quality of their firm's CM services is the amount of experience they have in performing similar work. Clients, however, feel that it is the type and scope of the experience of the firm's personnel that is the primary determinant of the firm's CM quality. Clients scan the proposal for evidence of engineering innovativeness, technical expertise, and especially past-project–specific experiences of the proposed CM team members.

3. *Project Team.* Firms acknowledge that their proposed team is considered to be very important to the client. But they are afraid that the client may misunderstand their proposal. The firm offers its "best guess" that these team members will be assigned to this project if the bid is accepted, with the understanding that other work assignments may preclude this initial work assignment.

   Clients recognize the limitations of the firm's crystal ball: conflicting work assignments may prevent the firm from actually assigning the team to their projects. However, they insist that those key team members proposed actually be assigned.

4. *Flexibility.* In excess of 90 percent of the respondents' questionnaires indicated agreement on the fact that projects are seldom completed as initially planned. Unforeseen events, and a client's change of heart, occur regularly in construction. In evaluating the CM proposal the typical client searches for clues as to how changes will be addressed by the firm.

   Two types of information are critical to the client: (1) the specifications of alternative means, or alternative solutions, to the client's problems, and (2) a list of "special charges" that the firms will impose if and when changes are made. The CM client appears to be saying, "Give us a bid on your standard model, but include a description and price list for the options you suggest we may need." CM firms generally do not feel that the inclusion of either type of information in their proposals is necessary or desirable.[15]

With an understanding of what clients seek in the selection of a contractor, management can better select the right people for the marketing effort.

NOTES

[1]Peter F. Drucker, *Management: Tasks, Responsibilities, Practices,* Harper & Row, New York, 1974, p. 63.

[2]Aubrey Wilson, *The Marketing of Professional Services,* McGraw-Hill Book Company (UK) Limited, London, 1972, p. 24.

[3]Philip Kotler, *Marketing Management: Analysis, Planning, and Control*, 4th ed., Prentice-Hall, Inc., Englewood Cliffs, NJ, 1980, p. 176.

[4]Arnold P. Richter, "IBM's Needs in the 1980s." Speech given at the 1983 *ENR*/Tecton Media Construction Marketing for the Eighties Seminar.

[5]Quoted by F. J. Depkovich, "J. C. Penney's Approach to Contractor Evaluation and Selection," in speech given at the 1983 *ENR*/Tecton Media Construction Marketing for the Eighties Seminar.

[6]Ibid.

[7]Warren J. Wittreich, "How to Buy/Sell Professional Services," *Harvard Business Review*, March–April 1966, p. 128.

[8]Richard L. Lang, "How A/E Firms Evaluate Contractors and Construction Managers." Speech given at the 1983 *ENR*/Tecton Media Construction Marketing for the Eighties Seminar.

[9]Edward C. Holland, "Owners View Industrial Contractors," *Constructor*, May 1982, p. 33.

[10]Charles B. Thomsen, *CM: Developing, Marketing, & Delivering Construction Management Services*, McGraw-Hill Book Company, New York, 1982, p. 10.

[11]D. Burt Carmody and James C. Haney, "Owners View Industrial Contractors," *Constructor*, May 1982, pp. 30–31, 34.

[12]Thomsen, op. cit., pp. 18–19.

[13]L. William Murray, Ron Woywitka, Evelyn R. Gallardo, and Sunil Aggarwal, "Marketing Construction Management Services," *Journal of the Construction Division, Proceedings of the American Society of Civil Engineers*, December 1981, p. 669.

[14]Ibid., p. 665.

[15]Ibid., pp. 666–667.

7

Organizing and Staffing for Marketing

The approaches to business planning and marketing considered up to this point have focused on the total enterprise. We have looked at the company from the viewpoint of its overall financial performance, its inherent strengths and problems, the external environment, and various means to chart its future.

We now turn to the implementation and administrative aspects of marketing: putting the plans into action. Action requires people, and people require organization to be fully effective. Successful construction companies organize and control their marketing efforts in a well-planned and disciplined manner.

Of prime importance is that the contractor's marketing organization fit the company's overall organization in size, degree of formality, style, structure, and level of professionalism. A highly structured, formal marketing department in a small, informally managed construction company would be a fish out of water. The opposite situation would be equally unproductive. Whatever the type of organization, however, the responsibility for marketing must rest with a single person—the president, a vice president, a director of marketing, or a sales/marketing person.

Prior to defining the marketing function, management needs to determine the type of organization it will function in. In other words, what type of organization exists in the overall company? The right choice will spotlight the right issues, foster a congenial work atmosphere, place events in the proper perspective, and emphasize strengths.

The small company needs the right structure just as much as the big one does, but it will find it more difficult to achieve. Organization becomes critical when a small business grows into a medium-sized one and a simple business into a complicated one. The construction company that wants to grow has to think through and work out the organizational structure that will enable it to function best as a smaller business *and* to grow into a larger enterprise.

TYPES OF ORGANIZATION STRUCTURES

There are four basic types of organization structures: entrepreneurial, functional, divisional, and matrix.

Entrepreneurial.   There is typically a lack of formal organization chart or structure in an entrepreneurial company. If one were to be developed, however, it would be very simple (Figure 7-1).

The principal advantages of this type of organization are flexibility, innovation, responsiveness, initiative, and informality. Its principal disadvantages are critical dependence on the president, the need for employees to be flexible in assuming many responsibilities, and nonspecialization that can lead to inefficiency. The marketing function in this type of organization would consist of the president, at least part-time, and one secretarial or marketing coordinator/assistant, and/or one salesperson, each reporting to the president.

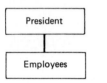

FIG. 7-1   Entrepreneurial organization.

Functional.   As a company grows, the organization often formalizes into a structure along functional lines (Figure 7-2). In this type of organization, there are centralized control of policies and procedures, managers with specialized knowledge, and functional areas staffed and managed effectively. The disadvantages are problems in coordinating functions, overspecialization, tight controls that stifle creativity, and an overload on the chief executive. In the functional organization, marketing is given equal stature with other important company areas and can be better organized to perform effectively.

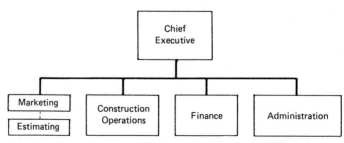

FIG. 7-2   Functional organization.

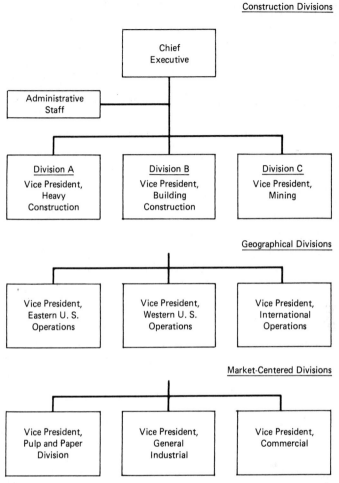

FIG. 7-3 Divisional organization.

Divisional.   The divisional organization structure is decentralized, with division managers related to a specific construction service area. There are at least three variations of this type of organization (Figure 7-3). The divisional organization has the advantages of decentralized authority and responsibility, and faster response to changing external and market conditions. Specific performance of a construction type or geographical area can be measured. The chief disadvantage of this type of organization is that divisions may become too independent and competitive, with the result duplication of effort and larger staffs.

Marketing can be centralized in the divisional organization to provide support services. Salespeople can operate out of the divisions to sell individual construction or geographic area capabilities, or out of the central marketing department to sell national accounts and the company's total capabilities.

As a construction organization grows into a major enterprise, it may have numer-

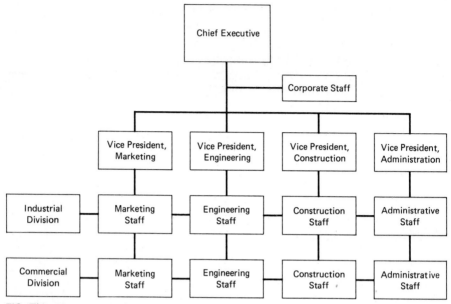

FIG. 7-4   Matrix organization.

ous divisions that can be arranged in logical groupings or strategic business units (SBU). Each SBU can be headed by a group vice president. In some of the largest construction organizations, an SBU can be a separate company headed by a president, as is the case with Bechtel Power Corporation.

Matrix.   A new organizational form that has evolved among major corporations in recent years is the matrix organization (Figure 7-4). In this structure there are major corporate functional areas that a division draws on as needed. The matrix organization allows for efficient use of personnel, but it can result in problems caused by dual command and multiple responsibilities. Staffs become resource pools for specialized construction or geographic divisions to draw on for personnel and services.

ORGANIZATIONAL LIFE CYCLES

As organizations grow and mature, they pass through changes in structure, roles, relationships, and interactions, often called the organizational life cycle. The four basic stages of growth are:

1. Entrepreneurial (initiation)
2. Bureaucratic or functional (specialization/standardization)
3. Divisional (market orientation)
4. Matrix (combination of service/geographic)

Organizations enter each successive stage when certain needs arise. As the organization grows, the founders may be burdened with unwanted management responsibilities, which leads to the need for skilled managers to introduce effective controls.

As the company's operations become more efficient and centralized, another need arises. Middle-level executives find themselves restricted by centralized authority and seek greater freedom in their decisions. Top management faces the choice of giving up some responsibility or losing talented middle managers.

In the third stage of the organizational life cycle, the divisional or decentralized structure, middle managers are given greater responsibility. In some cases, problems develop when top managers sense they are losing control over an operation that is becoming more diversified, and they attempt to regain control over the total company. The extended divisional organization, the SBU concept, allows for greater coordination of plans, money, technology, and personnel with the rest of the organization. It permits a high degree of centralized control, while retaining the advantages of decentralized decision making.

The fourth stage, the matrix structure, is characterized by participative management and adaptability to change. One organizational specialist believes that future organizations will need to be adaptive, rapidly changing temporary systems organized around problems to be solved by groups of relative strangers who represent a set of diverse professional skills.

From a management standpoint, it is important for the construction executive to be aware of the company's organizational stage, and how it might evolve and be improved upon. From a marketing standpoint, the introduction of a formal marketing effort in the company will be most successful if it is structured in a manner consistent with the overall organization.

SELECTING THE MARKETING ORGANIZATION'S STYLE

Just as company organizations vary from small and informal in the entrepreneurial phase to large, structured, and complex in the matrix phase, marketing organizations vary from the part-time executive or project manager to the fully staffed corporate department with scores of field salespeople. The small local contractor represents the former, and the major international design constructors, such as Fluor Corp., The Parsons Corp., Brown & Root, Inc.,and Daniel International Corp., the latter.

Of at least equal importance are the philosophy, climate, and style of the marketing organization. The combination of structure and style, and their interrelationships, determines the organization's functioning, staffing, and overall performance.

Organizational styles have contrasting elements:

- Formal versus informal
- Centralized versus decentralized
- Autocratic versus democratic

- Mechanistic versus organic
- Vertical versus horizontal
- Effective versus efficient
- Carrot versus club
- Specialist versus generalist
- Work-focused versus people-focused
- Individual versus group
- Calm versus conflict
- Climate versus system[1]

Following are guidelines for developing and maintaining a style of marketing organization:

- The style of marketing organization selected should be appropriate to the company, the marketplace, the industry, and the competitive arena.
- The style of the marketing organization needs to be in harmony with the management style of the overall business.
- The style should be compatible with the vision, character, and image of the business.
- The style must be consistent to avoid confusion and conflict.

DEFINING MARKETING SCOPE AND FUNCTION

In developing the marketing organization for the company, management must consider the scope of marketing and the functions to be performed. The scope, responsibility, and purpose of marketing in the construction company are:

1. To formulate and recommend to top management long- and short-range marketing plans for the business in terms of project types, geographic areas, clients, and services.
2. To formulate, execute, and measure sales and marketing programs to achieve these plans, and to integrate the performance of these activities with other functions of the business.

It is important to understand the difference between structure and function. Structure is the arrangement and assignment into organizational positions of work to be done. Function is the work to be done. In Figures 7-5 and 7-6 are examples of the organizational structures, including the marketing and sales functions of two construction companies.

The evolution of the marketing organization relates both to size of the construction company and to the level of marketing orientation. A large company may remain sales oriented, whereas a smaller contractor may have a greater degree of company-

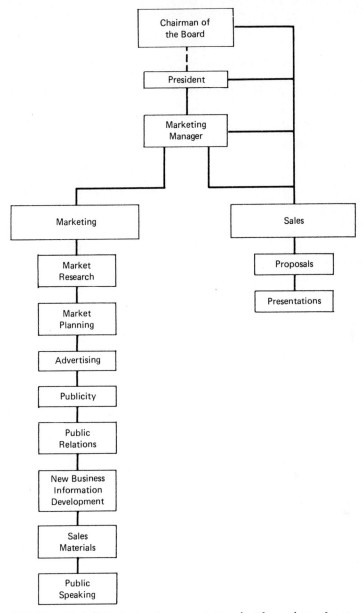

FIG. 7-5   Kitchell Contractors, Inc.: organization chart for marketing function.

wide customer orientation, which is the basis of modern marketing. Marketing evolves in the following five stages.[2]

Stage 1: Simple Sales Function.   All construction companies start with three simple functions. Someone raises and manages capital (finance), provides the service (con-

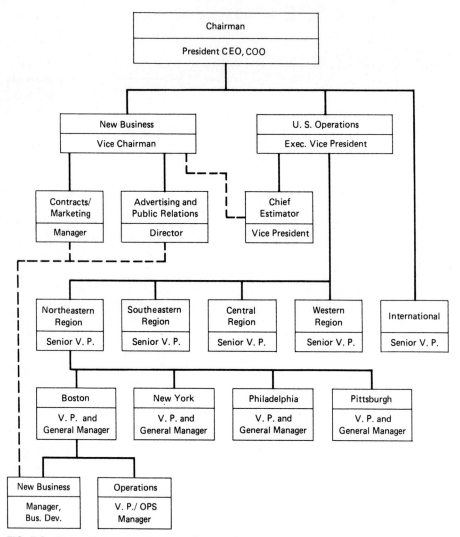

FIG. 7-6   Turner Construction Company: business development organization.

struction operations), and sells the service to customers (sales). For public-sector projects, sales consists of estimating and submitting bids. For private-sector projects, sales comprises the entire process from lead finding to customer contact and follow-up through contract award. The selling function is performed by the president or founder, a vice president, a salesperson, or a small sales force. Some basic marketing tools, such as brochures, are developed.

Stage 2: Simple Sales with Additional Functions.   As the company expands, it will require other marketing functions—market research, additional marketing tools, a public relations effort, systematic proposal preparation, and improved lead generating. The company may hire a marketing director to report to the president, vice president, or sales manager.

Stage 3: Separate Marketing Department. As the company continues to grow, these other marketing functions increase in importance relative to sales. The president or other top executive sees that sales can be facilitated by a separate marketing function with its own budget. The marketing department will be headed by a marketing director or vice president and will report, along with the sales vice president, to the president. At this stage, sales and marketing are viewed as separate and equal functions and are supposed to work together.

Stage 4: Modern Marketing Department. The modern marketing department differs from the above separate functions in that the marketing vice president is placed in charge of everything, including the sales force. This may occur by design as a marketing decision of top management, or it may be a decision forced on management because of an irreconcilable—and common—rivalry between the sales and marketing vice presidents. The sales vice president tends to be short-term oriented, seeking to maximize current sales. The marketing vice president tends to be long-term oriented, planning strategies and developing services to meet the needs of future markets and customers.

Stage 5: Modern Marketing Company. Being a modern marketing company means being a company with a widespread orientation to customers and internal support for marketing. This requires that all company departments work together to satisfy clients. Too often, the finance department is unsure of the return on marketing investment, and the areas of construction operations may be jealous of high salaries paid to sales and marketing people for efforts they don't fully regard as work (the only type of work being the management of physical construction). The solution requires a lengthy process of education, communication, and reporting of marketing successes and results, and the unwavering commitment of top management. Few construction—or other—companies have achieved the status of a modern marketing company.

STRUCTURING THE MARKETING EFFORT: SIMPLE TO COMPLEX

In the design of the appropriate marketing organization, the intent is to develop a structure that will implement defined marketing objectives and strategies. The process consists of five interrelated steps that are convenient and productive. Each succeeding step influences and modifies earlier ones. The five-step process for designing the marketing organization is:

1. Determining the work to be done.
2. Establishing the marketing structure.

Analysis Level   Date: _____

Companywide

_____

Branch Office (name)

_____

Division (name)

_____

Sales/Marketing Task	Time Required (Person – days)		
	Currently Performed	Needed, Projected	Total
1. Planning (Marketing)			
Overall Business			
Detailed Marketing Planning			
Strategies			
Target Markets			
Client Groups			
Tactics			
Market Research			

FIG. 7-7   Evaluation of marketing work to be done.

   3. Defining the individual positions.

   4. Reviewing and documenting the proposed organization.

   5. Communicating and implementing the organization plan.

DETERMINING THE WORK TO BE DONE

An inventory of current marketing work being performed and an estimate of anticipated work is needed. More than any other factor, the marketing tasks to be per-

	Currently Performed	Needed, Projected	Total
2. Lead Generating Cold Calling Follow-up to Rumors, Tips, Leads Qualifying Prospects Publications Review			
3. Selling Existing Accounts (Sales)			
4. Developing Relationships with Decision Makers (Sales) Owners, Corporate and Other Real Estate Brokers Architects, Engineers Business, Community, Government Leaders			
5. Developing Conceptual Estimates (Sales)			

FIG. 7-7   *(Continued)*

formed will determine the number, capabilities, experience, and characteristics of people who will be needed for the marketing effort.

Figure 7-7 presents the essential tasks that need to be performed in a well-rounded marketing program. This form is designed to present a realistic assessment of the number and type of personnel required to maintain an effective program to increase the contractor's business. It can be used in a variety of ways, and by a wide range of sizes and types of construction organizations.

First, it can be used as a time analysis for companies where some part-time sales

	Currently Performed	Needed, Projected	Total
6. Administration (Sales, Marketing)			
Internal Reporting System			
Meetings			
Internal Communications			
Files, Records, Etc.			
7. Community Participation (Sales, Marketing)			
Social			
Civic			
Professional			
8. Public Relations (Marketing)			
Developing Relationships with Editors (Local, Regional, National)			
Developing, Distributing Press Releases			
Ground Breaking			
Reprints			

FIG. 7-7   (*Continued*)

are being performed by the founder or other executives. Second, the form will allow a contractor with an existing marketing team to evaluate how the company's time is being spent, and what areas of activity are inadequately covered. Third, it can be useful to the larger construction organization in evaluating the marketing efforts of the company as a whole, as well as of its various components, such as branch office or division sales and marketing.

	Currently Performed	Needed, Projected	Total
9. Marketing Tools (Marketing)			
Brochures			
Newsletters			
Photographs			
Mailing Pieces			
Advertising			
10. Proposals, Presentations (Sales)			
Proposal Strategies, Development			
Presentation Strategies			
Presentation Rehearsals			
Presentation Performance			
11. Other Activities (Sales, Marketing)			
Trade Shows (Attendance or Participation)			
Exhibits			
Speaking Engagements			
Entertaining			
Working with Outside Public Relations, Advertising, or Market Consulting Firms			
12. Contract Negotiation and Closing (Sales)			

FIG. 7-7 (*Continued*)

The form presents tasks that are pure sales, pure marketing, and a combination of the two. It is important to understand the distinction, for several reasons. Position labels and titles are used in many different ways and have different meanings. Marketing titles are used to cover a broad range of activities and are not always well understood.

Often a contractor will want to hire a "marketing person," when in fact it is a salesperson that is needed. One medium-size construction company hired a "marketing person" and expected him to spend 75 percent of his time in direct sales to new accounts. The man's background was in behind-the-scenes marketing in an architectural/engineering firm, but he thought he could sell. The result was that he spent nearly 80 percent of his time in the office on marketing tasks. Management was unhappy, because they were expecting a sales-oriented person.

The problem started with the seemingly unimportant issue of the position title. The contractor called the position director of marketing, thinking it sounded better than director of sales or sales representative, but the new employee took the title literally. Other titles, such as director or vice president of business development, can be confusing also, unless the tasks to be performed are clearly defined and a person is hired who has the capabilities, experience, and desire to perform them. Figure 7-7 can help.

Several additional points should be kept in mind. One individual can deliver about 20 person-days in a single month. If a company's marketing tasks add up to more than that, then additional staff will be required. The skill and experience level of the new marketing staff depend on which tasks will be assigned to the primary sales or marketing individual. For example, if sales to new accounts will require 18 person-days per month, it is unrealistic to expect one person to fulfill that sales role and also be responsible for such office tasks as planning, administration, and public relations. However, a marketing coordinator or top-flight executive secretary could perform some of the office tasks.

The Start-Up Marketing Effort.   Generally, the start-up of a formal marketing program will apply to the smaller construction company or to the lump-sum, competitive bid, public-sector–oriented contractor seeking to diversify or expand. In the public-sector-only construction company, virtually no sales or marketing activities exist. The company may have had a brochure produced, but it is probably being utilized on a haphazard basis if at all.

Since organized sales and marketing will be new to those companies, they will want to proceed with caution. That will mean a limited budget, with room for one person with some possible clerical assistance. With the almost limitless amount of marketing work needed to be done in a company devoid of marketing but constrained by limited resources, a compromise must be reached (see "Budget," Chapter 13). Time could be listed as needed for nearly every item on Figure 7-7; however, the total person-days would indicate a need for two to three people. Therefore, management should focus on the most important tasks that can be achieved realistically by a single individual, with some clerical assistance and support in estimating from top management and others.

The most vital tasks are planning, lead generating and follow-up, proposals and presentations, and contract negotiation and closing (items 1, 2, 10, and 12 in Figure 7-7). A degree of planning should be accomplished by top management, with input from others in the company and possibly an outside consulting firm, prior to the assignment or hire of a sales-oriented person.

At this point we are concerned only about work to be done, not about who is going to do it. But it is limited work, to be done initially by a limited staff. A well-planned and well-organized sales effort, with face-to-face contacts and proper follow-up, is the first order of business.

The analysis of work to be done will point up needs for personnel to be either reassigned from within the company or brought in from outside. Effective marketing of construction services demands more of a companywide effort than one person can deliver. Time should be allotted for estimator, senior executive, and project manager involvement in the sales and marketing work to be done. In the smaller company, such tasks as contract negotiation and closing will still be the province of top management.

On-Going Sales/Marketing Effort.   As a construction company expands, it will need to expand its marketing activities. Greater demands will be made on a salesperson's time for proposals, presentations, and other follow-up work. Also, marketing tools will need to be prepared and a public relations effort facilitated (Figure 7-7, items 9, 10). All those activities will require time, and a shift in responsibility for certain marketing tasks may be necessitated.

Prequalifying of prospects, day-to-day contacts, and other sales work can be covered by others, which should free some top-executive time for such tasks as strategic, business, and market planning. Although top executives will continue to be involved in larger contract presentations and closings, the president and other top executives won't be able to relieve themselves of sales and marketing duties, except for planning, until the enterprise becomes a major construction company.

Figure 7-7 can be used to ensure that the time allotted for the sales or marketing function is being spent properly. For example, an analysis might show that only 25 percent of the company's effort is going into sales (items 2, 3, and 4). More than one form may be needed—one, a master, to show the total company requirement, and others to show individual assignments.

As a construction company grows and becomes more experienced in marketing, it will need to communicate with a widening array of architects, engineers, owners, and real estate brokers. Soon, the person in charge of the company's sales/marketing effort will be overloaded and will need assistance. Some help will be needed in the main office, but as new geographic areas are targeted, more salespeople will be sought. The form can be used for staffing decisions on branch offices as well.

In the growing company, there is the potential pitfall of adding salespeople to staff without proper marketing coordination and clerical support. Sales tasks must be balanced with marketing tasks. The two areas are interdependent. Strong salespeople want and need high-quality marketing tools, such as brochures, newsletters, and proposal and presentation formats, and the direction that only strategic planning and proper market research can provide. Since preparing these requires substantial time, people with more specialized talents will be needed.

In general, the smaller the company's sales or marketing staff, the more well-rounded or flexible the people hired will have to be. A construction company's first sales/marketing person should be a jack-of-all-trades, with an emphasis on sales ability. As the marketing department grows and specialists come on board, the business development effort will divide along sales and marketing lines.

Marketing in the Larger Construction Company. The larger construction contractor, one with several hundred million dollars in annual revenue, has a fairly complex corporate organization. In general, the company operates through divisions or groups, subsidiaries, branch offices, and numerous departments.

If the company is a heavy contractor primarily serving the public sector on lump-sum contracts, the company could be as lacking in sales and marketing experience as the smaller contractor. This type of company—exemplified by S. J. Groves & Sons Co., Peter Kiewit Sons Co., Guy F. Atkinson Company, and until the early 1970s Morrison-Knudsen Co., Inc.—could follow the work-to-be-done analysis of the smaller contractor at first, then accelerate rapidly in sales and marketing tasks and staff needs. For this type of company, several Figure 7-7 charts can be developed to cover headquarters and various branch offices and divisions.

For example, for sales, the company will need to call on large national and multinational corporation headquarters located in major cities. Branch-office salespeople could call on large manufacturing and process plants in their areas. Construction contractor prequalification, preparation of bid lists, and contractor decisions are made, depending on the client company, at headquarters or at the plant locations. The contractor's coverage of both requires a national accounts staff, operating out of the contractor's headquarters, and full- or part-time salespeople in branch offices, depending on the task analysis.

The large, mainly public-sector contractor requires planning, overall sales/marketing program management, marketing tool development, and other functions filled nearly from the outset. These tasks should be estimated for person-day requirements (Figure 7-7).

The large, mainly private-sector contractor building commercial and industrial structures, process and power plants, and other facilities will already have a sales and marketing team in place. Using Figure 7-7 forms for evaluation at various levels in the organization, from headquarters to subsidiaries and divisions, management in these companies can evaluate:

- Whether the number of people involved in sales and marketing is adequate for the tasks it wants performed.
- Which sales or marketing tasks are not being performed, or are not being performed adequately.
- Which divisions or branch offices are performing adequate sales and marketing tasks.

- Which markets will require special emphasis and what the staffing implications are.

The Role of Estimating.   Estimating is not a direct sales or marketing task, but it plays a pivotal role in the success or failure of the contractor's business development program. Sales and marketing in the private sector place demands on the company's estimating capability. Conceptual estimates, ballpark estimates, and free estimates are part of sales and marketing. To be considered for projects, the contractor must provide them to owners who request them.

Contractors with estimating departments will find it easier to meet the demands for estimated construction costs made by salespeople eager to satisfy potential clients. In companies where project managers do the estimating, problems may arise. These people are tyically overburdened and will not take kindly to new sales/marketing people seeking quick estimates. On the other hand, if the salespeople do not deliver the promised estimates to the waiting owner, they will quickly lose credibility and the company will miss valuable opportunities.

ESTABLISHING THE MARKETING STRUCTURE

Earlier in this chapter we reviewed the various forms of organization and their evolution. Since the sales/marketing function is an integral part of the construction company, it has to fit the organization it is serving. Organizational structures are basically a plan for determining who reports to whom and who works with whom.

The reason for designing an organizational format for marketing is to ensure that all marketing tasks, construction service areas, and markets are adequately covered. A good starting point is to review the key elements to be served by the marketing organization:

- Construction services to be sold: buildings, heavy, mechanical; CM, negotiated, design/build, lump sum; or specific capability such as concrete work or slipforming
- Markets to be served: commercial, industrial, health care, power, institutional
- Construction buying influences: owners, architects, engineers, real estate brokers, bankers
- Geography to be covered: local, home state, nearby cities or states, new regional locations, national, international
- Sales and marketing tasks, including work to be done with others in company, purchased externally, or other
- Support required from individuals or departments in company, such as estimating, construction operations, accounting (for cost reports, for example), and top management

The number and diversity of these elements, their interdependence, and the size of the overall company will determine the size of the marketing operation and its organizational form. As in any effective organization, there must be clear definitions of roles, responsibilities, and accountability. While there are almost limitless variations on and combinations of organizational structures, it is possible to narrow the choices to a couple of practical solutions.

Each marketing operation needs emphasis on different marketing tasks. To determine whether the preliminary marketing organization structure is appropriate, pose the following questions:

1. How well will the marketing organization provide for client service, market coverage, and competitive advantage?

2. Will the structure provide for achieving the contractor's corporate and marketing objectives and strategies?

3. Are all marketing tasks assigned for each market segment?

4. Is the marketing organization compatible with the company's organizational style?

5. Are planning and day-to-day marketing operations given proper emphasis and balance?

6. Are marketing functions and other organizational elements combined in a way that will facilitate—or at least not inhibit—work flow?

7. Are proper relationships established in reporting and between marketing and other construction company functions to foster teamwork?

8. Are supervision and control requirements met?

9. Can the structure be staffed and provisions made for performance evaluations, training, and development?

10. Will sales, advertising, public relations, proposal and presentation preparation, and other functions be well integrated?

11. Is the structure simple, clear, and unified so that it can operate effectively, efficiently, and economically?[3]

Applying these criteria to alternative marketing structures will lead to the selection of one that can be used to design individual positions.

Marketing Structure in the Smaller Construction Company. In the simplest form of organization, the president or founder performs numerous functions, including sales, and has a number of employees reporting to him or her. If the work-to-be-done analysis does not indicate a need for an expanded sales effort, then no additional staff or change in organization is required. That is not to say that the sales/marketing effort cannot be more organized. It can. However, no changes in *organization* are required. If the work-to-be-done analysis points to the need for additional staff, the person will most likely report directly to the president (Figure 7-8).

The more informal the organization, the less the likelihood that organization

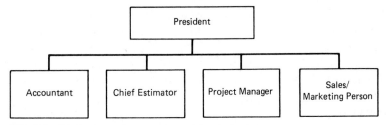

FIG. 7-8 Marketing in the entrepreneurial organization.

charts exist, so this, too, will be a new experience. It may seem impractical or useless to develop an organization chart for a small contractor, but it is an invaluable step in defining roles, relationships, and responsibilities. It is instructive to see on paper where the sales/marketing function fits within the company. It may have side benefits in airing and clearing up long-running misunderstandings in the organization. It may also reveal a chief executive stretched too thin with too many people reporting to him or her.

The smaller contractor who operates in a more formal manner with policies and procedures faces the question of where in the organization to place the sales/marketing function (Figure 7-9).

Marketing Structure in the Medium-Sized Construction Firm. As a construction company grows, its internal organization expands, and the markets it serves become multifaceted. Consequently, the marketing organization required to support the company's growing business developments will be more substantial and will demand greater attention to clearly defined roles and responsibilities with regard to sales, marketing support functions, geographical areas, construction services, and owner- or client-oriented markets.

As an example, Can-Do Construction Co. is a fictitious medium-sized contractor with a building division and an industrial division based in Chicago, with branch offices in Atlanta and Dallas. There are several ways that Can-Do can structure its marketing organization, depending on the number of marketing functions and people needed, the level of marketing experience (start-up or in-place), the diversity of markets and their requirements for specialized coverage, and the level of effectiveness needed to achieve corporate objectives.

The company can begin with a simple functional marketing organization (Figure 7-10). The main advantage of this functional marketing organization is its simplicity. Two specialists—one in sales and one in marketing support services (such as public relations and marketing-tool production)—can report to a vice president who has overall responsibility for business development. The marketing vice president would play a role in sales on larger accounts and at later stages in the selling process. He or she would report to the president and would have planning as his or her other main responsibility.

Geographical Organization. Can-Do Construction established one of its branch offices originally by bidding a public job, and the other by obtaining a contract to construct a plant for an existing client from its home area. To capitalize on the new

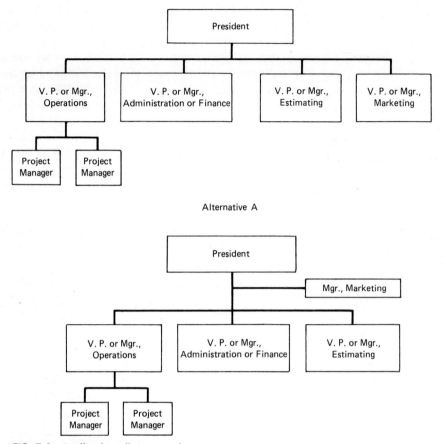

Alternative A

FIG. 7-9   Smaller, formally organized contractor.

locations, Can-Do wants to add local sales/marketing specialists to provide an expanding flow of projects for each office. The specialist in Atlanta would know everything there is to know about the Atlanta market and would prepare short- and long-range marketing plans for the Atlanta area, which could be incorporated into the company's overall marketing plan.

Can-Do's marketing organization would reflect this geographical emphasis and would be structured as shown in Figure 7-11.

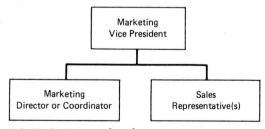

FIG. 7-10   Functional marketing organization.

FIG. 7-11   Geographical marketing organization.

Construction Services Organization. With further growth, Can-Do will require more specialization to fully cover markets served by the company's divisions. Salespeople will begin to specialize in either buildings or industrial, for example, and additional salespeople will be added to staff. As another layer of management is introduced, the sales/marketing manager's role is to be a focal point for developing the plans and strategies for each of the company's divisions. The sales/marketing manager will become involved in the sales process at later stages and will stay in contact with major accounts.

The advantages of the construction services marketing organization (Figure 7-12) are that each of the company's service divisions is well represented in the marketplaces served, and the company is in a position to respond quickly to changes in those marketplaces. The vice president of marketing receives valuable information from the sales managers and representatives to aid in overall company market planning.

There are disadvantages, however, since conflicts can develop centered around reporting. Does the Atlanta regional buildings sales representative report to the Atlanta regional office manager or to the buildings division sales manager? In some construction companies the salesperson reports to both, but primarily to the division sales manager. To avoid or minimize conflict, roles, relationships, and responsibilities must be clearly defined and continually reviewed. Open communication is vital.

Another disadvantage is cost. The expense of maintaining two full-time sales representatives in one branch office may be high, particularly if the market shrinks.

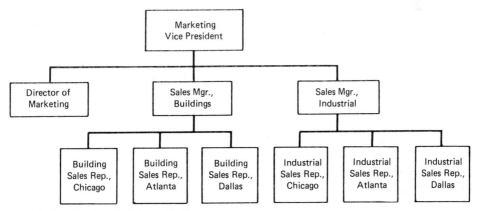

FIG. 7-12   Service-oriented organization.

Owner or Client-Oriented Marketing Organization. Each of Can-Do Construction Company's two divisions, buildings and industrial, serves a number of submarkets. For example, buildings includes offices, retail stores and malls, health care facilities, banks, and public buildings. Industrial covers unit manufacturing, chemical processing, food, power, petrochemical, pulp and paper, and other plants.

Each type of facility Can-Do builds takes in a specific set of owners and specialized design firms. One way to sell effectively to these owners is to organize the company by client (market-oriented division). In the medium-sized construction company, it is impossible to create a division to serve each submarket. However, this is commonly done in the larger construction company, with Morrison-Knudsen Co., Inc. and Brown & Root, Inc. as just two examples.

The medium-sized contractor can select two or three of its major project types and organize divisions to serve them. The selection would be based on those segments of the company's project mix that represent the highest percentage of its volume, or those segments with owners requiring a higher degree of specialization in their project type. Pulp and paper, chemical process, and health care are good examples of the latter. Each is a distinct client group with its own vocabulary, needs, buying practices and preferences, and intricacies. A number of construction companies are reorganizing their management around the markets they serve.

Marketing Structure in the Larger Construction Firm.   Marketing structures vary greatly in the larger construction companies. However, they tend to fall into two major categories. First, there is the geographical marketing structure, primarily evident in the larger building contractors, including Turner Construction Company, Gilbane Bldg. Co., and Huber, Hunt and Nichols, Inc. Second, there is the owner or client-oriented marketing structure, typified by the more industrial contractor and design builders such as Brown & Root and United Engineers & Constructors, which has power, steel, chemical, and general industrial divisions. Brown & Root's divisions are more segmented, including a pulp and paper division.

A typical marketing structure for a larger, market-centered contractor is shown in Figure 7-13.

The construction company considering a reorganization around its markets should recognize that reorganization can be a shock to any company. But there are ways to ease into such a reorganization and accomplish it by degrees.

According to Mack Hanan, market-centering the sales force is the first way, and it requires the least commitment and the least alteration to the business's basic structure. "In addition, it succeeds in establishing the central relationship that earmarks all forms of market-centered organizations: contact between customers with many varying needs and a sales force that can prescribe the most beneficial systems for those needs."[4]

Market-centering a company gives it two avenues for growth. First, by establishing a center of business for each of its major markets, the firm can serve them more intensively. Second, the company can search those markets for submarkets of closely related needs and establish new centers of business around one or more of them.

Designing a marketing function that is suitable to the contractor's organization is

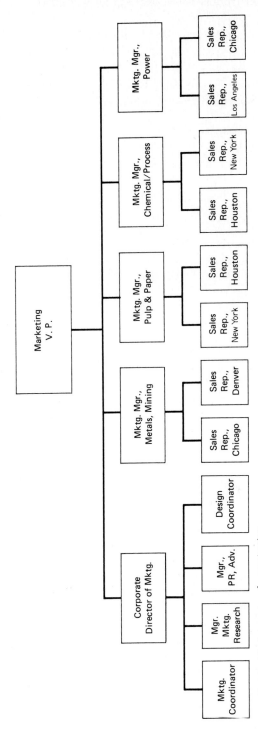

FIG. 7-13 Market-centered organization.

an important step toward ensuring success in business development. The organization-designing process itself will bring to the surface existing organizational problems and allow them to be discussed and solved. Unsolved, those problems will only be magnified with the addition of a marketing person or department. Many emerging marketing departments have been sunk when caught in an organizational cross fire. With proper overall and marketing organization design, the business development effort will operate in an environment conducive to producing the results management wants and the company needs.

NOTES

[1]Adapted from Edward S. McKay, *The Marketing Mystique*, AMACOM, division of American Management Association, New York, 1979, pp. 41–43.

[2]Adapted from Philip Kotler, *Marketing Management: Analysis, Planning, and Control*, 4th ed., Prentice-Hall, Inc., Englewood Cliffs, NJ, 1980, pp. 581–583.

[3]Adapted McKay, op. cit., pp. 60, 61.

[4]Mack Hanan, "Reorganize Your Company Around Its Markets," *Harvard Business Review*, November–December 1974, p. 66.

8

Defining Individual
Marketing Positions

Regardless of the size of the construction company, one person will have to be responsible for the company's marketing activities. All other positions will support that individual in carrying out his or her responsibility for the company's new business acquisitions. The larger the contractor, generally, the broader the range of marketing activities required, and the more people and positions needed. In using Figure 7-7, managers can approximate the amount of work to be done and the number of people required for the marketing effort. This chapter presents the titles and tasks associated with various positions.

It is important to define all the marketing positions. This includes new positions and existing positions that warrant redesign because of changing needs. In addition, some positions that are no longer justifiable may be eliminated.

With the expansion of marketing in the construction industry, there has been a profusion of titles to denote people with sales and marketing responsibilities. The most common titles in use are vice president of marketing (or business development), marketing director (or manager), marketing (or sales) representative, and marketing coordinator. In larger companies, there are specialists with such titles as director of market research, director of design (or marketing tools), director (or manager) of public relations, and director (or manager) of advertising.

These titles cause confusion, especially to firms hiring their first full-time marketing person. The same titles in different companies will carry different position descriptions and responsibilities. Further, there is a substantial difference in the responsibilities and tasks to be performed for identical titles in companies of different sizes.

The vice president of marketing in a small construction company may function primarily as a sales representative, in contact with prospects and clients as much as 80 percent of the time. In a large construction organization, a person with the same title may have virtually no client contact, except on the largest of projects for the biggest of clients, and will have several divisional market managers reporting to him or her. Much of that vice president's time might be taken up with strategic and market planning. While lieutenants focus on the day-to-day tasks of winning new contracts and maintaining high visibility for the company through marketing support services, the vice president of marketing in the larger construction company is peering into the future to determine where tomorrow's markets will be and how the company can best serve them.

When a contractor of any size hires a marketing person for the first time, the marketing role must be carefully defined. The confusion centers primarily around the main tasks to be performed. The prevailing attitude among smaller contractors is, "Titles don't mean much around here."

That view can have a crucial impact on the success of the new marketing employee. Titles *do* have meaning. That same company would not hire someone as a project manager and then assign him or her to a foreman's job. Often the first marketing person to be hired will be given a title of marketing director or vice president when, in fact, the contractor may be seeking a sales representative to contact prospects and design firms and to generate leads. The problem stems from the "marketing" title, which may imply marketing-support, office-bound tasks. The contractor is using the "marketing" title to sound more impressive than "sales representative," but in reality he or she may expect the employee to be a salesperson.

To a person with a sales or marketing background, especially someone with experience in a larger industrial or commercial corporation, titles do convey certain tasks and responsibilities. Marketing is not sales. The confusion between the two can be eliminated through communication, a clear understanding between the parties, and a precise position description. If this is done, the new staff person in the smaller company can have a marketing title and function as a sales representative.

The position descriptions in Table 8-1 represent various marketing and sales titles in the smaller, medium-sized, and larger construction company. Note how similar titles have widely differing responsibilities and tasks.

The larger construction company will have people in some or all of the following positions:

- Director of marketing, a corporate position reporting to the vice president of marketing. The person's responsibilities and tasks will be similar to those outlined for this position in the medium-sized construction firm. The main difference, however, will be in size of the staff and in the degree of their specialization. Reporting to the director of marketing may be specialists in proposal writing and preparation, market research, graphic design, public relations, advertising, and information and records.
- Division director of marketing or sales, a division-level managerial position

TABLE 8-1 Marketing Positions

	In the smaller construction company
I. Title:	Vice president of marketing (*note:* In this and other titles, "business development" or "sales" will sometimes be used in place of "marketing.")
Reports to:	President or CEO
Responsibilities:	1. Overall responsibility for success of marketing program 2. Achievement of company's growth objectives by obtaining sufficient flow of new business 3. Sales—entire process from lead generating through follow-up 4. Market planning and research 5. Public relations 6. Marketing tools 7. Marketing budget 8. Client relations
Tasks:	1. Develop overall marketing plan. 2. Contact prospects and clients through phone, mail, and primarily face-to-face meetings; requires half to three-quarters of time. 3. Plan presentations—strategy, orchestrating, rehearsing, participating. 4. Prepare proposals. 5. Initiate internal communication through meetings, reports. 6. Conduct meetings, develop reports, set up filing systems for prospective clients, photographs, project information, résumés. 7. Centralize all business development information. 8. Oversee preparation of articles for media. 9. Oversee preparation of brochures, newsletters, etc. 10. Join associations, clubs. 11. Prepare and update marketing budget.
Works with:	1. President, other executives (for communication, project pursuit selection, assistance in presentations, closing) 2. Estimators (for conceptual and other estimates) 3. Project managers (for assistance in gathering lead information and in interviews, proposals, presentations)
Comments:	The primary focus of this position is on sales tasks. After a period of familiarization with company, the vice president can set up internal systems and develop brochures or other basic marketing tools. Outside firms will be used extensively for consulting, marketing tools, and public relations, since there is no in-house staff. After six months, or less, an assistant will be needed to handle office tasks so that outside contact time can be maximized.
II. Title:	Director of marketing
Reports to:	President
Responsibilities:	Same as above
Tasks:	Same as above
Works with:	Same as above
Comments:	In the smaller construction company, this position is virtually identical with the above vice presidential one, without the

TABLE 8-1 *(continued)*

	In the smaller construction company
	corporate officer title. The title of director is used where (a) the person hired has a minimum of full sales and marketing experience; (b) a company employee, most likely a project manager, is given new responsibilities in marketing, but lacks experience; (c) the company has no other vice presidents; (d) the company has a policy that vice presidential titles are conferred only after many years of loyal service. After the director of marketing proves himself or herself, it could be in the company's interest to promote him or her to vice president. It gives the marketing role greater stature internally and with prospects and clients.
III. Title:	Marketing (or sales) representative
Reports to:	Director or vice president of marketing, if position exists, or to president
Tasks and responsibilities:	1. Develop new-project opportunities. 2. Coordinate client relations. 3. Sell by contacting prospects, presenting company's capabilities, persuading, answering objections, bringing company to presentation or select-bid stage. 4. Stimulate internal communications through reports. 5. Follow up with past clients and those recently sold.
Works with:	1. Estimators 2. Project managers
Comments:	The marketing or sales representative is hired when (a) management of the smaller construction company chooses to hire a salesperson rather than a director or vice president to generate new business opportunities for the president or other key executives to follow through on; (b) the director or vice president of marketing finds that spending time in the earlier prospecting stage of sales is no longer cost justified, and he or she and management agree that the better use of available time is in the later stages of raising prospects to clients, for example by improving proposals and presentations; (c) the company is growing and one or two new markets need to be explored so that the new sales or marketing representative can be assigned to them, or the director or vice president needs to be free to focus efforts on the new markets while turning over current market prospecting to the new person. Some smaller construction companies operate with two or more marketing representatives reporting to a vice president of marketing. This type of relatively large sales force in comparison to the size of the company can be found in design/build firms in the commercial and light industrial fields, where every project is the result of an intensive sales effort.
IV. Title:	Marketing coordinator
Reports to:	Director or vice president of marketing
Responsibilities:	Creation and maintenance of marketing support systems

TABLE 8-1 (*continued*)

In the smaller construction company	
Tasks:	1. Maintain marketing files and sales reminder systems. 2. Assist with writing and coordination of proposals. 3. Maintain slide and photograph files. 4. Develop public relations material. 5. Centralize project lead information. 6. Produce internal reports.
Works with:	Director of marketing, clerical personnel
Comments:	Marketing coordinators can be anything from a typist to a full administrator. The functions and levels of responsibility depend on the existence of a marketing director, the size of the company, and the capabilities of the individual.

In the medium-sized construction company	
I. Title:	Vice president of marketing
Reports to:	President
Responsibilities:	Same as above for smaller company
Tasks:	Same as above for smaller company, if the person is the only executive in marketing. If not, the same tasks will become more managerial, rather than direct performance. This is especially true in sales. With support people in the areas of sales and marketing, the tasks of the vice president of marketing are to:

1. Develop the overall marketing plan, with input and assistance from staff.
2. Manage the marketing department, consisting of one or more marketing representatives, a marketing coordinator, and, depending on company size and need, a director of marketing with his or her own staff.
3. Become involved in sales by (a) following up on leads generated by others and assisting on larger projects and more important clients; (b) contacting and maintaining relationships with major accounts—occupies half his or her time or less.
4. Plan presentations—strategy, orchestrating, rehearsing, participating.
5. Initiate proposals—strategy and review.
6. Stimulate internal communication through meetings, reports.
7. Join associations and clubs and obtain speaking engagements.
8. Select (with others) projects to pursue and set other priorities.
9. Prepare and update marketing budget.
10. Review marketing tools, public relations materials.
11. Attend conferences, conventions, exhibits.

Works with:	1. President, chairperson of board, other executives 2. Vice president of estimating and heads of various construction departments or divisions
Comments:	The medium-sized construction company is more likely to have two or more managers on the vice-presidential level. For both internal and external stature, the senior marketing person should carry the

TABLE 8-1 *(continued)*

In the medium-sized construction company	
	title of vice president. More often than not, in this size company, he or she will be head of a three- to ten-person department.

II. Title: — Director of marketing

    Reports to: — Vice president of marketing (or president, if no vice president of marketing)

    Responsibilities: — If no vice president of marketing exists in the company, responsibilities will be the same as above. If the company has a vice president of marketing, responsibilities include all marketing-support activities.

    Tasks:
1. Review public relations materials and maintain good relationship with press.
2. Stimulate marketing tool development.
3. Initiate market research.
4. Centralize information.
5. Prepare proposals.
6. Assist in presentations.

    Works with:
1. Managers of estimating and construction departments or divisions
2. Vice president of marketing
3. Marketing coordinator

    Comments: — Only the higher-volume medium-sized construction company has both a vice president of marketing and a director of marketing who oversees many of the office-developed support services and materials.

III. Title: — Marketing representative

    Reports to: — Vice president of marketing

    Responsibilities: — Same as in III, p. 112

    Tasks: — Same as in III, p. 112

    Works with: — Same as in III, p. 112

IV. Title: — Marketing coordinator

    Reports to: — Vice president of marketing or director of marketing, if one exists

    Responsibilities: — Same as in IV, p. 112

    Tasks: — Same as in IV, p. 113

    Works with: — Same as in IV, p. 113

In the large construction company	

I. Title: — Vice president of marketing

    Reports to: — President or CEO

    Responsibilities:
1. Overall responsibility for success of marketing program
2. Achievement of corporate and marketing objectives by obtaining a sufficient flow of new business in all areas

TABLE 8-1 *(continued)*

In the large construction company

	3. Strategic and market planning 4. Policy and procedures for marketing 5. Public, community, and corporate relations 6. Market expansion and corporatewide sales
Tasks:	1. Develop strategy and review corporate marketing plan. 2. Continually update plan and monitor market and economic data. 3. Manage corporate marketing department, including administration, support, personnel. 4. Develop budgets and financial commitments. 5. Develop tactics, themes for corporate advertising and public relations programs, and work with outside agencies. 6. Appraise marketing performance. 7. Communicate internally with top-level executives, managers, marketing staff, and others. 8. Communicate externally with clients, general businesses, community, and other groups. 9. Set policy on sales and marketing matters.
Works with:	1. Top corporate executives 2. Vice president of sales 3. Vice presidents or managers of divisions 4. Vice presidents and directors of marketing for subsidiaries
Comments:	This is a high-level corporate executive position, similar to ones in other major corporations. The vice president of marketing in the larger construction company is quite removed from day-to-day operations and becomes involved primarily in establishing policies, plans, and strategies and matters of importance as they relate to the company's communications with major media and client groups. The vice president may, however, become involved in sales of major contracts to large clients.
II. Title:	Vice president of sales
Reports to:	Vice president of marketing (or possibly, directly to the CEO)
Responsibilities:	Overall responsibility for the sales efforts of the company
Tasks:	1. Develop strategy, review corporate sales plan. 2. Manage, through divisional sales managers, the company's sales force (typically 10 to 50 or more sales or marketing representatives). 3. Plan and attend sales meetings. 4. Motivate and review performance of sales or marketing representatives. 5. Remain in contact with major accounts. 6. Set policy and procedures for sales.
Works with:	1. Vice president of marketing 2. Vice presidents or managers of divisions 3. Vice presidents or managers of sales for subsidiaries

reporting to the vice president in charge of the division, or directly to the vice president of sales, or in some companies to both—to the division manager on a day-to-day basis and to the sales vice president on sales policy matters.

- Marketing or sales representative, a front-line sales position with primary responsibility for increasing new business through prospecting, client contact, follow-up, and possibly contract closing. In the larger construction firm, particularly the industrially oriented one, sales representatives tend to be specialists in certain industry groups, such as pulp and paper, power, steel, process, metals, mining, etc. In some larger building construction companies, the sales representatives are construction generalists with broad responsibilities. Turner Construction Company, for example, employs a business development staff in each of its domestic branch offices. They may be selling Turner's construction services to a hospital board one day, to a major developer the next, and to a manufacturer the next. Each manager of business development has broad responsibilities, running from initial contacts with prospects, through proposal preparation, contract writing, and follow through during construction.

REVIEWING, COMMUNICATING, AND IMPLEMENTING THE MARKETING ORGANIZATION PLAN

After the marketing organization plan has been designed and positions described, it is ready to be reviewed to ensure that it is clear, simple, well-defined, and workable within the overall company organization. This will require further detailed descriptions. The marketing organization plan should be a document complete with:

1. An introductory statement of purpose, principles, and reasons for proposing it.
2. Organization charts showing both the old and the new formats.
3. Position descriptions for all managerial and specialist positions.
4. Job specifications, including skill and experience requirements.
5. A staffing plan for recruitment.
6. A list of services to be provided to the marketing organization by others, including shared sales, estimating, and other services; employment of agents; and use of outside advertising and public relations firms, market research services, management or market consulting firms, and others.
7. A sequential timetable for implementation of the plan.
8. A cost-benefit analysis covering the plan and alternatives.
9. A concluding statement summarizing the reasons for the proposed plan, and an outline of implementation recommendations.[1]

The final review process should ensure that accountability is defined for each position, and that responsibility is clear for monitoring, supervising, and appraising marketing work. Also to be answered in the review are questions of the organization's adequacy in scope and emphasis to accomplish the company's objectives and strategies.

Another review question is: Does the organization structure mesh with the rest of the business and does it provide for flexibility and growth? Finally, will components operate as independent empires or as cooperating units in an effective, efficient, and economical marketing operation?

After documenting and reviewing the plan, management will need to communicate it to current staff and assign or recruit people to fill new positions. The objective is to obtain acceptance, approval, and support from general managers and people in marketing.

Change always causes resistance, so there will be obstacles to implementing the plan. With proper introduction, communication, discussion of benefits, and orderly implementation, the plan should prove successful. One of the best ways to earn acceptance and support is to encourage everyone's participation, ideas, opinions, and suggestions.

NOTES

[1] Adapted from Edward S. McKay, *The Marketing Mystique*, AMACOM, division of American Management Association, New York, 1979, pp. 69–70.

9

Recruiting and Compensating Sales and Marketing People

To this point we have discussed the marketing organization plan in planning terms, which is the first vital ingredient for the success of the marketing effort. The second vital ingredient is the people to make it work.

Management has to recruit, select, train, compensate, supervise, motivate, and evaluate sales and marketing personnel. As in any phase of the construction company's business, at the heart of a successful sales and marketing program is the selection of good people. The techniques, approaches, and level of management involved will vary greatly with the size of the contractor and the position's relative place in the organization.

By far the most unfamiliar ground is trod by the top management of the small to medium-sized contractor in hiring the company's first sales or marketing person. The most common questions are:

1. Do we need a marketing person or a salesperson?
2. Should we select a person from within the company or hire from outside?
3. Should the person have a professional (engineering or architecture) degree?
4. Should the person know the construction industry, or should he or she be a professional sales or marketing person with experience in another industry?
5. How much should we pay the person?
6. What title should he or she have?
7. What is the best way to find a top individual?

8. What characteristics should we look for in the person?

9. How many years of experience should he or she have?

10. Should we have a marketing plan before hiring, or should the new person develop it?

This chapter address each of these questions.

MARKETING PERSON VERSUS SALES PERSON

If management has performed the overall business analysis described in several earlier chapters, the choice between a marketing or a sales person will become clear. Typically, the contractor's basic need, after the business and marketing analyses have been performed, is for a person to tackle the arduous, time-consuming task of face-to-face contacts with prospective clients—or sales.

The first marketing person assigned or hired, however, has to be somewhat like the president of a small construction company: multitalented and capable of doing many different jobs. Sales ability is important, but the person should be capable of growing into a manager and have a knowledge of, or at least a feel for, marketing.

SELECTING FROM WITHIN VERSUS HIRING FROM OUTSIDE

If there is a person on staff interested in communicating and persuading, who can be relieved of field or office construction duties, he or she could become an effective sales/marketing person. There are advantages and disadvantages to this. On the plus side, the staff member will have construction experience, possibly a professional degree, and will be familiar with the company's projects and personnel. On the negative side, he or she will not have the knowledge and experience to practice the disciplines of sales and/or marketing. Like other disciplines, however, these can be learned through years of formal training courses, reading, and experience.

The other negative factor is risk, both for the person and the company. Any person performing in an entirely new role is an unknown quantity. Performance ability, as well as response to the new situation, will only be proven with time. If the person fails to perform well or does not like sales or marketing, he or she may find it difficult to readjust to the old position, if it still exists.

The contractor is risking time. It will take months if not years for the sales/marketing neophyte to reach a high productivity level, if ever. By hiring a sales or marketing professional with a proven track record, the company is acquiring a better-known quantity. There is some risk here, too, in that the person may not be as capable as he or she appears, or may not mesh with management or with others in the company. Again, valuable time could be lost and the risks have to be weighed.

One major point should be considered. Sales and marketing skills are very different from other jobs in the construction company. They require a certain personality and psychological makeup. The tasks involved are not as tangible as management of bricks and mortar, and most situations are not as controllable as coordinating subcontractors or arranging deliveries to a job site. The intelligent, friendly, well-groomed project manager may look the part but may not enjoy the rejection and other aspects of sales. And there will be no one in the company to teach the necessary new skills.

There is no right answer to this question, and contractors have had success with both approaches. On balance, though, there is less risk and earlier results can be expected with a sales or marketing professional. Once the marketing program is rolling and additional people are needed, on-staff construction people can be assigned. If they do not perform, the marketing program will not grind to a halt. If they do perform, the company will have two solid sales/marketing producers.

ARCHITECTURE OR ENGINEERING DEGREE VERSUS GENERALIST BACKGROUND

Clearly the person with a professional degree has an advantage in sales and marketing of construction services. The reason is twofold: first, this person will have a better grasp of the construction process and will not require an education in that area; second, he or she will find it easier, personalities aside, to earn the respect of peers inside the company and of prospective clients. Many construction companies only recruit salespeople from the ranks of their graduate architects or engineers. The Austin Company is an example. That company has over 100 salespeople and has found that while a small portion of their professionals do not perform well in sales, the company is large enough to absorb a percentage of turnover, and so it has developed a successful sales force.

Although the ideal person is one with a professional degree and a high level of sales/marketing ability, such people are relatively rare. The ideal person may not be available to the contractor who is ready to launch a marketing program. For the contractor facing a choice between a generalist with a sales/marketing track record in construction and a professional with little or no sales/marketing experience, the nod should go to the generalist. Many construction companies have had success in generating new business with experienced sales/marketing generalists, with those having a Bachelor of Arts, and in some cases with those having no degree.

KNOWLEDGE OF CONSTRUCTION VERSUS RECORD IN OTHER INDUSTRIES

This question is related to the one above, professional versus generalist. If the ideal candidate—with a professional degree and construction knowledge combined with sales/marketing experience—is not available at the time the company is prepared to hire, another decision must be made. Since businesses in general have sales/marketing people in far greater numbers than does the construction industry, there are simply more such employees available at any given time and place. The person trained in sales and/or marketing techniques can be effective in construction, particularly if he or she has previously sold professional services or major industrial products.

If someone shows an aptitude for learning construction concepts and has functioned on an executive sales level, other things being equal, that person can be successful in construction. This is truer in building construction than it is in specialized construction, where the purchasers of construction services are more technically oriented and want to discuss projects on that basis.

One northeastern mechanical contractor experimented in sales with a bright, energetic young man who had been involved in the sale and manufacture of men's slacks. The man learned the basics of the company's piping capabilities and functioned effectively in prospecting and leading the contractor to many new business opportunities. The company's engineers and other technical personnel followed up after the door was opened.

Many industrial companies in electronics, such as IBM and Xerox, or in heavy equipment, such as Clark and Caterpillar, have excellent sales and marketing training programs. People with that kind of background can adapt to construction sales and perform well.

COMPENSATION FOR THE SALES OR MARKETING PERSON

Compensation for sales or marketing people covers a broad range, based on the individual's past performance, experience, education, age, and personal perception of his or her own value in the marketplace. At the lower end of the scale is a recent college graduate who wants to enter the field of construction sales or marketing. If the going rate for college graduates is $12,000–$15,000 for generalists and $18,000–$22,000 for architects or engineers, that is a fair compensation level.

At the high end of the scale is a person with twenty years of sales or marketing experience in the construction industry. This person can point to a record of selling $5 to $20 million or more worth of construction projects per year. In relative dollars, this record commands an annual compensation of $80,000 to $120,000 or more. (The figure is a combination of a base salary of $40,000 to $80,000 and an incentive arrangement, commission, bonus or other.)

Management must weigh a number of factors, including:

- The importance of marketing to the company's future
- The importance of the position in the marketing effort
- The company's growth, profit, or marketing objectives and the perceived ability of the person to help achieve them
- The compensation the person requires to take the position
- Compensation levels in the company
- The person himself or herself and the probability of working well in the company's style and environment

Only top management can evaluate the priorities and potential benefits. Very often the desired construction-experienced person requires higher compensation than most executives in the smaller to medium-sized construction company. The typical initial reaction of top management is to say no to this salary level because it could cause a great deal of strain and resentment in the company. This need not occur if discussions with other managers center on the sales/marketing person's importance to the company's—and therefore everyone's—future. The new person is to be a generator of new business, not a drag on overhead, who could pay for himself or herself hundreds of times over in new business won.

Two companies serve to illustrate the point. Both are midwestern contractors, primarily in the industrial and general buildings areas. Both were replacing vice presidents of marketing, primarily sales positions. One company, with an annual volume of $40 million, planned to pay up to $45,000 in total compensation. When an ideal candidate was presented to the company, one who had specialized knowledge in its field, since he worked for a competitor, the company decided to hire him at $70,000. The decision came after much soul searching and agonizing. The situation is working successfully.

Another larger contractor, in the $100 million-plus range, originally planned to pay about $65,000, the same as was paid to the long-time company project manager turned marketing vice president, who was being replaced. After more than a dozen interviews with qualified candidates ranging from young sales representatives with construction or design firms to vice presidents, top management hired a person at a $70,000 base salary, with anticipated additional incentive compensation of $30,000 to $50,000 or more, a potential total of $120,000—about twice the planned level and far higher than other executives in the company.

Certainly other contractors have hired their first or top sales/marketing person at lower compensation levels of $25,000 to $35,000 including incentive, and they have had varying degrees of success. As a rule of thumb, that level person can be effective, if it is early in his or her career and he or she is not expected to produce the same way as a high performer. The less experienced person requires more guidance, time, and involvement on the part of management and can function well as a second or third addition to the marketing staff.

The matter of incentive compensation can often cause a dilemma for the contractor about to hire a first sales/marketing person. It can also be an ongoing dilemma for contractors with a marketing department and a sales force.

At the heart of the question is the fact that most construction companies pay people based on a fixed salary and a more or less company standard benefits package. Often there is a company bonus arrangement, where higher-salaried employees share in a bonus pool during good years or receive a discretionary bonus based on evaluated performance. The idea of a guaranteed incentive tied to a dollar-based performance is unheard of. Opposed to this ingrained system is the fact that most salespeople are accustomed to receiving a base salary plus benefits, plus a bonus or commission for new business secured through their efforts.

What typically occurs when these two compensation cultures bump up against each other, is that the contractor makes an exception in the company policy to accommodate the sought-after sales-oriented person. This does not happen without difficulty; change rarely comes easily. Not only must top management veer from a long-honored course, but it must confront loyal employees—who are bound to learn of it anyway—and explain the aberration in policy.

There are several arguments in favor of an incentive arrangement for sales personnel:

1. Salespeople are generators of new business, a driving force for growth and expansion.

2. They are not strictly an overhead item, unless they are not producing.

3. Sales and marketing are different and unusual functions in a construction company and can be treated in a unique way.

4. Incentive compensation is a well-established method of rewarding salespeople in construction and most other businesses. If the high-producing construction salesperson does not obtain the desired incentive package from one construction company, he or she will get it from another.

5. Incentives provide the fuel for motivation. A strongly motivated salesperson or sales team can have a major impact on the growth plans of an entire company. Everyone in the company can benefit. In a rising sea, all the boats go up.

Incentive compensation packages can be relatively simple or complex, an exact formula or a vaguely defined reward for overall performance. The methods include:

- A small percentage, 0.25 percent or less of project value for new contracts obtained largely through the person's efforts

- A guaranteed annual bonus of an exact dollar amount to be paid for a generally agreed upon high level of performance

- A small percentage of the annual increase in the company's gross volume

- A bonus commensurate with salary level as offered to other highly productive company employees (This requires no special arrangement and would be more acceptable to existing employees, providing the new salesperson or persons will accept it.)

TITLE

Like compensation, a first sales or marketing person's title will depend on:

- The company's title-giving policies
- The new person's experience level and/or requests
- The level of authority the person is to have externally and in the company's organization

The rule of thumb that applies to other company titles is in effect here: the higher the title, the greater the weight the person carries in dealings within the organization and with outsiders—in this case, with clients and potential clients. In practice that translates into a vice presidential title. If the company has no other vice presidents, or if it has them but they have worked their way up through the ranks after many years, or if the person does not request it or does not seem to be officer-level material, a lesser title will do.

Possible titles include:

- Vice president of marketing (or business development)
- Director of marketing (or business development)
- Marketing (or sales) representative
- Project engineer or planner, contract manager, or manager of business development (Some companies such as the Austin Company and Turner prefer a nonsales title.)

Before actively recruiting sales or marketing people, management should decide on a title. That title could change with unforeseen factors; however, people seeking new positions want to know early on what the title will be. It gives them an idea of the position's desirability and suitability to them. A person already functioning as a vice president at one company would probably want to retain that title, for example, whereas someone with a marketing representative's title at one company would view a director's title as a step up and would be eager to pursue the new job.

HOW TO FIND A QUALIFIED SALES OR MARKETING PERSON

Very much the same employment channels exist for seeking a sales or marketing person as exist for other management-level people. One or more of the methods shown in Table 9-1 can be pursued simultaneously. There is more than one way to recruit a qualified person. The table assumes that either there are no potentially qualified people in the company or management has decided to recruit a sales or marketing professional.

Following are several examples of newspaper advertisements for marketing positions with varying levels of responsibility.

CONSTRUCTION BUSINESS DEVELOPMENT MANAGER Mid-Atlantic and Midwest areas. Gilbane Building Company, a leading general contractor and construction management firm, has an immediate career construction opportunity for an experienced Business Development Manager. Candidate will be responsible for respective regional areas. Degreed individual with a minimum of three years experience in the construction industry, including exposure in selling, securing and negotiating construction management services. Comparable experience in architectural engineering services will be considered. Excellent starting salary, company car

TABLE 9-1 Methods of Recruitment

Methods	Cost	Advantages	Disadvantages
Local newspaper advertisements	$100–$300	Low out-of-pocket cost. Attracts local person with no relocation needs.	Publications cover small area. Best possible candidates may be located elsewhere. Could attract person with local focus only. Could take a long time to find the right person.
Regional or national newspaper or magazine advertisements (regional construction magazines, ENR, *Wall Street Journal*)	$300–$1000	Low out-of-pocket costs. Attracts person with construction background.	Publications read only by people looking for new positions, misses others. Could attract a too-large number of applicants, requiring significant staff time for screening.
Word of mouth (friends of employees, salespeople calling on company, architects or engineers, other business acquaintances)	Nil, except for possible reward to employee or business acquaintance.	No or low cost. Results in candidates known to trusted employees or acquaintances. Could smooth the way for internal acceptance.	Limited exposure for position, limited number of candidates to select from. Best-qualified people may never learn of opening.
Executive recruiters	$5000 to $20,000 or more.	Pinpoints potentially best qualified people. Attracts high-performance people, not seeking new position at time. Saves time of top management. Should result in earlier hiring. Management receives advice of experienced personnel counselor.	High cost.

and paid fringe benefits package including profit sharing and dental plan. Call or send resume with salary history to . . .

BUSINESS DEVELOPMENT MANAGER Rapidly-growing CM firm with projects in 32 states has immediate opening for aggressive individual with marketing experience. Engineering/Architecture degree and construction experience preferred. Will locate in St. Louis or Florida. Relocation reimbursed. Excellent benefit package includes profit sharing. Send resume or call . . .

DIRECTOR OF MARKETING Creative, aggressive position with dynamic, fast-paced construction management firm (ENR rating No. 27) headquartered in Phoenix, Arizona. In charge of acquiring new business opportunities, proposal preparation and presentation interviews. Good communications and writing skills, construction management background desired. Our company is public sector oriented, well-established, very anxious to find a positive team member. Send resume and salary history to . . .

What Qualities to Look For. The ultimate success of the company's marketing program will hinge on the quality of the people selected for the task. The larger construction company will have a number of individual sales and marketing positions requiring specialists. The smaller contractor places the burden of marketing and sales responsibility on one or two people, who require a broader range of skills.

The office-bound marketing positions need people possessing an ability to:

- Plan and organize a marketing effort.
- Gain exposure for the company in media.
- Understand, but not perform, the sales function.

In the related field of marketing design services, Gerre Jones points out the following desirable characteristics for a marketing person:

- A combination of technical, administrative, and human relations skills of a high professional order. . . .
- A knowledge of the technical and professional aspects of [construction] is of course to be preferred, but is not a mandatory requirement. . . .
- Ability to program and coordinate his work on a practical day-to-day basis for the timely accomplishment of approved business development and public relations objectives.
- Creative human relations skills and the personal characteristics needed to develop and maintain, both externally and internally, those relationships of confidence and cooperation necessary to the fulfillment of his function.
- An intimate, first-hand knowledge of the major sources of [construction] work. Also an understanding of current practices in real estate finance and leasing would be desirable.[1]

Success in marketing and sales depends on a variety of personal and psychological characteristics and abilities. Those are subjective qualifications that go beyond the background and skills set forth in a job description.

John Simonds looks for these personal characteristics not found in a résumé:

- *The entrepreneurial instinct* is of singular importance; unfortunately it's a rare quality and not well understood. That sixth sense of seeing opportunities that others fail to recognize is what sets the entrepreneur apart . . . a marketing director must have an almost instinctive grasp of key variables (financial, technical, political, social, competitive) and of what clients want. Since the heart of the job is the development of a strategic marketing plan, he must have an entrepreneur's vision—an eye for what's coming in the next three to five years.
- A close second to the quality of entrepreneurship is *superior communication skills*, both oral and written . . . a special gift for persuasion. [Marketing directors] must be able to address a variety of media—letters, brochures, proposals, newsletters, presentations, and seminars. . . . Even if the marketing director does not

make client contacts, he needs the ability to train others in the art and science of persuasion.

- The third essential attribute is *optimism,* or the willingness to take reasonable risks. . . . The individual should have a strong belief in the firm's capability, which gets translated into confidence and aggressive strategies that present the firm as competent to handle the tough jobs. In the marketing position, a low-risk taker can be a disaster.

- Another important attribute is basic *competitiveness.* The ideal marketing person derives a strong sense of satisfaction from winning . . . at bridge . . . tennis . . . or in [construction]. A person who is highly competitive by nature will put more energy, thought, and creativity into getting and keeping clients—which is, after all, what marketing is all about.

- The last trait in this picture is *conceptual ability.* This is the ability to see patterns or trends in seemingly unrelated facts or events, to look beyond the separate parts and see the situation as a whole.[2]

One of the reasons that good marketing directors are so rare, Simonds points out, is that those characteristics are either innate or developed early in life. They are not something an individual can decide to learn at mid-career. Nor are they the characteristics necessarily found in successful technical people. For that reason many construction companies look beyond the industry for the ideal marketing director.

Many of the attributes needed for a successful marketing director are similar to those required for a successful salesperson. Mayer and Greenberg[3] studied more than 7000 salespeople on the basis of tangibles and intangibles and have drawn several conclusions about the basic characteristics necessary for a salesperson to be able to sell successfully.

Their theory is that a good salesperson must have at least two basic qualities: empathy and ego drive. "*Empathy,* the important central ability to *feel* as the other fellow does in order to be able to sell him a product or service, must be possessed in large measure," the authors state. "Having empathy does not necessarily mean being sympathetic." The salesperson must be able to understand how the other person feels but does not have to agree with that feeling. However, a salesperson cannot sell well without the ability to get strong feedback from the client through empathy and to adjust to the client's reaction.

The second basic quality that is absolutely needed by a good salesperson, according to the same authors, is "a particular kind of *ego drive* which makes him want and need to make the sale in a personal or ego way, not merely for the money to be gained." Because all selling involves failing to sell more often than succeeding, the salesperson's ego must be strong enough to withstand the failures or rejections and use them to trigger motivation toward greater efforts.

Empathy and ego drive are separate dynamic factors. Someone can have a great deal of empathy and any level of ego drive. Someone with poor empathy can also have any level of ego drive. A person may have a high degree of both empathy and drive, or little of either.

Before hiring a person for sales and spending time and money to train him or her, the contractor should find out in advance whether the person has the basic dynamics to be successful. Psychologists, industrial psychologists, and psychological tests are helpful in determining the person's attributes. The psychology department of a local university is a good source for information and advice.

Age and Experience.   There is no right age for a marketing director or salesperson. A person may seem too young for a marketing or sales position with one construction company and be appropriate in another. Some of the factors to consider are:

- *Age of top managers within the company.* A youthful management team in their thirties or forties would want a younger marketing person to be consistent with the company's image and internal dynamics.

- *The position.* If the person is being hired for the top marketing and/or sales position in the company, a more seasoned veteran (thirty to fifty) would be appropriate. If the position is for one of two or three or more sales representatives in the company, a younger qualified person will serve well. If the person is to have client contact, but not closing responsibility, a younger person would also qualify.

- *Average or typical age of decision makers in client organization.* If the people buying construction services in particular types of targeted client organizations seem to be in their fifties, a more mature sales or marketing representative who could relate better to prospective clients would probably be more effective. One contractor serving utility companies in California, for example, found that many of the purchasing people were in their forties and fifties and determined that they needed a more mature sales representative. Age tends to carry greater credibility, given salespeople of equivalent abilities. The "voice of experience" has more impact on some prospective clients.

- *Career path.* Regardless of age, a person's career history is a good measure of past performance and success. A talented person should have advanced in position, compensation, and responsibility during his or her working life. If the person appears to have stagnated for several recent working years, that could indicate a potential problem. This is particularly true in direct sales, where good performers advance rapidly in compensation and responsibility. One highly successful sales representative for a major design constructor was earning in excess of $100,000 per year in his early thirties.

  Part of career-path analysis is observing the person's length of time in a position or a company. A person who has had a new job every year or two can be considered a "job hopper" with very little staying power. There are people who make a career of seeking new jobs every year. Their instability and chronic dissatisfaction will probably not be cured by getting one more job. Many of these people are intelligent and highly capable. They present themselves well and score high in interviews. They usually have seemingly logical reasons for leaving each previous position. However, there is a high risk of quick turnover in hiring them.

- *Experience.* Experience relates both to age, in terms of quantity, and to skills, in terms of sales, marketing, and construction knowledge. In their studies of thousands of salespeople, Mayer and Greenberg have found a "fallacy of experience." "Many sales executives feel that the type of selling in their industry (and even in their particular company) is somehow completely special and unique. This is true to an extent. . . . Differences in . . . the special qualifications for a particular job can easily be seen in the applicant's biography or readily measured. What is not so easily seen, however, are the basic sales dynamics . . . which permit an individual to sell successfully, almost regardless of what he is selling. . . . What companies need is a greater willingness to seek individuals with basic sales potential in the general marketplace. Experience is more or less easily gained, but real sales ability is not at all so easily gained."[4]

Thus, the salesperson's possession of the two characteristics of empathy and ego drive are more important than direct or specialized experience in permitting him or her to sell successfully.

MARKETING PLAN OR MARKETING PERSON FIRST?

To the contractor who has reached a decision to organize a strategic planning and marketing effort, this becomes a chicken-and-egg question. Would the company be better off developing a marketing plan before hiring a marketing director, or should the marketing person be hired and given the task of preparing the plan?

The company that has performed some strategic or marketing planning, however imperfect or with whatever outside assistance, is far more assured of success. Some of the reasons are:

1. Marketing is a discipline, and marketing people can be successful only when operating in an environment where they are providing the means for the company to achieve its objectives. Objectives can be determined only through the careful analysis required by a planning process.

2. The planning process will expose major issues facing the company and force top management to make important business decisions regarding them. This difficult process requires months of time. If that time is taken during the marketing person's first months of employment, it can lead to a frustrating period for all parties.

3. The planning process will raise and provide answers to questions regarding the type and level of compensation of the marketing person to be hired, marketing budgets, overall direction of the company, markets to pursue, and so forth. The new person will be entering a planned business, rather than one with little direction.

4. A previously developed marketing plan can be a useful tool in recruiting a talented person. Management will be better organized and will be able to

spell out the anticipated future of the company and the marketing person's opportunities within it.

5. Through the planning process, management will have a good understanding of strategies, marketing, and sales, and their place in the company and its future. Without this understanding, managers of construction companies tend to think only in terms of sales. A problem typically occurs when the new marketing person is asked to develop the plan, which requires months of office work. Management expects to see the new person out of the office contacting prospects and becomes uneasy when the person remains in the office, not recognizing that the office work is in response to their own request for a plan.

The need for a marketing function to operate in a planned and organized environment cannot be overemphasized. An organized approach will attract better-qualified people, and better-qualified people are the keys to successful marketing and profitable business.

WHY MARKETING DIRECTORS SOMETIMES FAIL

Even in planned and organized environments, however, situations do not always work out as anticipated. This can be particularly true in the more subjective areas of marketing, and especially with the contractor starting up a marketing program.

John Simonds has identified six causes for the failure of marketing directors:

- First: The key decision makers do not accept the need for a strategic plan or the applicability of modern marketing techniques to [construction services].
- Second: The principals fail to communicate by word and deed to others in the firm that a marketing director is critical to the firm's continued success.
- Third: The principals fail to agree on the scope and authority of the marketing position.
- Fourth: The individual selected lacks the unique constellation of attributes and skills necessary in order to market intangible professional services, as opposed to tangible products.
- Fifth: The principals assume they can delegate marketing to one person and thus free themselves from any substantial role in marketing the firm's services.
- Sixth: The marketing director is not included as an equal in the key group of top decision makers.[5]

Marketing is too vital to the success of the company's business not to be done right the first time. The success formula is simple.

Success = commitment + definition + selection + support

NOTES

[1] Gerre L. Jones, *How to Market Professional Design Services*, McGraw-Hill Book Company, New York, 1973, pp. 36, 37.

[2] John Simonds, "Why Marketing Directors Fail," *SMPS News*, Society for Marketing Professional Services, Alexandria, VA, December 1981, pp. 1, 2.

[3] David Mayer and Herbert M. Greenberg, "What Makes a Good Salesman," *Harvard Business Review*, July–August 1964, pp. 119–125.

[4] Ibid.

[5] Simonds, op. cit.

10

Developing the
Marketing Budget

In any aspect of the contractor's business it is important to have control over expenditures. While marketing costs should be viewed as an investment in the company's future, they are a considerable investment and must be monitored.

A marketing budget determines the resources that will be made available for the company's business development program. The start-up marketing effort requires a proportionately higher investment than would an expansion of an established program. Even the contractor about to start a formal marketing function, however, is very likely to have existing expenditures for items that are sales related. Many of those expenditures are distributed among job-related travel and entertainment, and general and administrative expenses.

INITIAL BUDGET AUDIT

A good first step in establishing the marketing budget is first to assess what the company's real sales-related expenses are. These include:

1. Salaries (portions of people's time spent in business development activities)
2. Travel for business trips to explore project possibilities, or to visit an owner or design firm
3. Entertainment, including country clubs, dinners, lunches, football or other sports tickets, etc.

4. Brochures or newsletters

5. Mailings, promotional films or tapes, and miscellaneous items

6. Lead services and publications

PROJECTED BUDGET

Many managers will be surprised to learn what their current expenses amount to. The next step is to approximate the additional expenses required for the organized marketing program. By far the major item will be salaries. The formation of a marketing department will add the compensation and expenses for the marketing director, as well as full- and part-time support people.

One cost that will be increased as a result of aggressive marketing activities is estimating. An already hard-working estimating department or group will need additional assistance. That could be considered a marketing cost. Some construction companies factor an increase in estimating costs into the marketing budget; others do not. Similarly, other indirect sales or marketing costs are factored into the business development budget by some companies and not by others. For that reason it is difficult to devise an exact formula for expressing the marketing budget as a percentage of overall volume.

A rule of thumb, based on experience with construction companies of various sizes and on the survey of the top 400 contractors conducted in 1980–1981 by *Engineering News-Record* and Tecton Media, is that marketing can consume up to 2 per-

TABLE 10-1 Marketing as a Percentage of Volume

Key findings: Both large and small companies appear to be spending similar *percentages* of their annual revenue on marketing, though the companies with greater growth rates are spending a larger percentage on the average. The larger companies are spending significantly more *dollars*, with annual budgets ranging up to more than $6 million. Smaller companies have median growth rates of 15 to 20 percent, while those of larger ones are 8 percent.

		Growth rate, %	Amount spent for marketing, %[*]
$20–$50M	Range:	2–72	0–1.5
	Average:	19	0.38
	Median:	15	0.25
$51–$100M	Range:	0–44	0–2
	Average:	19	0.54
	Median:	20	0.4
$101–$500M	Range:	5–58	0–1
	Average:	21	0.24
	Median:	16	0.13
Over $500M	Range:	3–22	0–2
	Average:	11	0.46
	Median:	8	0.4

[*]Percentage of annual revenue expended on marketing
Source: ENR/Tecton Media Survey of top 400 contractors

TABLE 10-2 Typical Marketing Budgets for Design Firms

The following is based on a 1980 survey done by the Society for Marketing Professional Services and *A/ E Marketing Journal*. Note that marketing expenses do not include any fringe benefits or overhead, and they are expressed as a percentage of total annual revenues.

Overall mean	6.2 percent
Overall median	5.5 percent
Firms 1–25 employees mean	8.5 percent
Firms 26–75 employees mean	6.2 percent
Firms 76–200 employees mean	4.6 percent
Firms 201–499 employees mean	4.4 percent
Firms over 500 employees mean	4.6 percent
Architects employees mean	7.3 percent
Engineers employees mean	5.2 percent

In the opinion of the survey firms the above figures are somewhat low because most firms do not charge all appropriate expenses to marketing (particularly principals' salaries). They suggest adding 1 to 2 percent to each figure.

cent of gross volume (Table 10-1). The larger the company, the closer to the 0.5 percent figure or less it will be in its marketing expenditures. Architectural and engineering firms spend up to 10 percent of gross fee volume on marketing (Table 10-2), including overhead and salaries.

A contractor with an annual volume of $20 million could be spending between 0.5 and 1.0 percent or $100,000 to $200,000 on marketing. The expenditure percentage can be calculated as follows:

$$\frac{\text{Marketing budget}}{\text{volume}} = \frac{\$150,000}{\$20 \text{ million}} = 0.75 \text{ percent}$$

The minimum amount of business required to cover marketing budget at 3 percent gross profit is:

$$\frac{\$150,000}{0.03} = \$5,000,000$$

Thus, a $150,000 marketing budget will pay for itself with additional revenue of $5 million.

After start-up or major expansion, marketing should be a declining portion of overhead. Figure 10-1 shows that, as the company grows, marketing expenditures will not need to grow at the same rate. With increased repeat business, through satisfied clients and improvements in marketing efficiency, the marketing budget becomes a declining percentage of overhead.

Another way to measure the marketing budget's reasonableness is to compare it to anticipated gain. If the same company increased its volume from $20 to $30 million, as planned for in its corporate objectives, then a $150,000 marketing investment should return an additional $300,000 in gross profit.

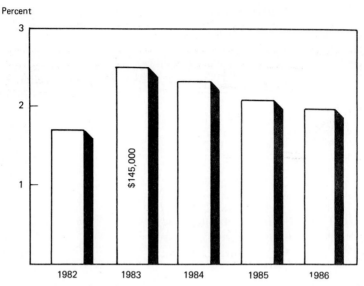

FIG. 10-1 Marketing budget: a declining portion of overhead.

BUDGET FACTORS AND ALLOCATION

What is the right marketing budget for a construction company? There is no exact answer, not even for two construction companies of similar size performing similar types of work, as the survey of the top 400 contractors shows. There are several key elements in a marketing budget and the allocation of funds to those elements will depend on the company's needs and priorities as well as on the total budget.

The marketing budget—backing planning decisions with dollars—is the acid test of management's commitment to the company's planning and business development efforts. The biggest component in the budget is salaries and benefits. The analysis of positions needed for the marketing program is the starting point for determining the overall budget's magnitude. Salaries and benefits will make up about 70 percent of the total.

The remainder of the budget covers such items as travel and entertainment, marketing tools, advertising, public relations, etc. All are to support the marketing staff. Marketing is a people-intensive function, and it is important that the major investment be made in acquiring good staff. It would be unwise for a contractor to invest heavily in marketing tools in the belief that they can substitute for effective personnel.

It would be equally unwise, however, to invest in top-notch sales and marketing people and not support them with high-quality marketing tools. Whatever the budget, a balance must be struck between quality people and quality support materials to ensure a successful marketing effort.

Management should strive for another balance in the marketing budget: a total dollar figure that adequately takes into account priorities, degree of importance to the company's future, and marketing tasks to be done, weighed against the risk management is comfortable taking in its marketing investment. From a cash flow stand-point, management should consider that the total annual budget will be expended over 12 months, and that there may not be any new revenue results for that period of time in the start-up or expanded marketing situation.

The rule of thumb on survey percentages of marketing budget to total company revenue can be used as a guide. Since any new addition to overhead is distasteful, management may understandably not want to reach that level in its first year. How-ever, unless the company is offering a proprietary service, management can recognize that it will eventually need to invest an amount in marketing not too dissimilar from what other successful contractors in its league are spending.

Table 10-3 shows a sample marketing budget for a medium-sized construction company. For the purposes of example, it is assumed the company is starting up a marketing effort. The company does an accounting of its current expenses related to business development and project expenditures for the first and second years of oper-ation of the marketing department.

From the analysis of percentages of expenses to gross revenue, it seems that the budget is too high for the $50 million company, about right for the $100 million company, and somewhat low or inadequate for the $200 million contractor.

For the sake of comparison, the smaller contractor can scale down all the budget items, since it will be spending less and in fewer categories. For example, that com-pany's chief marketing person may not be a vice president and would be earning $35,000 to $45,000 per year. His or her expenses will be less, since the company's

TABLE 10-3 Sample Marketing Budget for a Medium-Sized Construction Company

Item	Current	Increment	Total first year	Total second year
1. Marketing V.P.	—	$60,000	$60,000	$70,000
2. V.P. expenses and incentive	—	30,000	30,000	35,000
3. Sales rep	—	—	—	30,000
4. Sales rep expenses and incentive	—	—	—	18,000
5. Marketing assistant	—	17,000	17,000	20,000
6. Travel and entertainment	$23,000	20,000	43,000	50,000
7. Marketing tools				
a. Corporate brochure (amortized four years)	—	10,000	10,000	10,000
b. Newsletter	5,000	10,000	15,000	20,000
c. Public relations	7,000	11,000	18,000	20,000
d. Advertising	5,000	5,000	10,000	15,000
e. Proposal system	1,000	7,000	8,000	8,000
f. Presentation materials	2,000	4,000	6,000	7,000
g. Audio visual	4,000	7,000	11,000	13,000
8. Lead sources, publications	4,000	3,000	7,000	8,000
Total	51,000	184,000	235,000	324,000
Percent of volume ($50M)	0.1	—	0.48	0.66
Percent of volume ($100M)	0.05	—	0.24	0.33
Percent of volume ($200M)	0.03	—	0.12	0.16

geographic range is smaller and less money will be needed for travel and entertainment. Accordingly, less will be spent for marketing tools and miscellaneous items. The total first-year marketing budget for the $20 million construction firm could be $100,000 to $150,000, or 0.5 to 0.75 percent of volume.

One item not included in Table 10-3 is the cost of time other than that spent by those specifically assigned to marketing. That would include primarily principals or other company executives and staff who play a part-time role in business development. Another significant item not accounted for is estimating. Management can decide whether or not to include factors for these items in developing the marketing budget. Including them can yield a truer picture of actual marketing costs.

CONSIDERATIONS FOR THE MARKETING BUDGET

To the contractor taking the first plunge into marketing, the expenditures will seem to vary from high to outrageous. The primary reason is not that management is unaccustomed to dealing in those terms, since one piece of heavy equipment could easily cost more than a year of an aggressive marketing program. The reason is that marketing is an intangible. To the construction executive, experienced in working with bricks and mortar and project costs that are easily quantified and evaluated, marketing is a difficult area to commit sizable funds to. It is not easy to see the value obtained for the money spent.

The trend, though, as contractors gain experience in successful marketing operations, is to spend the money. This fact was demonstrated in the survey of the top 400 contractors, in which nearly 100 percent of those with organized marketing programs planned to increase their budgets.

This is not to say that money should be lavished on a marketing department. In developing the marketing budget, management should start with a realistic minimum, consistent with quality, the work to be done, and the objectives to be achieved. Quarterly or semiannually, the budget should be reviewed and trimmed or expanded as either can be justified. Once a year, prior to the start of the following fiscal year, management can thoroughly analyze the marketing department's budget on a zero-base approach and relate it to overall performance and return on marketing investment.

Part 2

ADVANCING PLANS INTO
ACTION

11

The Effective Sales Process: Phase 1

Effective selling is the art of acquiring and holding key clients. It is the result of a systematic and coordinated effort guided by the contractor's objectives and the potential client's needs to have construction problems solved. The steps involved in the selling process are shown in Figure 11-1.

In the marketing of construction services, sales performance is the most important contributor to marketing success. In the world of consumer and some industrial products, advertising, promotion, and merchandising can have a powerful influence on the buying decision. Many purchases are made without a salesperson's ever meeting the customer. That is never true in the marketing of construction services.

Of course, marketing tools such as brochures, advertising, and promotion are important for communicating the company's image or services capability, and thus for breaking ground for the sales contract. But by themselves these tools can never close a sale. Only the salesperson can carry through the lengthy transaction characterizing construction sales and get the final commitment to buy.

OBJECTIVES IN SALES

The primary objective in selling is the building of long-term business relationships with key clients. Since that requires not only selling construction contracts but performing well on them, sales is everybody's business in a construction company.

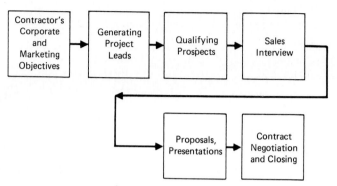

FIG. 11-1   The sales process.

A company's most valuable asset is its reputation, to which everyone in the company contributes. If a project manager performs well for a client and develops a good working relationship, he or she has also performed a selling function. If that client has the potential for more than one project, the contractor will be well positioned for future work. If the client company has only the single project for a while, it can still serve as a good reference for another sale.

Selling, planning, and marketing have to be in harmony. The company's overriding corporate and marketing objectives plot the course for those involved in selling. Salespeople, in turn, play a role in planning and marketing by transmitting valuable information about the marketplace and customers back to the company's marketing or management executives.

The effective salesperson's objectives are to help carry out the company's marketing plan and contribute to its success. If management has targeted the health-care field as a marketing objective, that is where the company's salespeople need to focus their efforts. They seek opportunities, learn about individuals in the hospital field, and communicate the benefits of the construction company to hospital boards, planners, and administrators.

That means a disciplined and planned sales effort, as opposed to the haphazard chasing of leads whenever they turn up. One way management can be certain that sales representatives are performing in accordance with company objectives is to design and administer a compensation plan that:

- Ensures a balanced selling job that pays off with new clients in targeted markets, new work from existing clients, new-capability sales, and other sales development activities essential to strengthening the company's short- and long-term position.

- Provides attractive earnings potential for both entry-level and career salespeople, so that there are skilled, trained, and motivated people serving on the leading edge of the marketing effort.

- Rewards salespeople for feedback to management on market conditions, competitors, clients, and prospects.

- Determines that the salespeople are pursuing projects that offer the greatest profit potential.
- Requires that the salesperson know cost and profit history for various project types and clients.

CONSULTATIVE SELLING FOR KEY CLIENTS

In their book *Consultative Selling*, Hanan, Cribbin, and Heiser point out that "One of the few universal facts of selling is the 80–20 rule . . . 80 percent of almost every company's sales may come from fewer than 20 percent of its customers. . . . As long as a business lives it must respond to its key accounts."[1]

But how can key accounts be won? After they are won, how can they be maintained? The answers lie in developing a special strategy, based on creating long-term, mutually beneficial relationships with major clients by helping them improve their profits through the use of the company's services.

The consultative salesperson regards himself or herself as the manager of a personal service business, treating accounts not as customers but as clients. The objective is to help them maximize the profitable operation of their business.

The consultative salesperson plans an entire business relationship with key accounts. He or she develops a series of short-term plans that move into the long range of the client's business. The aim is ultimately to embed himself or herself, with the construction company's services, into the client's business.

In the process, the salesperson transforms a customer (someone to be sold) into a client (someone to be served). The conversion of a customer into a client is the consultative salesperson's continuing and most demanding task. Hanan, Cribbin, and Heiser give the following landmarks as evidence that the conversion process is working:

- A customer is a buyer of [services]. When he becomes a client, he will be a *consumer of services.*
- A customer is price sensitive. When he becomes a client, he will be *profit sensitive.*
- A customer is also competitor sensitive, with a keen awareness of the salesman's rivals. When he becomes a client, he will be *less sensitive to the salesman's competition.*
- A customer operates with the salesman within a relatively short time frame. When he becomes a client, he will operate within a *longer time frame.*
- A customer applies controls to the salesman's performance. When he becomes a client, he will *share the development of the relationship's controls* with the salesman.[2]
- In construction, sales are turned into a problem-solving service to the client. The construction salesperson needs to learn as much as possible about the client's business in order to translate the project's bricks-and-mortar aspects into service ben-

efits. The client is made to feel that ABC Construction Co. is genuinely interested in that client's profit when ABC delivers a facility that will be built in a shorter time frame, will function better (if the construction firm can influence the design), will be built economically, and will cost less to maintain (if value engineering can be provided). Each client or business or organization will have its own special requirements, but a consultative selling approach will determine them and show the client how they will be met.

FINDING PROSPECTS

The first and one of the most important steps in the selling process is identifying prospects. A prospect is a person or organization that has the need and ability to pay for services offered by a construction company. Identifying prospects requires a planned program on the part of the salesperson. Maintaining a steady and growing supply of prospects or leads is a critical element in the sales process. Leads are the fuel that powers the contractor's marketing engine. Today's prospects are business opportunities that will be tomorrow's construction contracts.

Prospects by definition have a need and an ability to pay, but those criteria are not always found together. This section will focus on discovering people and organizations with the need for construction services. Determining their ability to finance potential projects will be discussed in the following section on qualifying prospects.

Finding the prospect is only the first step in the long journey to closing a contract. Many of those journeys will lead nowhere because:

- Funding could not be obtained.
- The owner, responding to conditions in his or her business, postponed or canceled the project.
- A competitor was selected.

Even prospects with an ability to fund a project and who select the contractor exist in widely varying stages of readiness. Some prospects may be thirty days away from contracting for construction services; others may be three years away. The aggressive construction salesperson needs an ever-expanding list of prospects to ensure a steady flow of new construction contracts. It is not uncommon for a contractor to have 50 or more prospects at any given time and to have that list result in fewer than five contracts in a one-year period.

An aggressive prospecting effort is the company's "offense" in relation to the marketplace. It allows for the contacting of owners before they are committed to a contractor, construction manager, or design firm. It also gives the contractor the opportunity to influence the construction process and to build a relationship with the prospect at an early stage in the thinking and planning of the project. Prospecting allows the contractor to be of service to the owner in providing early cost and other information. It places the contractor in a preferred position with the owner by the time the owner is ready to commence the project.

Fortunately, there are a number of sources of prospects available to the construction salesperson, limited only by the salesperson's imagination and energy. These sources can be divided into two main categories, primary and secondary. Primary sources are those obtained through direct contact with people who have knowledge of planned construction projects. Secondary or indirect sources are those who can provide names of people or organizations that may or may not have a need for construction services.

PROSPECT SOURCES: PRIMARY

1. Current and Former Clients.   Current and former clients can be one of the best sources of prospects. People in organizations change, so former clients should be contacted regularly. Current and former satisfied clients can also be a source of referrals and of names of other potential buyers of construction services.

2. Networking.   Networking is the development of an ever-widening circle of friends and acquaintances who are willing to provide information about potential projects. It takes time and community involvement to build a network, and it takes cold calls, visits, lunches, referrals, and other means to establish an effective network. Networking sources include:

- Architects and engineers
- Real estate brokers
- Subcontractors
- Suppliers
- Bankers
- Accountants
- Attorneys
- Business executives
- College alumni

Architects, engineers, and real estate brokers can be excellent sources of early project leads. Since most new construction projects require the purchase of land, a real estate broker may have the earliest knowledge of a potential project. One contractor in the Midwest has formed a "Tip Club," a group of local businesspeople who meet regularly for breakfast and exchange information of potential value to other members of the group. A construction sales representative learned of a major project in another city through an architectural firm he had developed a good relationship with. He visited the city and selected a capable contractor to team up with, and the joint venture won a project worth more than $100 million.

3. Outside Organizations. An important part of networking is joining organizations in which there is a high probability of meeting or learning about prospects. Organizations fall into the following major categories: (a) service, fraternal, religious organizations (Rotary, Kiwanis, Lions, and various charitable and religious groups); (b) business organizations (chambers of commerce—local, state, national; sales and marketing executives clubs; Jaycees); (c) professional organizations (Associated General Contractors, Associated Builders & Contractors Inc., National Electrical Contractors Association, American Subcontractors Association, Society for Marketing Professional Services, various associations of client groups, such as American Hospital Association and Technical Association of the Pulp and Paper Industry); (d) college and university alumni groups and boards of trustees; (e) cultural organizations, including museums, symphony societies, and other groups; and (f) political organizations.

4. Staff Information. Often an excellent source of project leads are the people already in the contractor's organization. Once alerted to the need, people from secretaries through superintendents and project managers can be reliable and continuing sources of information. They will obtain information through friends, spouses, property signs, newspapers, magazines, and organizations they belong to. One contractor relies almost entirely on supers and project managers for new project leads.

5. Cold Calls. The cold call has two primary purposes. The first is to determine whether the person or organization has any thoughts or plans regarding new construction, expansion, or renovation. The second is to obtain an appointment with the person to discuss those plans. Using the telephone to make cold calls on persons and organizations is known as telemarketing. It has several advantages: prospects for construction services can be uncovered; wasted prospecting time can be eliminated; and selling efforts can be concentrated on the most likely prospects.

The first step in cold-call prospecting is to decide what type of individual or firm constitutes the best prospect. Then develop a list for that classification. Possibilities include commercial and industrial corporations, hospitals, real estate developers, service companies, banks, and authorities. Lists can be compiled from telephone directories, local trade association membership lists, chamber of commerce listings of local industries, and business services and directories such as Standard & Poor's, Dun & Bradstreet, Thomas' Directory of Manufacturers, *The Red Book* (for banks), and the *Insurance Almanac* (for insurance companies). Professional list brokers can provide a specialized list.

The list can be sorted according to business type, size, location, financial condition (if known), number of employees, and so forth. Unlikely prospects can be weeded out. Then, using index cards or computer code, the list can be further sorted alphabetically or geographically.

The following six-step procedure will increase the effectiveness of cold calls:

    a. *Plan the Call.* Organize information about the person and plan the approach. Avoid memorized sales pitches. One method is to send an introductory letter first and follow it up with the call.

b. *Introduce Yourself.* Keep it simple, clear, and firm, introducing yourself and your company. Do not use gimmicks.

c. *Create Interest or Qualify.* Ask a leading question or make an interest-creating comment and wait for the prospect's response.

d. *Mention a Benefit.* Since the purpose of the call is to sell the value of an appointment, say just enough to whet the prospect's appetite. One way is to mention a benefit—in terms of cost or time saving, or of problem solving.

e. *Sell the Appointment.* Assure the prospect that your visit will be brief and ask for a definite time to see him or her. Have a reason to come in person—some photographs you want to show, examples of project ideas, or the like.

f. *Confirm the Appointment and Express Thanks.* After scheduling the date, express thanks and confirm the time. If the prospect does not consent to an appointment, he or she may not be a prospect, or not at this time, though conditions change. Whatever the response, express thanks.[3]

6. Cold Visits.   Dropping in cold on some owners can be an effective, though time-consuming, method of generating project leads. In some industries, where the buying of construction services is done by the plant manager or company purchasing agent or on the facility director level, cold visits are an accepted procedure for sales. Many of those people will not make appointments to see salespersons, so dropping in and waiting to see them is the only method.

7. Speaking and Writing Activities.   Speaking and writing are good ways to increase the salesperson's visibility. Giving talks on the construction process or pitfalls in construction, or on major or interesting projects known in the area, gives the salesperson stature, credibility, and recognition. Good platforms for such talks include some of the groups listed in item 3 above.

Writing articles about similar topics for publications that will accept them is another way of reaching prospects and generating inquiries.

8. Planning or Zoning Boards and Utility Companies.   Early in the construction process, owners contact zoning boards and utilities for information, file requests for permits or zoning variances, or request data on power costs and availability. It may be difficult to obtain lead information directly from utility companies, but planning and zoning boards are public agencies that are obligated to disclose the names of owners who have filed a preliminary site plan, which generally precedes design services.

9. Direct Mail.   Successful marketing requires maintaining a presence in the mind of a prospect at the time he or she is ready to initiate design or construction. A proven method for achieving this presence is through periodic mailings to lists similar to those approached in cold calls. Direct mail can be in the form of a series of letters, a newsletter, advertising flyers, project case history sheets, or similar literature. The format

LUEDER CONSTRUCTION COMPANY

SUITE 500   11128 JOHN GALT BLVD.   OMAHA, NEBRASKA 68137   TELEPHONE 402-339-1000

May, 1979

Dear Friends & Customers:

Building construction costs continue to escalate at a pace faster than 1% per month. Thus, the cost due to inflation of twelve per cent per year on a one million dollar project would be as follows: Per minute: .23¢ - Per Hour: $13.70 - Per Day: $329 - Per Week: $2,308 - Per Month: $10,000 - Per Year: $120,000. As a consequence, customers are turning to us increasingly for "fast track" construction. Comprehensive management of design and construction is truly the quickest way of bringing a building to an early completion. If you want to avoid further cost increases, call us today.

On six of the last jobs that we have competitively bid, the low bid has exceeded the owner's budget. By working with us at an early stage, this problem can be avoided.

We were most pleased to be selected as the general contractor for the new Richard H. Young Memorial Hospital. It represents the newest and most modern approach to the treatment of this area's emotionally disturbed citizens. The Hospital Board believes it will be looked upon as a standard to be studied and copied by other psychiatric hospitals.

We continue to stress the fine quality of our craftsmen in remodeling work. Recent renovations include a new Jerry Leonard Store, remodeling of three Walgreen's, a refurbishing of the Royal Inn, numerous offices in the Medical Arts Building, three jobs for Hinky-Dinky, and work for Sears-Roebuck, Coca Cola and D H Foods.

The quality of a contractor is usually reflected in his repeat business. Currently, we have underway, work for the following customers. We have built for these firms ten times or more.

        Hormel   Valmont   Mercy Hospital

One of the jobs we are most proud of is the President Ford Birthplace Memorial, and we are currently adding to it a magnificent Rose Garden. It already is one of Nebraska's major tourist attractions.

Is there anything we can do at this time to be of help?

                            Sincerely,

                            Robert G. Lueder
                            Robert G. Lueder

An Equal Opportunity Employer, M/F

FIG. 11-2   Sample letter for direct mail campaign.

should be consistent, because the objective is to promote name recognition and generate inquiries.

Figures 11-2 and 11-3 show some of the letters used in a successful direct mail campaign conducted by Lueder Construction Company in Omaha. Each letter describes benefits obtained by the owner who selected Lueder and a brief description of recent projects. The projects lend credibility to the Lueder story and provide an

LUEDER **CONSTRUCTION COMPANY**
SUITE 500   11128 JOHN GALT BLVD.   OMAHA, NEBRASKA 68137   TELEPHONE 402-339-1000

September, 1980

Dear Friends and Customers:

    Although the construction industry, in general, is definitely in a recession, Lueder Construction Company is fortunate to be going contrary to the trend.

    We owe this to a loyal and dedicated group of office personnel and field craftsmen who are using tight controls, critical path scheduling and most importantly, a large measure of creativity and ingenuity.

    As an example, on the new Millard Senior High School, the Architect asked in the bid proposal for voluntary suggestions to reduce costs. One suggestion of ours saved the School District $150,000. With the start of this construction, we have now built for seven School Districts in the Omaha vicinity.

    Karnett's were forced to move by condemnation to make room for the new MAT bus depot. Working closely with the Owner and the Architect, we will complete construction in approximately four months of working time.

    We love repeat business! When Montgomery Wards decided to remodel their Westroads location, they awarded the work to us on a time and material basis because of their good experience with us on past construction. We have completed or are currently doing repeat business for: The Prudential Insurance Company of America, Keebler Company, Weyerhaeuser Company, Baker's Supermarkets, Omaha Public Power District, Packaging Corporation, Control Data, Ash Grove Cement, Mercy Hospital and Sears Roebuck.

    Speaking of repeat business, in 1962 we built a major addition for the Cornhusker Motor Club. At that time, the Bureau of Contract Information solicited comments from owners on the completion of their job. Frank Malm, the owner, wrote as follows: "We could not have picked a better contractor. Quality workmanship and materials throughout. Excellent cooperation every step of the way. No cutting of corners. Final cost was 5% under original contract price." We have just commenced construction on their new headquarters building.

    We were pleased that both President Ford and his wife could be present for the dedication in July of our new Betty Ford Rose Garden.

Sincerely,

LUEDER CONSTRUCTION COMPANY

Robert G. Lueder

Robert G. Lueder, President

An Equal Opportunity Employer, M/F

FIG. 11-3   Sample letter for direct mail campaign.

opportunity for the prospect to associate the Lueder name with a project he or she may be familiar with.

10. Referrals.   The best opening, particularly for the one-time sale, is through a third party—a fellow contractor, an architect, an engineer, a real estate broker, a friend, or some other person familiar with the owner and the contractor. This kind of referral, related to "networking," enables the seller to gain recognition and credibility, avoid making a cold call that puts him or her at a disadvantage, and obtain information without announcing one's intentions. Some contractors have developed proven third parties into a second sales force. Through the second sales force, referrals can work in reverse in the form of inquiries to the contractor.

11. Trade Shows. The use of exhibits at trade shows by design and construction firms has been increasing in recent years. Exhibit areas at conference and conventions draw a large number of potential buyers together in a concentrated area. Contractors offering construction management services have been exhibiting at such conventions as the American Hospital Association. The contractor has an opportunity to meet hundreds of decision makers face to face in an informal manner and before they select a building team.

Trade shows or conventions are held on a local, state, and national basis. By contacting associations related to targeted markets—whether hospitals, real estate development, utilities, or manufacturing—the contractor can obtain information regarding dates, exhibit costs, and requirements.

PROSPECT SOURCES: SECONDARY

1. Information Sources: Business and Trade Publications. A number of reference books, directories, and periodicals are available for compiling mailing lists or cold-call lists.[4]

Standard & Poor's Register of Corporations, Directors and Executives. Published annually by Standard & Poor's Corporation, 25 Broadway, New York, NY 10004. Price $298 on a lease basis. About 40,000 United States corporations are listed, with the names of officers and directors, annual sales, number of employees, and products. Standard Industrial Classification is indexed.

Reference Book of Corporate Management. Published annually by Dun's Marketing, Parsippany, NJ 07054. Price $165 on a lease basis. Contains biographical data on executives in 3000 major businesses. Some 50,000 officers and directors are shown by company affiliation. Lists companies on an alphageographic basis.

National Trade & Professional Organizations of the U.S. Published annually by Columbia Books, Inc., 777 14th Street, NW, Suite 236, Washington, D.C. 20005. Price $40. Contains data on more than 5800 national trade associations, labor unions, and professional and educational national societies.

ProFile 1983/Official Directory of the American Institute of Architects. Published by Archimedia, Inc., 3715 SW 29th Street, Topeka, KS 66614, under the sponsorship of the American Institute of Architects. Price $86 softcover, $100 hardcover. Contains listing of architectural firms and principals.

Who's Who in America. Published biennially by Marquis Who's Who, Inc., 200 East Ohio Street, Chicago, IL 60611. Price of the 42nd edition $118.50. Carries 74,500 biographies of important persons, including business and government executives. There are *Who's Who* regional editions for the East, the Midwest, the South and

Southwest, and the West. *Who's Who in Finance and Industry* is also available from the same publisher.

Polk's World Bank Directory, North American and International Editions. Published by R. L. Polk & Co., P.O. Box 1340, Nashville, Tennessee 37202. The North American Edition is $80 a copy on a five-year contract. A single issue is $108. The International Edition is $60 a copy on a five-year contract. A single issue is $100. Contains information about officers, balance sheets, and correspondent banks for more than 15,000 banks and almost 25,000 branches.

Dun & Bradstreet Reference Book. Published every two months by Dun & Bradstreet, Inc., 99 Church Street, New York, NY 10007. The reference book contains nearly 3 million listings for commercial enterprises in the United States and Canada. Listings are alphabetical by business name and town within the state or province. Included is the business's estimated financial strength and corporate credit appraisal. Cost of the service is determined by the coverage.

Thomas' Register. Published annually by Thomas Publishing, One Pennsylvania Plaza, New York, NY 10001. Price $160. Seventeen-volume directory of industrial manufacturers throughout the U.S.; includes names of officers, annual sales, products, and services.

National Real Estate Investor. Published monthly by Communication Channels, Inc., 6255 Barfield Road, Atlanta, GA 30328. Price $41 per year. Contains information about developmental and investment trends in the real estate industry.

2. Sources of Project Leads

Dodge Reports. Published by F. W. Dodge Division of McGraw-Hill Information Systems Company, 1221 Avenue of the Americas, New York, NY 10020. Price varies according to subscription. Daily packet of bid lead information about new projects, renovation, and alteration work, edited by project type, cost, geography, and/or project stage.

Herb Ireland's Sales Prospector. Published by Prospector Research Services, Inc., 751 Main Street, P.O. Box 518, Waltham, Boston, MA 02254. Reports on commercial, industrial, and institutional projects planned, in design, and under construction throughout the United States and Canada. Issued in 15 monthly regional editions. Annual rate for one region is $98; additional regions, $88 each. Full nationwide coverage costs $695 per year.

Engineering News-Record. Published weekly by McGraw-Hill Publications Co., 1221 Avenue of the Americas, New York, NY 10020. Price $31 a year. The "Pulse" section carries the week's significant projects in planning and bidding stages. Occasionally a job is listed before the A/E has been selected.

Million Dollar Project Planned Lists. Published monthly by Live Leads Corporation, 200 Madison Avenue, New York, NY 10016. Lists projects of more than 50,000 sq ft and/or $1 million in the planning stage. Projects listed by state and building types, including commercial, educational, recreational, residential, medical, and governmental types. The *Industrial/Engineering Project Planned List* covers industrial, manufacturing, power, warehousing, transportation, and engineering projects.

Costs per list for nationwide coverage, $900 annually; territorial subscriptions, $480 annually; single-state subscriptions, $120 annually.

Hotels & Restaurants International. Published by Cahners Publishing Co., 1350 E. Touhy Avenue, P.O. Box 5080, Des Plaines, IL 60018. Free to qualified readers. Includes a regular feature listing hotels, restaurant chains, industrial caterers, and tourism facilities planning new construction or expansion worldwide.

Commerce Business Daily. Published daily by the U.S. Department of Commerce. Available from the nearest Department of Commerce Field Office or the Superintendent of Documents, Government Printing Office, Washington, D.C. 20402. Price $100 a year; by air mail $175 a year. Contains unclassified requests for bids and proposals, procurements reserved for small business, Postal Service construction-leasing proposals, contractors seeking subcontract assistance, upcoming sales of government property, prime contracts awarded, research and development leads, current foreign government procurement offers in the United States, and nongovernmental export opportunities for American firms.

Who's Who in American Politics. Published biennially by R. R. Bowker Co., 1180 Avenue of the Americas, New York, NY 10036. The 1983–1984 edition is $89.95. Contains biographical data on 25,000 political leaders and government officials—city, county, state, and national.

3. Miscellaneous Sources

Clipping Services. Clipping services will read all periodicals in markets subscribed for and supply pertinent articles. Such services can be a useful means of staying abreast of land purchases or options, corporate personnel changes, zoning board variances or applications, community and business related events, and legislative changes over a wide geographic area.

Newspapers. Local newspapers will yield similar information in a town, county, or city.

The Wall Street Journal. The *Journal* is the only national business newspaper. It contains news of broad economic interest, trends in real estate and various industries, changes in corporate organizations, corporate finance data that could indicate capital expenditures, and information about individual companies.

Corporate Annual Reports. Annual reports can be particularly useful in developing background information about prospects. Annual reports provide data on the company's financial condition, product lines, short- and long-range goals, capital expenditures, and organizational changes. Annual reports can be used to research a company to determine whether it should be pursued as a prospect.

Business and Trade Magazines. General magazines such as *Business Week*, *Forbes*, and *Fortune* are valuable information sources for the marketing effort. In addition to news about business and economic conditions and about individual companies, these magazines publish special issues on corporate earnings and roundups of various industries.

QUALIFYING PROSPECTS

After identifying potential project leads, the next step is to determine whether a sale can eventually be made. This process has been described as "separating the suspects from the prospects." Unfortunately, many contractors spend too much time selling to prospects who have no intention of buying or who do not have the ability to sponsor a construction project. While the number of prospects a company has is an important measure of new business potential, the quality of those prospects is a more important criterion. The salesperson should consider questions like these:

- Does the prospective buyer really have a need for construction services?
- Do top managers recognize that need?
- If they don't, is it likely that I can educate them?
- Can I justify my company's services as a response to that need?
- Can I identify influential buyers and others who may affect the decision to buy?
- Does the prospect appear to have the ability to finance a potential project?

Basically, there are two important issues: (1) Can my company be of service to their organization? (2) Can I bring the two together? To answer the above questions, the contractor's salesperson can obtain information through some of the reference sources listed in the previous section and through brokers or designers who may have knowledge of the owner. What the salesperson must learn is that if the lead is not likely to become a sale, he or she should not pursue it. If the owner organization passes the screening questions above, however, the next step is to qualify the project itself. The salesperson should then ask such questions as:

- Where will the project be located? Is it within my company's geographic range?
- What is the proposed size of the project? Is it within the capability of my company to manage a project of this size?
- Can my company do a good job on this type of project?
- Do we have the personnel to assign to the project?
- Can we be competitive on the project?
- Who is the architect or A/E on the project? Can we work well with them?
- How will the project be contracted for? Will it be low bid only, or will the owner consider a negotiated, CM, or other approach?
- Who is the competition? Are they contractors that the owner has had good experience with in the past? Are they local firms without the expertise to manage the project? Is there a contractor with a special relationship or family tie? Have there been problems on previous projects that will make the owner receptive to a new company?

Prequalifying prospects and projects can be accomplished by telephone. AT&T has a program called Phone Power, offered by Bell System affiliates throughout the United States. Phone Power representatives offer seminars and course workbooks on telephone sales and prospect qualification techniques. Other sources of telephone and general sales training include the Dale Carnegie Institute, Xerox Learning Systems, and the American Management Association.

Through the prospect qualification process, the salesperson will learn whether the lead is likely to become a sale. If not, he or she should not pursue it—even if that means breaking off a friendly relationship because it holds no promise of business.

RECORDING, REPORTING, MANAGING SALES INFORMATION

The accurate maintenance of records and information in business development is as important as it is in accounting or job execution. People involved in sales are in an ideal position to gather information about a variety of matters of concern to marketing and company management. Their daily contact with "suspects," prospects, clients, competitors, and others allows them to accumulate a great deal of first-hand knowledge about what is going on in the marketplace.

The sales call report or initial contact form is the basic information source in a sales/marketing information system. An example of a form used by one firm is shown in Figure 11-4. A form of this type could be completed in the lead or "suspect" stage of the sales process. It can be updated as the prospect and project are qualified.

On an individual prospect basis, the form is useful in:

- Providing information and timing for follow-up contacts, whether by phone, personal visit, or mail.

LINBECK
CONSTRUCTION CORP.

LEAD CONTACT LOG

DATE	ACTION & RESULTS

FIG. 11-4 Lead contact log.

- Keeping management and others informed of potential projects, client activity, and other matters.
- Having a reference source for future interviews, proposals, and presentations.

From management's standpoint, prospect forms are useful in:

- Monitoring the salesperson's activity and performance.
- Providing information for sales forecasts, operating plans, marketing strategies, and other planning.
- Gauging the overall sales effort.
- Learning of the needs, plans, and satisfaction of existing clients.

Like other managers, those in sales and marketing rely on information to maintain control over their operations, to establish objectives and policies, and to become alerted to and resolve problems. Many construction companies that have developed computer expertise in other areas of their businesses are using the computer for a sales and marketing management information system.

As the sales effort gathers momentum, the number of project possibilities and prospects begins to multiply. Many companies have found it useful to develop lists of prospects arranged by time and the probability of the project's materializing. Prospects can be rated as short (thirty to ninety days), medium (ninety to one hundred eighty days), or long term (six months to two years). Within those lists, prospects can be ranked by the likelihood of the project's going ahead and by the contractor's chances of obtaining it.

Through this system of dividing prospects by projected timing and ranking them by likelihood of obtaining the contract, a program of effective follow-up can be developed. Short-term (thirty to ninety days) prospects should be contacted every one to three weeks, depending on whether they are close to the thirty- or ninety-day mark. Medium-term prospects (ninety to one hundred eighty days) should be contacted every two to four weeks. Long-term prospects (six months to two years) should receive a visit or call every one to three months, and a brochure or other company mailing should be sent every two to three months.

Because highly ranked prospects are the likeliest to become clients, more sales and other company time and resources should be focused on them. The lower-ranked prospects receive proportionately less time, care, and attention.

LEAD GENERATING, RECORDING, AND FOLLOW-UP: A CASE HISTORY

Linbeck Construction Corp., Houston, a growing medium-to-large general contractor, uses the following approach to generate, record, and follow up leads and prospects.

- *Priority contacts* are a very limited, very specific group of architects, owners, and developers for each city or geographic location. They are contacted monthly. This list is reviewed each month at the marketing meeting and, if necessary, updated.

- On the *contact list* by category (owners, developers, architects, etc.) are all companies that should be contacted regularly. There are entry columns for a code number, name of contact (company), address, phone, name of individual, date entered/adjusted, action taken, and individuals assigned to the contact.

- There are physical *files* for each contact that hold letters, annual reports, brochures, and memos regarding the contact.

- A *mailing list* is available via the contact list, since the address information is updated regularly. This is rarely used in its entirety, but it is often used for individual categories.

- *Leads* become available through reading the various reports, magazines, and newspapers, and through the contact system. Each lead is entered on a lead form (Figures 11-4 and 11-5) and a copy sent to the vice president of marketing. Immediate action can be called for, or the decision on the lead can be held for the monthly marketing meeting. At the meeting, the lead is either discarded, held for another month and assigned to someone who pursues further information, or put on the prospect list.

- The *prospect list* is for those projects that do warrant further and immediate action. Projects are divided into "Negotiated" or "Bid" categories and subdivided into "Priority" and "General." Entry columns are for the code, project name, description, location, dollar amount, date information was first entered, date information was adjusted, comments, and action assignment. This prospect list is reviewed at each meeting. Individuals assigned to the particular project will have researched the project and contacted the individuals in charge. The new information is entered. If the prospect has not become a reality, it is moved to the general listing or removed.

- *Prospect files* are also maintained for the project as it develops. These hold letters and memos. There are occasions when a lead becomes a prospect so quickly that it skips the list and goes straight to the prospect file.

- The next stop for a potential project is a *proposal.* If in the request for proposal a pro forma estimate is given, the prospect will be assigned an estimating number. It is then a definite enough project to pass from the marketing group to estimating/operations for further action. There are many prospects that must be pursued for several months, even several years. It is the responsibility of the marketing team to stay with the prospect until such time as it no longer qualifies or becomes an operation responsibility.

As the Linbeck procedures state, "Leads become available through reading the various reports, magazines, and newspapers, and through the contact system." While those methods are valuable sources, they should be considered as supplementary to a basic program of face-to-face visits with potential prospects.

LINBECK
CONSTRUCTION CORP.
Box 22500 • Houston, Tx 77027 • 713 621-2350

LEAD ORIGINATION FORM

DATE:

LEAD ORIGINATOR:

Company:_____Phone:_____

Person Contacted:_____ Address:_____
_____

Decision Maker:_____

Name of Project:_____Address:_____

Project Type:_____

Architect:_____ Address:_____

Engineers/Subcontractors:_____

Size: $_____ S/F_____

Start Date:_____

Source of Lead:_____

Competition: None_____Yes _____

Identify:_____

Bid_____ Nego_____CM_____ PM _____GMC_____Open_____

Probability Rating:

Project Certainty:_____%

Linbeck as
Contractor: _____%

Remarks:
_____
_____
_____
_____
_____
_____
_____
_____
_____
_____
_____

Action Required:_____
_____
_____
_____

LCC Communications 11/77

FIG. 11-5   Lead origination form.

SALES PLANNING

An effective sales program begins with a sound plan for the use of each salesperson's time. Several steps are involved in sales planning. Following is the procedure utilized by salespeople in one large design and construction company.

Step 1: Territory.   Defining the salesperson's geographic area of coverage is the first step in sales planning. For a contractor with operations in a single city or several counties, the territory will be relatively compact. The same holds true for a branch office of a national contractor. For a contractor covering a region or several regions in the United States with few salespeople, each one's territory might cover several states or more, with travel from major headquarters cities such as New York, Chicago, Houston, and Atlanta. Figure 11-6 shows the territorial areas covered by Turner Construction Company's branch offices.

Step 2: Sales Goals.   Sales goals are realistic goals, based on previous performance and projected activity in the sales territory. It is preferable for the salesperson to establish his or her own goals, for review by management. People tend to achieve goals they set for themselves, rather than those imposed on them. Goals can be set according to services or by project or geographic market. Following are sample goals for a given year, arranged in three different classifications.

Individual Sales Goals, 198X	
1. Service or contract type	
Negotiated contracts	$12,200,000
CM, fee only	700,000
Lump-sum bid (through placement on new preferred-bid lists)	7,500,000
	$20,400,000
2. Geographic area	
Georgia	$8,000,000
Florida	9,000,000
South Carolina	3,400,000
	$20,400,000
3. Project or industry classification	
Photographic/printing	$3,400,000
Manufacturing, electronics	5,000,000
Food and beverage	4,200,000
Utilities	4,800,000
Hospitals	3,000,000
	$20,400,000

Step 3: Prospect Analysis.   Develop a list of prospects in the territory. A prospect can be defined as a company or owner with the potential for becoming a client. Companies are designated as A, B, or C prospects, depending on their size and probable need for a contractor's services. Smaller companies and branch offices or plants may

Turner   DOMESTIC OPERATIONS

FIG. 11-6   Turner Construction Company's domestic operations (regions and offices).

represent some potential but may not by comparison warrant a major portion of available sales time.

If the territory has 300 prospects, the list can be arranged as follows:

1. *A* prospects (63), companies with $40 million or more in annual sales (including Fortune 500 companies)

2. *B* prospects (119), companies with $10 million to $40 million in annual sales, banks with deposits between $200 and $400 million, newspapers with more than 100,000 circulation, TV broadcasters, and all colleges

3. *C* prospects (118), companies with less than $10 million in annual sales, banks with deposits between $100 million and $200 million, and hospitals

The prospects can then be summarized by category:

1. Manufacturing companies (183) (automotive parts and manufacturing, building products, electrical equipment, appliances, food and beverage, machinery, machine tools, metal products, paper products)

2. Newspapers, publishers, and broadcasters (12)

3. Insurance companies (5)

4. Banks (23)

5. Utilities (4)

6. Colleges (18)

7. Hospitals (47)

8. Miscellaneous (8)

_______ District Assigned To _______

Territory Prospect List for _______ Sales Plan _______

_______ Category Prospects for Zone _______ Date _______

Prospects	Sales, in Millions						Personal Calls						Mailings					

FIG. 11-7 Gerard Construction Company's sales planning form.

The next classification of prospects is by section of the territory, or zone. Figure 11-7 is an example of a form that can be used in sales planning.

1. Zone 1—Atlanta and vicinity	114
2. Zone 2—Tampa, Orlando, Miami	126
3. Zone 3—Charleston	60
	300
"Suspects"	100
Total	400

Step 4: Sales Time Allocation.   In this step the salesperson determines the realistic amount of time available for sales in a given year and establishes priorities for use of that time.

Available time for sales calls per year	
Total working days	260
Less:	
Vacation days	15
Holidays	9
Serving present clients	20
Average 1.5 days per week in office for establishing scope, developing conceptual estimates, preparing proposals and presentations	75
Average 1 day per month for presentations, association meetings, miscellaneous	12
Days available for sales calls	129

Averaging three calls a day, it will be possible to make about 387 sales calls per year. These calls will be distributed as follows:

A Prospects @ 2 per year × 63	126
B Prospects @ 1 per year × 119	119
C Prospects @ 0.5 per year × 118	59
"Suspects" @ ⅓ per year	33
	337
Extra calls on top prospects or design firms	50
Total calls	387

The prospect and "suspect" lists can be used for organizing mailings. Everyone on the list should receive at least one mailing and one follow-up mailing after every sales call. This will result, in the above example, in more than 750 additional contacts per year with the prime sources of business in the salesperson's territory.

First or cold calls are used to acquaint prospects with the contractor's services and capabilities. Second or follow-up calls are used to deliver more specific or tailored company materials. These give the salesperson an opportunity to introduce more technical personnel. For the company's desired potential clients, this system makes efficient use of available sales time, and it ensures maximum economy in the sales effort.

The cost of maintaining salespeople in the field is rapidly rising. It has been estimated that the cost of an industrial sales call rose from $71 in 1975 to $100 in 1977, and to $150 in 1980. Since the contractor cannot pass these costs along, it is important to plan the sales program for optimal benefit.

FACE TO FACE: THE INITIAL SALES CALL

Selling is not a neat package of predictable actions. It is a freewheeling, dynamic set of interactions between the salesperson and others, with a number of things going on at once—and the balance between the players in a constant state of flux. Feeling, riding with, and controlling the flow of the action provides much of the challenge in selling.

The most basic element of interaction is human contact. That begins with the initial sales call, when those all-important, and rarely reversible, first impressions are formed. They alone will not make the sale, but they could break it.

The sales process begins before the initial sales interview and proceeds through several phases to closing. The phases in the sales process are:

1. *Prospecting.* Finding the right organizations, companies, and people to call on.

2. *Precall Approach.* Learning as much as possible about the owner organization, its needs, and its decision makers, and the buyers, their personal characteristics, styles, and objectives.

3. *Sales Interview.* The first face-to-face contact with the prospect, greeting the person, making a good first impression, gaining the prospect's attention, learning his or her needs, building credibility for the contractor, and relating the company's services to the buyer's situation.

4. *Proposal/Presentation.* Developing the contractor's sales strategy and presenting to the decision makers in the owner organization.

5. *Closing.* Overcoming objections, negotiating, and signing the contract.

The initial sales interview can take place as the result of a prearranged appointment, made by telephone or letter, or without an appointment, depending on the prospect's preference. In addition to information gathered in the precall phase, there are a number of items to keep in mind as to how the salesperson should act, what his or her role is, and what the nature of sales is.

These are guidelines used by salespeople at one national contractor:

- Construction services are a means to an end for the owner. The owner is not interested in them per se but is concerned with the role the facility will have for his or her organization.

- The prospect is busy; have objectives set for the call and specific points to cover. Act like a guest, and don't stay too long.

- Treat each business and each individual differently. Be aware of the person's background, education, personality, behavior, and motivation.
- If a person is dominant, let him or her talk; if quiet, draw the person out. A banker's interests are different from an engineer's.
- The owner always wants to know: "What's in it for me?" Stress the benefits your company offers, rather than features. A benefit is an advantage the buyer desires. A feature is a characteristic of the service.
- Rehearse the first five sentences; they are critical to the success of any sales call. If possible, include a benefit you can offer or any other attention-getting statement. The opening line should be positive and pleasant: "Ms. Richards, I am Jim Brown from ABC Construction Company. I appreciate your willingness to see me. I will do my best to make this visit profitable and worthwhile for you and your company."
- Ask questions; probe for owner's needs, orientation, and prime interests.
- Be a good listener. Try to have the owner or prospect talk 85 percent of the time. It is said, "When you're telling, you're not selling."
- Keep it simple and straightforward. Owners buy because their needs are fulfilled and trust has been established.
- Remember these points:

  1. Act professionally.
  2. Play the part of an educator with a valuable contribution to make—a big part of selling is educating the client to be able to make the best decision.
  3. Remember you represent a high-quality firm.
  4. Remember you are not going to the call to sell—rather to diagnose and discuss.
  5. Act like a detective, observing every detail and seeking facts to use in your sales strategy.
  6. Everybody likes to buy but nobody likes to be sold.

- Understand the psychology of selling. All people have four areas of personal need:

  1. Need to feel comfortable, not threatened—find ways to ease the buyer's fears.
  2. Need to be needed—seek to make the buyer feel important.
  3. Need that is underlying—determine the buyer's "hot button."
  4. Need for recognition—assess the buyer's ego and find ways to feed it.

- Don't intrude into sensitive areas.
- Never argue with the prospect or criticize his or her method of doing business.
- Never criticize the competition.

- It may take two, three, or four exposures to the salesperson's message before the owner begins to pay attention to it.
- Remember that most contractors are capable of executing the building process. What makes the difference in securing new clients is the quality and effectiveness of the contractor's salespeople and their ability to develop and communicate the right sales strategies.

Establishing Credibility.   Questions to the prospect, to stimulate talk about the organization and the specific project they may be planning, should be the thrust of the salesperson's approach at the initial sales interview. However, the salesperson at some point will need to establish his or her company's credibility. In other words, the company's construction services must be related to the prospect's situation. There are several ways to accomplish this.

A third-party endorsement is one of the best ways to ease the buyer's innate skepticism. That endorsement can be a reference to a mutual friend, an architect, a past client, or another impartial person.

Another good method is to discuss a successful project similar to the one being sought. By demonstrating the outstanding features of one or more similar projects and the contractor's role in their successful completion, the salesperson can begin to distinguish his or her company from the competition.

If the owner is interested in the earliest move possible, discuss projects completed on or ahead of schedule. If the owner is interested in a "monument," discuss projects of high quality. If cost is a prime factor, discuss projects completed within budget, or value engineered to lower costs.

Other methods include discussing the contractor's financial capability, showing a general knowledge of costs and familiarity with local officials, suppliers, and subcontractors. The salesperson should make the prospect aware of the contractor company's capability of organizing, planning, and scheduling the work. Finally, the salesperson should show how the company builds competitively.

The above points should be made as briefly as possible. The salesperson is not there to hard sell but to listen and take notes. The salesperson should find out what business the prospect is in (if he or she does not already know), what the buyer's influences are, who the competition is, what the project is about, whether it is funded, and who will be at the presentation interview (if there will be one).

After the meeting with the prospect, the salesperson should always write a follow-through letter. This will help the buyer remember the salesperson's name, company, logo, and courtesy.

FINDING THE DECISION MAKER

A study by a sales executives' organization revealed that 60 percent of all industrial sales calls are made on people who do not have purchasing responsibility. Often a salesperson will present an effective story for his or her company only to learn later that the person was not a key decision maker. Every organization is different. At some companies, decisions are made at corporate headquarters; at others, they are made at the plant. Company divisions and subsidiaries sometimes have the responsibility for facilities. Then, too, it depends on the project. A plant expansion project may be decided at the plant or divisional level, whereas a new corporate headquarters facility could be decided by top management.

There are several approaches to determining who the decision makers are. Talking to people in the organization is one way. They can be asked who would be interested in a project of this type. Another way is talking with other salespeople who call on the organization. These are not necessarily people in the construction industry, but they would be familiar with the prospect's organization, its people, and its influence centers. Talking with architects or engineers who have performed design services for the organization can be helpful in learning who were decision makers in design selection and what was important to them.

In some organizations the sale will have to be made on several levels and may require a team from the contractor. People involved in the facility decision may be from production, finance, and top management.

Once the decision makers have been identified, the salesperson will have to judge the best way to reach them. If another initial interview with a person higher in the client organization is needed, the salesperson can ask the lower-level person for permission to contact the higher executive, or the information can be held and used for a presentation or sales interview later.

This chapter has focused on the initial phases of the sales process—planning, prospecting, handling the initial interview, and finding the decision maker. If these phases have been executed thoroughly and professionally, the salesperson will have placed the company on a solid foundation for securing a new client. The next phases, building the sale through to closing, follow.

NOTES

[1]Mack Hanan, James Cribbin, and Herman Heiser, *Consultative Selling*, rev. ed., AMACOM, division of American Management Association, New York, 1979, p. 1. Excerpted by permission of the publisher. All rights reserved.

[2]Ibid., p. 15. Excerpted by permission of the publisher. All rights reserved.

[3]Adapted from Charles Bury, *Telephone Techniques That Sell*, Warner Books, New York, 1980, pp. 35–39.

[4]List of reference sources adapted from Gerre L. Jones, *How to Market Professional Design Services*, McGraw-Hill Book Company, New York, 1973, pp. 80–87.

12

The Effective Sales Process: Phase 2

Having identified a prospect and a possible sale, the salesperson needs to develop a plan for directing his or her own efforts and to deploy the company's resources to make the sale and develop the client relationship.

The way the salesperson proceeds will be governed by the method the owner chooses to do business with contractors. Many utility companies and large industrial and commercial companies select a small group of contractors from the many approaching them to place on a preferred bidders' list. Once a contractor has "sold" the owner on its having the qualifications to bid on the project, the balance of the sales process consists of submitting a lump-sum or cost-plus-fee bid. The private owner can then negotiate with any of the bidders to obtain the best contractor for the project based on price or performance, or both.

When the owner selects a contractor based more on qualifications than on price, as with projects in the predesign stage, the sales process is more complex, requiring elaborate proposals and formal presentations.

DOING ADDITIONAL HOMEWORK

Once the salesperson and other executives determine that a prospect has a project that seems "real" and that the company will pursue it, there is a selection process involved and further homework is needed.

Using the lead or sales call report (Figure 11-4) as a starting point, the salesperson can compile a Prospect Profile that will help map out a strategy and organize the sales effort so that all bases are covered. The profile contains separate forms for detailed information about the project, the owner, the decision maker follow-up activities, and any other intelligence gathered.

For example, the form on the decision makers will have space to answer such questions as: Is this person the sole decision maker? What kind of person is he or she? How does he or she fit into the organization? What is the person's background? Is it technical? Managerial? Where did he or she work before? Where did the person receive his or her education?[1]

The homework phase is the time needed to complete the intelligence gathering on the prospect. The salesperson who is calling on three potential prospects a day will not have the time to research each one thoroughly. For the initial sales call, the salesperson can obtain basic company information contained in the Standard & Poor's directory or the company's annual report. The salesperson may also talk briefly with an architect or engineer familiar with the prospect. But once the contractor decides to pursue a specific project, more in-depth information will be required. The salesperson should find out everything possible about the prospect, the project, the architect-engineer (if one has been selected), and the community.

For background information about individuals, as far as reference books are concerned, the *Who's Who* series, from Marquis Who's Who, Inc., is a good place to begin. (See Chapter 11.)

Any common areas of background—schools, fraternities, friends, clubs, hobbies, and past clients –can be important in the selling effort. Dun & Bradstreet reports, local newspapers, and business and real estate editors are additional sources of information.

A visit to the site, preferably scheduled with the prospective client, is a good way to maintain contact with the prospect and to furnish further data that can be used in the presentation or proposal. The visit provides an opportunity to photograph the site and to offer ideas or advice to the prospect as well.

During the selection process it is always a good idea to have as much contact with the prospect as possible. Additional meetings will allow that, and they will allow the contractor to clarify certain points while building a relationship with one or more people in the organization. It helps to get to know prospective clients and for them to get to know the contractor.

Charles B. Thomsen, in his book on CM, points out that every project has its "hidden agenda" issues. Each project has different ones, but these are the more common ones:

- A client may want bid packages structured to maximize participation by local contractors, minority contractors, union (or nonunion) contractors, etc. Or the client may want to bring in outside competition.

- A client may want a construction manager to absorb some of the responsibility and to minimize the risk if there are any problems. On the other hand, the client may be a bit of a risk taker and may want to take credit for the best possible results.

- If public money is involved, a key selling point may be cost predictability and budget containment, not necessarily economy. If it's private money, economy will probably be more important.
- Some clients place great value on professionalism, education, and sophistication; they want someone who understands advanced systems. Others view construction as a tunnel of horrors, and what they want is a tough construction manager with mud on his boots to protect them on the way through.
- Some clients want to relinquish responsibility for the project and get involved only in critical decisions. Others view the project as a major event in their lives, and they want to be directly involved, perhaps with the construction manager operating as an extension of their own staff.[2]

If the salesperson can discover these hidden agenda issues and other owner needs and desires, the contractor will know which capabilities to emphasize in the proposal and at the presentation interview.

DEVELOPING THE PROJECT SALES STRATEGY

Once the information-gathering phase is as complete as possible, the contractor will need to develop the sales strategy to secure the project. That strategy will largely be determined by facts gathered from a wide variety of sources.

At the core of the sales strategy is the prospect's needs and constraints. This may seem obvious, but often it is forgotten by the contractor's management, sales, and marketing people. In their eagerness to sell, throughout the sales process, from first call through proposal and presentation, they are oriented in the wrong direction—telling the prospect about their company and its capabilities.

A winning approach to strategy development is to:

1. Analyze all the information gathered prior to, during, and after the sales interview to determine what the prospect wants.
2. Analyze the competition and consider what they are likely to offer.
3. Identify the firm's strengths and weaknesses for the project and decide what it can offer. Be specific and document.
4. Develop a sales strategy and a theme for the proposal and presentation, which should stress the benefits the owner can derive from selecting the firm.

One approach to analyzing the contractor's relative strengths and weaknesses regarding a specific project is shown in Figure 12-1. This form can be used in several ways:

- To arrive at a go/no-go decision, if weaknesses far outweigh strengths.
- To develop the sales strategy, through matching the contractor's strengths to the owner's needs.

	Strength					Weakness						Rating
	10	9	8	7	6	5	4	3	2	1	0	
Project Characteristics												
Size												
Location												
Type												
Schedule												
Budget												
Technical Aspects												
Preconstruction or Other Services												
Contract Type												
Negotiated												
CM/Fee												
Design/Build												
Lump Sum												
Competition												
Success Against												
Capabilities (ours vs. theirs)												
Intelligence												
Owner												
A/E												
Local Area												
Proposal/Presentation												
Capability												
Time to Prepare												
Potential												
Profit												
Repeat Work from Client												
Total												

FIG. 12-1 Go/no-go decision and sales strategy form.

- To highlight areas of company strengths and weaknesses for future prospects.
- To point up areas of weakness to shore up for pursuing the project.

JOINT VENTURES

Some of the areas of relative weakness that the form shown in Figure 12-1 may reveal could relate to the project's size, which may be much bigger than any previously undertaken; or to its location, which may be an unfamiliar area; to the type of project, such as a hospital or some type of industrial plant, for example, that the company has little or no experience in; to CM services, which the contractor cannot provide; or to knowledge of the owner or design firm, or some other crucial aspects that the contractor does not have.

Any weakness in one or a combination of the above factors may indicate a need for a joint venture partner. A joint venture that combines the strengths of two or more companies can usually satisfy many of the prospect's requirements and concerns.

Often joint ventures are made between a reputable local contractor and a large regional or national one. Many owners want to select a national contractor for its nationwide experience in the project type, as well as its financial and technical resources, and select a local contractor with community ties and knowledge of the area's subcontractors, suppliers, labor, and officials and agencies. Many owners feel comfortable with local people and believe they will perform well to maintain their reputation. Many of the largest contractors form joint ventures with local or highly specialized ones to win projects that neither company would have won on its own.

SELLING OTHER PROJECT APPROACHES

One sales strategy is to persuade the owner to approach the project in a different manner from what he or she has in mind. The contractor who can convince the owner to approach the project in a certain way can be a front runner for the job.

If, for example, the owner planned to employ the traditional design/bid/build method and the contractor is a specialist in CM and fast-tracking techniques, the contractor can try to sell the owner on that approach. The message is: "Now that we've convinced you that you can save time and money with the CM approach, you see us as experts, and it would be natural for you to select us for your project."

That strategy, as we have seen in earlier chapters, worked very successfully with Barton-Malow Company, Gilbane Bldg. Co., R. E. Dailey & Co., and many other pioneers in CM.

Kugler-Morris General Contractors Inc., a general contractor based in Dallas, has developed a strategy of selling the design/build method. Its sales approach follows:

> The primary interest of Kugler-Morris in establishing its construction development services is in being able to offer a complete service with a single source of responsibility to an owner or developer. This single source of responsibility is the key

to cost-effective design, faster construction time, and less time-consuming paper work and administration.

The advantages of design/build are:

- Single source of responsibility
- Cost-effective, efficient design
- Analysis of major building systems based on use/cost/payback value
- Prearranged agreed-to fixed fee—known by owner
- General conditions (indirect costs) can be negotiated on a not-to-exceed-percentage-of-the-job [basis].
- Competitive direct costs
- Savings to owner at the end of the job
- Minimized change orders; in some cases only one is necessary at project completion.
- Early establishment of a firm budget price or guaranteed maximum price to allow for early bank financing
- Quicker completion, earlier occupancy
- Early material purchase at cheaper cost
- "Team" approach—not an adversary approach; all members of team are there to serve the client.
- The end product is important, not the process to get to it.
- Savings in time and money can be and usually are far in excess of any differential in bids that may exist through the competitively bid method.

With a negotiated project, an owner gets all of the same advantages, although he has, and may desire, the additional responsibility of administrating the contracts of both the Architect and Contractor rather than having single source responsibility. All other aspects of design/build exist, especially when the contractor is selected at the very early stages of a project. . . .

Finally, in concluding the review of what we sell, we should reiterate that in selling Kugler-Morris overall, and in selling design/build in particular, we must sell ourselves on the basis of *trust* and *reputation*. Stressing our percentage of repeat clients, illustrating successful case studies of projects completed, and emphasizing a sincere desire to provide a recommendable service and serve the client, are key to securing design/build work.

PREPARING EFFECTIVE PROPOSALS

Many projects are secured, in part, through the submission of a well-prepared proposal to the owner. On projects ranging from relatively small and simple to large and complex, proposals can be as little as an expanded letter or as large as a bound volume.

On negotiated projects, owners look not only at project costs but at the organization as a whole, how well equipped it is to handle the project, the experience of its people, its financial strength, and its assessment of and approach to the project. One contractor believes that "if an owner is impressed with all aspects of your firm, but your budget is high, it is likely that he will help you get low."

As a general rule, once the go decision has been made to pursue a project, the contractor stands the best chance of being selected by going first-class in everything—from initial follow-up through proposal, presentation, and after.

Kugler-Morris General Contractors, Inc. recognizes the importance of proposals for the initial impression it gives the potential client. In its marketing plan Kugler-Morris states, "It is extremely important that they [proposals] be clear, well-written, without error, and professional in appearance." The company is successful on a high percentage of its proposals, and it always places in the top three proposers. The company is often complimented by owners on the presentation and appearance of its proposals. Kugler-Morris follows these guidelines in the preparation of its proposals:

- Be highly professional in presentation, with cover letter; format should be consistent throughout; quality and care must show through.
- Have no mistakes—multiple proof-reading should be done to eliminate all typing errors.
- Cover the points addressed in the owner's request *specifically*. In addition, the proposal should cover these points in the order that the client presents them.
- Contain all information normally required by the A.I.A. Contractor's Qualification Statement.
- Address not only budget of potential project but Kugler-Morris key personnel, résumé of key field people to be assigned to particular project, schedule of project, analysis of project, and organization of the construction effort by Kugler-Morris, and financial stability of Kugler-Morris.
- Include brochure on major members of the team.

The proposal format designed is universally applied on all presentations. A right-hand-column format 4½" wide allows for notes in the wide left margin and does not overwhelm the reader with too much printed wording.

All presentations are divided into five sections. In some cases, therefore, what may be two sections in one presentation is only one section in another. For instance, a financial statement can be included with an AIA 305 or separately.

Every contractor should address two basic questions in a negotiated proposal: How do you control costs, and how do you control time? The Management Controls Section addresses this.

The Team Early Negotiated Project Procedure indicates a Kugler-Morris step-by-step approach to a project. It indicates that we have a process for doing this work and being an active team member.

TYPES OF PROPOSALS

There are two basic types of proposals. The prequalification proposal is essentially an expanded brochure, submitted to an owner to demonstrate the contractor's basic capabilities for the project. It is not project-specific and is used by the owner to narrow the list of eligible contractors to a few finalists.

The other type of proposal is in response to a request for a proposal (RFP), and it is for a specific project. This type of proposal is more detailed and focuses on the contractor's approach to the owner's project. It also contains a fee.

Prequalification Proposal.   Many contractors have a standard information package that they give to owners requesting basic information about the company. A common form for the prequalification proposal is a spiral-bound booklet with tabbed index sections. Linbeck Construction Corp.'s system contains the following sections:

- Introduction—company background, philosophy
- Approach—the team approach, scheduling system, cost control
- Experience—a list of completed projects tailored to the type of project planned by the owner, or a five-year and current project list
- References—clients, architects, and financial and trade organizations
- Agreement—standard form contract

The information sheets in the Linbeck prequalification booklet are typed and copied on a high-quality photocopier. This allows for updating of information wherever necessary at a relatively low cost. For responding to RFPs when longer and more detailed proposals are required, Linbeck uses its basic system and adds a set of numbered tabs to separate the added material from the basic sections.

The introduction should be a brief, concise description of the company, stressing areas that are important to the client. Linbeck's prequalification introduction is a good example:

> *Linbeck Construction Corporation stands for dependability and construction quality.* Formed in 1939 by Leo E. Linbeck, Sr., the company ranks as one of the largest general contractors in the nation. The range of Linbeck's professional talents and cumulative experience equips it for work on a diversified scale and on almost every size of project. Working primarily in Texas and the Southwest, Linbeck's construction credits include office buildings, health-care facilities, airports, high-rise residential buildings, industrial facilities, retail projects and quality interior work.
>
> *Linbeck serves the client's needs by providing a variety of comprehensive services to assist in project planning as well as project construction.* These services are incorporated into the team approach, a concept applied to virtually all projects. Implemented with the Guaranteed Maximum Contract, this approach assures the client the best value for the construction dollar.
>
> *Linbeck would welcome the opportunity of assisting you in the planning and construction of your next project.*

The RFP Response.   An RFP demands a fully planned and organized effort involving several people. The detailed RFP response aims to persuade the owner that the contractor's expertise is greater than that of its competitors.

According to proposal consultant Herman Holtz, these are the five most frequently evaluated items in proposals:

1. A demonstration of your clear understanding of the project

2. An offer of a reasonable plan, backed up with a logical, persuasive rationale

3. Evidence that your plan is likely to work out all right

4. The offer of a well-qualified staff for the project

5. A reasonable estimate of costs, presented in an understandable form[3]

One contractor uses this approach in organizing and planning a proposal:

> When a Request for Proposal (RFP) arrives, it is immediately reviewed by the marketing group for identification of items which need a long lead time for proper response. Then the organization of the response is planned. Occasionally, the RFP does require a set format, but usually the organization is open. We have a system that allows for the response to be tailored to each request. After this initial review, individuals work on the responses they were assigned. The Communications Coordinator assembles all responses and with the Assistant organizes the proposal (typing, special art, pictures, etc.).
>
> Although each RFP is different, certain questions are repeated regularly (items such as references, project lists, services, etc.). It has cut down on production time to keep a file of all past responses. Note that this is not the file on past proposals, which is also kept, but a file organized by type of question, i.e.—company description, craft/union affiliations, insurance/bonding references. For the specific response, this data bank can be used; sometimes only a few words need to be changed. The possibilities are excellent for the company with a word processor.
>
> Several copies of project lists are maintained to save on having to make copies when all the new information is photocopied for distribution. Also, we use color photocopies of previous projects. A large file of the most commonly needed pictures is maintained with a backlog of up to 50 available copies.
>
> When this system is used, it is important that the information in the files be updated regularly and reviewed carefully each time it is reused.
>
> After the Communications team assembles the proposal, the Vice President of Marketing, who has been monitoring the proposal from step one, reviews the proposal with the President, and if necessary, the Chairman of the Board.
>
> Any last-minute changes are done and the proposal is ready for delivery.
>
> We prefer for the proposal to be hand-delivered to the company requesting it. Sometimes this is done by the Marketing Representative; other times he and the Vice President of Marketing [go] together, or the President often decides to hand-deliver the proposal.
>
> There are many times when the proposal is presented along with a large interview presentation. Then the proposal becomes just another part of the presentation, but an important part, as it is left behind when the company representatives, their presentation boards and the slide show all leave.

PROPOSAL KICK-OFF MEETING

If, after an analysis using Figure 12-1, a preliminary go decision is reached, a proposal team can then be selected, consisting of business development representatives, a proposal coordinator, and operating department managers.

While the department managers review the RFP, the business development representative and proposal coordinator should develop a preliminary outline of the proposal, stressing important client and project requirements. Related past projects and proposals can be identified for use during proposal preparation.

The entire proposal team should then meet to:

1. Review and develop a general project strategy for the proposal.
2. Identify all unique client needs and critical aspects of the project that will require special attention in the proposal.
3. Develop a proposal outline and assign responsibilities and deadline dates for submitting each proposal section, including charts, project cost, schedule, and personnel estimates.
4. Summarize the meeting and confirm the proposal preparation schedule.

THE PROPOSAL

Table 12-1 is generally applicable to most types of proposals. It can serve as a guide when the outline is not fixed in the RFP, and as a checklist for proposal contents.

TABLE 12-1 Standard Proposal Outline

Cover
Cover letter (or letter of transmittal and executive summary)
Table of contents
Project description
Scope of work
   Summary and objectives
   Scope of services
Project execution plan
   Summary
   Project organization
   Detailed approach to the work
   Project schedule
Project team
   Personnel available
   Key personnel
   Position descriptions
Project control systems
   Overall computer operations
   Office and field systems
Qualifications and experience
   General
   Specific to project, location, client
Contractual terms
Appendixes
Résumés

STANDARD PROPOSAL OUTLINE

Cover and Cover Letter.   The proposal's cover and cover letter are two important selling elements. Both should be tailored to each client and project.

The cover should be of high-quality paper stock, professionally designed and printed, and contain the contractor's name, the client's name and logo, and the project title. Some contractors use a photograph or map relating to the project on the cover, but this should be done only if they are of professional quality.

The cover letter should provide a broad summary of the entire proposal. It should:

- Refer to the RFP by document number and project title.
- Provide a brief description of the scope, location of the project, and key dates.
- State any important items that have been excluded or included in the proposal, or any unique approach to the project.
- State any special terms and conditions of the proposal, such as an expiration date.

Some firms provide the above information in a letter of transmittal and more sales information in an executive summary. Whether they are all part of a single cover letter or split between the letter of transmittal and an executive summary, the following are important selling points to cover:

- Highlight specific aspects of the proposal that demonstrate why the firm should be selected—unusual and related project experience and qualifications, background and capability of key personnel, competitive contractual terms, and familiarity with unique technological or difficult aspects of the project.
- Summarize reasons why the firm specifically desires this project and what it would do if it were selected to ensure the project's success.
- List the information or services to be supplied by the firm and by others.
- Stress any unique approach to the job.

Charles B. Thomsen advises that the cover letter or executive summary should always be at the front of proposals and:

> should convey 98 percent of the message using 2 percent of the words so a busy executive can get the message without falling asleep and so the person who actually reads the whole proposal has a framework of understanding upon moving into the full version. . . .
>
> Short proposals are almost always better proposals. . . . Simple words, graphics, and a distinguished cover letter are the essential components to a good proposal. Most of the time you have to force yourself to be original and fresh, using good material only when it applies. The important parts of a proposal are the sections on (1) services, (2) qualifications, and (3) price. The rest is boilerplate. The most impor-

tant thing is not to let the support material smother the communication. Keep the issues up front and the backup where it belongs.[4]

Project Description.   The project description demonstrates to the prospective client that the contractor is fully aware of the scope of the project. The project is defined in terms of size or capacity, materials, technology, major quantities, or other aspects that may apply. This section should convince the prospective client that the contractor is familiar with the type of project and has the expertise to execute the job superbly from a technical standpoint. Any guarantees or assurances can be included in this section.

Scope of Work.   This section outlines the contractor's general responsibilities for the project and proposed services. It states the project's objectives and breaks down the work into clearly defined phases. It should be tailored to address all areas of client concern. List anticipated types of services—design or design monitoring, procurement, construction, and start-up. Cover project support services, such as labor relations, consultants, and financing services. Mention preparation of cost estimates and reports, bid books, record books, schedules, and other significant reports. If other contractors' or consultants' services will have an impact on the contractor's work, that should be discussed in this section.

Project Execution Plan.   This section is one of the most important from a sales standpoint. The way the contractor will approach and execute the actual project is explained in detail. Using *project organization charts*, the contractor describes senior management, project manager, project team members, and others involved in the prospective client's project.

If the proposal organization is similar to one used successfully on similar projects, say so. If the project involves several phases, show the organizational changes between phases, discussing the continuity of personnel between phases.

Show the relationship between the contractor's project team and the client organization. If appropriate, discuss the project manager's full responsibility to the client and to the contractor's management for the entire project. Also state the responsibilities of all key personnel.

As for the various project activities, say where the work will be done and describe the responsibilities of the contractor's operating departments—construction, estimating, engineering, accounting, and purchasing. Refer to specific objectives, tasks, and the way they will vary from phase to phase.

Mention regular client progress-review meetings, progress reports, major schedule milestones (completion of reports or design, final estimates, start of fieldwork, completion of construction, and start-up). Cover completion of the fieldwork—punch lists, final checkout, and coordination with move-in or start-up activities.

Describe the use of subcontractors, consultants, and other third parties, as well as labor surveys, probable labor availability, recruiting, training programs, site facilities, and logistics. Cover quality control and assurance in the office and in the field.

The *project schedule* portion of this section should present an overall proposed project schedule, including a ninety-day kick-off schedule, mentioning meetings, initial plans and budgets, first cost and schedule information, and so forth. This can be expanded to include a detailed schedule for the first six months.

The project schedule—with its key dates and schedule intervals, broken down by phases—should be presented as preliminary, based only on proposal information and subject to continuing review and development.

It is important to highlight critical client dates and activities, particularly input, approvals, and release of work. A separate client schedule could be prepared.

Project Team.   The project team description, too, is an important section for selling the client. While charts or curves of labor required and available versus time may be useful for certain major projects, of greater concern to the client are the specific key personnel, mentioned by name, to be assigned to the project. Provide résumés for named personnel, proposed positions on the team, and, possibly, personal references (past clients served) for key people. If possible, summarize the experience of the project team in terms of average number of years of experience in the industry and average number of years with the contractor.

Project Control Systems.   Clients are placing increasing stress on the subject of project control, which often becomes a factor in the prequalification process. Contractors unable to demonstrate an effective—and usually computer-based—control system may not reach the "short list" of firms to be interviewed. The project control section of the proposal should describe office and field computer operations and cover office and construction controls for costs, labor hours, materials, and schedules, including a description of monitoring and reporting systems. The contractor should emphasize the use of these controls in taking corrective action to meet the project objectives.

Qualifications and Experience.   While some information relating to past experience may have been included in other sections of the proposal, it should be understood that deliberate repetition can be useful in sales. Provide a general experience statement, emphasizing the reasons the firm is uniquely qualified for the job, through past projects, special expertise, an unusually well-qualified project team, or other factors.

For specific related experience, refer to similar projects or portions of projects, to knowledge of current factors and trends affecting the job (labor markets, materials procurement lead times, price trends), and to any other pertinent information, such as weather experience or prior experience with the A/E, subcontractors, or major suppliers.

Contractual Terms.   The contractor's or other standard form contract can make up the major portion of this section. Other items can include statements on the contractor's policies and procedures, comments on or exceptions to the client's proposed contract, and legal, tax, insurance, and personnel matters. In addition to total and fee costs, a critical area is the agenda of reimbursable and nonreimbursable items. Also to be included in this section are affirmative action, EEO, and safety programs or provisions.

Appendixes.   Other materials requested in the RFP that do not fall into the above sections can be included in appendixes. Such items could be a financial statement, an overall organization chart, information about security, confidentiality, and technical resources, and typical forms for drawings or reports.

Résumés.   Employee résumés should be held to one page and presented in a consistent format. The essentials are clearly visible name and title, one- or two-sentence summary of overall experience, summary of experience with the contractor and total years of employment, and other data, such as education and professional memberships and activities.

A well-planned, professionally prepared proposal focusing on the client's concerns and project requirements is an invaluable tool in securing new contracts.

NOTES

[1]Adapted from Benson P. Shapiro and Ronald S. Posner, "Making the Major Sale," *Harvard Business Review*, March–April 1976, pp. 68–78.

[2]Charles B. Thomsen, *CM: Developing Marketing, & Delivering Construction Management Services*, McGraw-Hill Book Company, New York, 1982, p. 10.

[3]Gerre Jones, *How to Market Professional Design Services*, 2nd ed., McGraw-Hill Book Company, New York, 1983, p. 174.

[4]Thomsen, op. cit., pp. 35–37.

13

The Effective Sales Process: Phase 3

As owners become more sophisticated in choosing contractors, their selection procedures become more formal. One key step is the contractor's presentation to the decision makers.

The presentation affords an opportunity for the client to meet face to face with the several semifinalist construction firms that have survived the rigors of prequalification, including sales interview, further contacts, proposal, and possibly reference checks. At this point, the client believes that any one of these semifinalist firms is capable of constructing its project.

The presentations will help the client decide which firm to entrust with its several-million- to several-hundred-million-dollar investment. The client will also see which firm it would like to work with for the next year or two, or longer, who the members of the project team are, and whether they are likable and believable. In addition, the client will need to be convinced that the contractor selected best meets its greatest concern for schedule, quality, budget, project difficulty, or hidden agenda items. The client wants to know what the contractor will do to enhance its project—what the benefits are in selecting Contractor A.

By the time of the presentation, the client has all the typewritten facts and figures on each of the construction companies. Now the client wants to size up the contractor as people. The selection committee will take their impression from the appearance of the contractor's team, their ability to communicate and speak persuasively, their personality, and their apparent honesty, commitment, intelligence, and amiability.

Rightly or wrongly, clients increasingly take strong impressions from the professionalism of the contractor's presentation. The perception in many cases is that if the contractor is professional in delivering a presentation, then the contractor will be professional in executing the project.

To many contractors the presentation is mostly hogwash. The attitude of many an otherwise astute contractor/businessperson is, "We're great contractors. The client knows it and we know it. We can do a fine job on their project. Why do we have to go through this ritual of acting?"

That was the attitude of one contractor who did not win jobs. His team—if he brought one to the presentation at all—was never prepared. They had no visual aids, stumbled over their words, were nervous, made statements relating only to their past experience, answered questions poorly, and generally were not in control of the situation.

The attitude of the winning contractor, on the other hand, was, "The presentation is our opportunity to win the job. We are going to do our homework by studying the selection committee and finding out what their concerns are. Then we'll prepare a professional presentation. It will be organized, coordinated, and well rehearsed. We'll carefully select a presentation team and back them with visual aids that address the client's project. We'll show why we're the best contractor for their job—in terms that benefit them.

"We want this job and we'll do everything we can to get it. We'll have our top people at the presentation and make sure they're well prepared. Our presentation will flow smoothly. We'll anticipate the client's questions and rehearse answers. We'll be in control. We are the best contractor for this job and we'll communicate that effectively. That's what we're going to do to win."

One general contractor, a Midwestern firm with an excellent performance record, took the first attitude toward presentations—so much hogwash. This contractor was consistently short-listed but won only about one in 25 jobs where a presentation was involved in the selection process. It regularly lost projects to contractors that had the second—more professional—approach. The result was that the firm was becoming in effect a subcontractor, bidding on portions of projects won by others.

SPEAKING TECHNIQUES

Not only are most people unaware of the image they project when speaking before a group, but surveys show that public speaking heads the list of people's greatest fears. Yet more and more a person's success depends on his or her ability to speak effectively and persuasively before groups.

One recently retired chairman of the board of General Motors, one of the world's largest corporations, has said that of his many responsibilities public speaking was the one he dreaded. He claims that he never overcame his fear of speaking and still feels slightly ill before every talk.

Presentations are entirely an exercise in visual and verbal communications. There are many techniques for improving both these, and it is important for everyone involved in presentations to improve the ability to speak. That includes top executives, project managers, estimators, and superintendents.

Speech consultant Sandy Linver describes the visual and verbal images we project this way:

> The choices we make about our visual image determine to a great extent how other people perceive us—until we open our mouths and speak. At that moment many of us destroy our carefully constructed façades. . . .
>
> Our spoken image consists of much more than the words we say. It's how we say the words, the sound of our voice, the way we use our body as we speak—all of which determine how effectively we convey our message. . . .
>
> Both our success in our work and our personal happiness depend a great deal on our speaking abilities. Sure, education, writing ability, job performance and personality are important, too. But what happens when we talk to people exerts such a powerful influence that it can destroy—or reinforce—all our other positive attributes and achievements.[1]

Improving one's speaking abilities and techniques is not an easy thing to do. It requires:

1. *Awareness.* Learn how you appear to others, what your speaking image is, what your individual strengths and weaknesses are.
2. *Techniques.* There are several basic techniques that can be learned immediately to improve your verbal image.
3. *Practice.* As in any endeavor in business, sports, or personal life, change is a process that requires constant practice.

Awareness.   The single most effective way to develop awareness of one's speaking ability is through the use of videotape. This is the fastest, most efficient, and best way to see yourself as others see you. Videotape reproduces your total image, visual and verbal. The best way to improve speaking ability quickly is to enroll in a speaking course that uses videotape. Some speaking consultants give in-house training courses using videotape, so that members of presentation teams, from estimators to top executives, can improve their speaking abilities.

The simple lack of awareness of speaking ability can be costly to a contractor required to make presentations. One construction company vice president who gave all the contractor's presentations finally received feedback from an architect friend that he was "turning people off" by the way he spoke. The company's success rate on projects requiring presentations for selection was one in thirty, representing hundreds of millions of dollars in lost business opportunities.

Techniques.   Books have been written on the pointers, rules, and how-to's of speaking. Many are helpful, but learning them and trying to apply them can cause more tenseness and self-consciousness.

Sandy Linver's philosophy is that speaking improvement involves the whole person and his or her relationship with the audience. Linver's four basic concepts are represented by "EASY"—Energy, Awareness (of self and audience), Strength (or self-esteem), and You.

- *Energy.* To make an audience listen, a speaker must have energy. Energy and power are closely related. . . . The energy necessary for effective speaking can best be defined as intensity or involvement. It is the force that impels a speaker to reach out to make contact with an audience. . . . The most common block to a speaker's energy is the desire to deliver a perfect, polished speech. When a speaker tries to be perfect, his energy is turned inward and transmuted into tension.

- *Awareness.* Many people—particularly business persons—place too much emphasis on the content of a speech. They organize their material carefully and stand up to speak with the attitude that the information they are about to convey is important enough to guarantee the audience's attention. They're enthusiastic and send out plenty of energy. But they are oblivious to the way their audience receives their information. The speaker—not the speech—determines how the message is received. If he is not super-sensitive to the way his audience responds, his energy may be wasted. . . . Authentic audience awareness . . . means relating to each member of the audience as an individual and opening yourself up to him. . . . If you're too wrapped up in yourself and your message, you will never develop audience awareness.

- *Strength.* One of the fears speakers express most often is of the person in the audience who is obviously out to get them. The important thing to remember when someone tries to intimidate you is that he is more interested in how you handle a hostile question than he is in your specific response. In other words, your delivery is just as important as what you actually say. . . . The most important thing is to answer coolly and directly and not become angry, emotional or irrational. . . . Strength, or self-esteem, means having a strong, secure sense of self which you will not allow your audience to threaten.

- *You.* Speaking success . . . all comes back to you and how much time and effort you are willing to devote to improving your spoken image. You can attend dozens of communications seminars and read a stack of books on the subject, but if you don't deal with yourself and your own personal speaking strengths and weaknesses, you will have wasted your time. . . . The right way for *you* to speak effectively will not be quite the same as the right way for anyone else.[2]

PLANNING THE PRESENTATION

While it is important for each member of the contractor's presentation team to have good speaking abilities, it is equally important for the entire presentation to be a well-coordinated performance. That begins with planning.

Proper planning, an essential first step in an effective presentation, should include:

1. *Gathering complete intelligence* on the project, the prospect, the competition, and the decision makers or selection committee.

2. *Reviewing the proposal submission,* if one is required, and its coverage of the prospect's main concerns and areas of interest.

3. *Selecting the presentation team,* including the team leader, top executives,

and key project personnel (including project manager, superintendent, and chief estimator).

4. *Visiting the site*, if this has not been done before, to gather additional information, trigger ideas, and take pictures.

5. *Preparing a rough outline of the presentation*, complete with order of speaking, client-benefit points to be covered, timing of each person's comments, question and answer period, and visual aids to be used (slides, flip-charts, videotapes, handouts). Assign responsibilities for each task.

6. *Developing content*, including a theme, answers to client concerns and interests, specific visual support (slides and charts), and text for handouts. Check to ensure use of "you" more than "we" throughout: focus on the client.

7. *Checking the presentation room* for size, acoustics, arrangement of furniture, location of electric outlets and light switches, and places for slide projector and for presentation team to speak from.

8. *Preparing visual aids and handouts as professionally as possible*, using graphic artists for charts and professional photographers for slides. Have a one-page agenda.

9. *Anticipating tough questions* by developing a list of those likely to be asked and assigning presentation team members to answer them.

10. *Rehearsing and evaluating the presentation*, if possible using a video recorder and videotape, to review for overall flow and coordination, coverage of client concerns and needs, consistent use of theme, speaking skills, audience interest and awareness, timing, use of visual aids, and handling of questions.

11. *Revising and rehearsing*, if necessary—it's worth the extra time. Then organize all materials for transportation to the actual presentation.

THE PRESENTATION TEAM

Owners surveyed as to key selection criteria always rate the actual project team high on their list. Clients want to meet the people who will have significant impact on the success of their project. They also want to meet the people they will be working with for many months.

One of the problems that the contractor faces in selecting the project team members and presenting them to the prospective client is that good project managers and superintendents are usually committed to other projects. If the project is out of town, it may involve a relocation for them, and if the start of the project is delayed, they may be reassigned. Despite these problems, other things being equal, clients tend to select the contractor who presents an actual project team.

Generally, project managers and superintendents are not good at making presentations, so their speaking skills need to be improved through training and practice.

For the presentation team, a leader should be selected to coordinate the effort, make decisions, and act as the quarterback during the presentation, introducing people, fielding questions, and assigning people to answer them. He or she is the spokesperson and the focal point for the prospective client to direct questions to.

CASE HISTORY OF A WINNING PRESENTATION

The board of a hospital in a southern state was about to select a contractor to work with the board's architect on a new $14-million facility. Part of the selection process called for a formal presentation to the eight-member board.

The competition essentially came down to two contractors: one—call it Family Constructors—had a total annual volume of scarcely more than the value of the project. The other was a $100-million-a-year contractor whose executives knew members of the board through business and community activities. The larger contractor, more or less taking the project for granted because of its own size, reputation, and contacts, delivered a canned presentation consisting of a discussion of its credentials.

The smaller contractor took a different approach. Family Construction executives learned all they could about each member of the board and about the project. They selected a presentation team composed of the president and vice president, a project manager and an estimator. Family Construction settled on a theme of saving money for the hospital. The presentation team went on to develop their presentation around seven features of their company that translated into potential savings for the client. Each feature of the company was a selling point they wanted to communicate to the hospital board. The idea of turning each into a client benefit kept the board's interest and attention.

Family Construction used a 2 × 3-foot easel pad and placed one feature on a page, along with the line; "This advantage will save you $———." The features or advantages were:

1. Experienced hospital builders
2. Open-shop revolution
3. Good building-team members
4. Job site productivity
5. Full-service organization
6. Top management support
7. Quality work

Family's handout material consisted of an outline of the presentation and a sheet with the name of the client at the top and pictures of each of the four team members, along with their individual project responsibility.

After several rehearsals, the team was ready. At the presentation, the vice president was the leader and spokesperson. He introduced himself and the team members, expressed appreciation to the board, and outlined the presentation. Each team member spoke twice, for five minutes each, discussing one of the company's advantages and writing in, where possible, the dollar amount of savings to the hospital.

Family's vice president told the board what their fee would be, then summarized the advantages and their cost-saving benefits.

Family Construction won the job. One key to its success, according to its vice president, was its honest and sincere approach. "Once you get to the table, you've got to get them to trust you," he said.

SOME SUCCESSFUL TECHNIQUES

One small Midwest contractor successfully uses a slide presentation to win contracts. The first half of the slide program is tailored to the client's needs and project. The second half describes the building process, so the owner is less confused and more knowledgeable about the endeavor.

Some contractors employ graphic aids for presentations to break the project down into sections and describe details, make value engineering recommendations, or suggest money- or time-saving alternatives.

One business development manager identified the decision maker his construction company was to make a presentation for. He read *Fortune* and other publications to understand the executive's business philosophy. He determined what the client wanted to hear. He learned that the man was extremely conscious of quality and geared his presentation to that characteristic. He won the contract.

WAYS TO IMPROVE

The presentation can be thought of as a process with several phases:

- Preparation
- Beginning
- Middle
- End
- Follow-up

Preparation.   Match the size and experience of the presentation team to the project and the interview committee. Be sure all team members have good speaking skills and are well rehearsed and know their parts. Go through dry runs until the presentation is sharp. Anticipate tough questions and rehearse answers. Have all materials organized and test all equipment, such as slide projectors.

Just prior to the presentation, be rested and allow plenty of time for getting set up and for psyching up (through deep breathing and giving yourself a pep talk) and for relaxing. Remain relaxed throughout by focusing on ideas and individuals in the audience. Review the first two to three minutes of the presentation. If possible, try to be the first or the last firm interviewed.

Beginning.   The presentation team leader or spokesperson introduces himself or herself (if someone has not already done this) and introduces other members of the team. The team leader does most of the talking and is the focal point for the selection committee. All materials are handed out.

The spokesperson expresses appreciation for being there, states the purpose of the presentation, and provides an overview. If possible he or she begins with an attention-getting statement, question, or appeal to the interviewer's interests.

Middle.   Have presentation flow from one team member to next. Each speaker should use primarily client-directed words such as "you" and "yours," as opposed to such self-directed words as "me," "my," "I," "we," "us," and "our." Use simple everyday language, not jargon. Involve the interviewers as much as possible through audience awareness techniques. Be sincerely enthusiastic and energetic. Remain natural, however, and don't fidget. Speak clearly, not too fast, and vary the pace and volume of your voice. Don't use a script. Adhere to the presentation's theme.

Use visual aids such as slides if they can be discussed in terms that apply to the client's project. Try to use "action" visual aids, such as easel pads, or chalkboards that are written on during the presentation.

Demonstrate the firm's familiarity with the client's type of project, and make clear the continuity of responsibility and the approach to the project. Identify the highest ranking executive who will have overall responsibility for the project and the person who will give full-time attention to the project all the way through to completion (usually the project manager).

End.   Stay within the time allotted by the client and leave time for questions and answers. The team leader should field questions and answers and direct them to the appropriate person. Always be honest, and if asked an embarrassing question, use silence to gather your thoughts and possibly gain audience sympathy. Don't belabor sticky issues or tell a client he or she is wrong. Have a well-planned and rehearsed closing that summarizes the presentation's theme and key client-benefit points. Refer to future and specific action. Thank the interviewers for the opportunity, be friendly, but do not apologize for anything in the presentation. And, most important, ask for the job.

Follow-up.   Write thank-you letters to members of the selection committee, summarizing key points made during the presentation. Reemphasize your strong interest in the project. Hold a debriefing with members of the presentation team, and if possible get feedback from the client.

CONTRACT NEGOTIATION

Even after a winning presentation, one final hurdle remains for the contractor before being selected—price. The client may have been impressed with the contractor's professional and benefit-filled presentation, may have liked the project team members, and may have believed that they could perform well on this project. But the fee proposed may have been the highest received by the selection committee. If fee was not first among the prospect's selection criteria—and it usually is not—the contractor will be invited back to "discuss" the price. At that point, the contractor is involved in a negotiating process.

What is negotiation? Gerard I. Nierenberg, a leading expert on the negotiating process, states:

> Whenever people exchange ideas with the intention of changing relationships, whenever they confer for agreement, they are negotiating . . . negotiation is a cooperative enterprise; common interests must be sought; negotiation is a behavioral process, not a game; in a good negotiation, *everybody wins something.* . . . The cooperative approach . . . is based on a simple but important premise. Negotiation takes place between human beings. . . . Therefore, to negotiate successfully, you must have a knowledge of people. . . . We learn by reading, by listening, by observing, by finding out how people react—and have reacted—in certain situations. . . . The satisfaction of needs motivates virtually every type of human behavior. . . . Needs and their satisfaction are the common denominator in negotiation. If people had no unsatisfied needs, they would never negotiate. Negotiation presupposes that *both* the negotiator and his opposer want something; otherwise they would turn a deaf ear to each other's demands and there would be no bargaining.[3]

Thus, if a prospect contacts the contractor to negotiate a price, it can be assumed that the contractor has impressed the client to the point that the client wants the contractor to perform on the project. The contractor, of course, wants the project, so there is basis for negotiation. If the negotiation process is successful, both sides will feel that they have won something, and the contractor will be awarded the job.

It is said that no sale ever takes place until the prospect feels he or she is getting benefits commensurate with the money he or she is being asked to pay. For the contractor, the negotiation process is a matter of bringing into balance price versus the benefits offered. If the contractor can convince the owner that the value of those benefits is equal to the price, he or she will not have to compromise on the fee. If the owner does not see that the benefits balance the price, the contractor may need to reduce the fee—if he or she wants the job.

KNOWING COST

To negotiate effectively the contractor must know what his or her costs are. A fee consists of two basic elements, overhead and profit. Since overhead is more or less fixed, any compromise in the fee will amount to a reduction in profit.

The contractor can propose a fixed overhead fee that is all-inclusive of overhead factors, such as estimating, project management, accounting, and data processing, with reimbursable items confined to field construction, from superintendent down. In this case, the fee might be 5 percent or 6 percent, which includes a 2 to 3 percent profit.

Another method of fee pricing is to propose a lower fee of 2 percent or 3 percent, which would be primarily profit. All other items, including project management, data processing, accounting, and estimating, would be chargeable to the cost of construction.

Some clients favor the higher all-inclusive fee arrangement; others prefer the lower fee with more reimbursable items. In proposing the fee, the contractor can ask the prospective client which method is preferred (if not stated in an RFP) or assess the client and the competitive situation and decide on that basis.

Factors that will affect profit and overhead in the contractor's fee include the market situation, competition, labor exposure, complexity of the project, and time schedule. It is important for the contractor to be prepared to explain to the prospect in detail the reasons for proposing a certain fee.

ANSWERING PRICE OBJECTIONS

Owners are motivated by one or more of several factors in objecting to a contractor's price:

- The prospect sincerely believes that the price is too high.
- One or more competitors have submitted a lower price.
- The owner is using the price objection as a brush-off.
- The owner is trying to save money.

It is helpful to find out what is motivating the owner to object. This can be accomplished by asking open-ended questions such as, "The fee is too high? In what respect?"

Price competition is one of the phenomena of a free-enterprise marketplace. The contractor should recognize that there will always be a market for high-quality services, just as there will always be one for lowest price. It is important for the contractor's business development people to be aware, too, that price is only one of the complex factors involved in the purchase of construction services. If that were not true in the private sector, the lowest bid or fee would always win the job, and that is not the case. Successful salespersons and negotiators of construction services know that owners must believe they are getting (in terms of benefits) at least as much as they are giving (in terms of money). The scales must be in balance.

Bringing the scales into balance in the owner's mind requires skillful sales and negotiating techniques. Essentially it is a matter of minimizing cost and maximizing benefits to the owner.

Establishing Understanding.   Early in the first meeting with the prospective client who has objected to price, the contractor must be sure that he or she and the owner are discussing the same issues. It is necessary to define the price objection so that it can be approached from the owner's point of view. First, does the owner understand exactly what the contractor is providing in services, what is included in the fee versus what is included in lower quotes from competitors? Does the owner understand all the reasons for proposing that level of fee or total cost? Take time to review the cost factors in detail so that any discrepancies or misunderstandings can be cleared up. If the contractor is providing additional services or proposing a more inclusive fee, the negotiation can center on those items to bring the price differential in line with a lower quote and perhaps eliminate the spread.

If it becomes apparent, after equalizing issues, that the contractor's price is higher, then the negotiating will become a matter of bringing the scales into balance by persuading the owner that the contractor is providing benefits that equal or outweigh the price difference.

Quality and Value.   Depending on the type of project, many owners are willing to pay more for quality if the features are pointed out to them. Quality may be reflected in the:

- Qualifications of the people assigned to the project
- Quality of subcontractors (or designers if it is a design/build project)
- Quality of work (if the contractor performs a portion of the work and is expert in some trades)
- Quality of management
- Quality of technology or technical know-how

Value to the owner can be shown by explaining that most money is saved during design and that the contractor will provide value engineering during that phase. In that way the owner can obtain the optimal facility, or value, for the money. If the contractor has a record of delivering savings to clients through value engineering, this should be mentioned. Just telling the owner about quality and value advantages is not sufficient, however. The results of those advantages have to be demonstrated through case histories and references—if possible on projects similar to the owner's. If available, case histories of savings paying for a portion of or all the fee would be most helpful to the contractor's cause.

Schedule and Performance Advantages.   If the contractor can assure the prospect that he or she will complete the project earlier than competitors, that will suggest substantial savings to the owner in lower interim financing cost or earlier generation of income from use of the facility. And if the contractor can compute the savings, it can have a strong impact on the client.

The client who requires guaranteed use of the facility by a certain date may be willing to pay a premium for the assurance. For example, industrial or manufacturing companies may need to bring a new product on the market as early as possible, or a retail owner may be committed to an opening date, or an institution may be geared to the start of an academic year, or a hospital may need beds, and so forth.

Service Advantages.   Additional services can often justify a higher fee. More frequent estimates during the design phase, cost reports tailored to the owner's formats, assistance with permits, and financing are examples.

Experience and Reputation Advantages. If the contractor has a considerable record of success on projects similar to the client's and enjoys an impeccable reputation, these can be seen as "peace of mind" benefits to the owner. Experience and reputation translate into dependability, which commands a higher fee. The contractor can provide references of clients who have hired the company repeatedly for many years because they have found it better in the long run to pay slightly more for high-quality projects delivered in a timely and budget-conscious manner.

Interest and Enthusiasm. Owners respond positively to business development people who go out of their way or display genuine interest and enthusiasm for the project and for their own organization. Clients also favor people who keep their word and follow through on details. Greater personal assistance and service during the selling and negotiating process can help overcome lower prices from competitors.

If the contractor's price is higher for sound reasons that are beneficial to the owner, and if the contractor can communicate those benefits effectively, he or she need not be the lowest bidder. The owner is usually seeking a balance between cost and benefit, not necessarily the lowest price. For the contractor, successful negotiating starts with an understanding of what is important to the client and creating a balance in the client's mind.

NOTES

[1]Sandy Linver, *Speak Easy,* Summit Books, New York, 1978, pp. 18, 19.

[2]Ibid., pp. 24–38.

[3]Gerard I. Nierenberg, *The Art of Negotiating,* Cornerstone Library, New York, 1968, pp. 8, 32, 33, 75, 81.

14

Marketing Communications Tools

Contrary to common opinion, successful marketing of construction services to private clients depends on more than efficient office and field operations, competitive prices, good salespeople, and well-prepared strategic plans. It depends to a great extent on the contractor's ability to disseminate information about the company, its capabilities and services, and the ways it can benefit its clients.

For the contractor seeking work in the private sector, the question is not whether to develop marketing tools, but rather which of these tools can produce an effective communications program and for how much. The contractor's information program, though geared to clients and prospects, must go beyond. The program must reach architects, engineers, real estate brokers, newspapers, trade and business magazines, possibly radio and television stations, the contractor's bank and bonding companies, and its own employees and in turn their families. Through a communications program, the contractor seeks to gain the confidence of its various audiences. Ultimately, owners' confidence in the contractor is a major factor in the company's being placed on select-bidders lists and in its being selected for projects.

A contractor without a communications program will still communicate through its projects, employees, and actions, but a planned program is a more controlled way of communicating and thereby gaining a competitive advantage. It helps to build a reputation for integrity, progress, and dependability. This chapter will deal with the planning that goes into the marketing communications program and the developing of effective tools to ensure its success.

MARKETING COMMUNI

Marketing tools are the specific media a contractor uses to reach audiences. Each marketing tool is designed to deliver one or more messages to prospects, clients, and others in a different way. At one time, the contractor's prime marketing tool was a photocopied list of past projects. Today, the marketing-oriented contractor uses an array of sophisticated tools, from four-color brochures to minimagazines to videotape cassettes.

The contractor's marketing tools support the company's salespeople and executives in their business-development efforts. They spread the word among target audiences, reaching them periodically and at a cost far lower than that of a sales call. While marketing tools can never close a sale in the complex construction buying process, they can reach thousands of people efficiently and periodically.

Which marketing tools the contractor requires depends on the company's needs, budget, activity level (number of projects or newsworthy events occurring in one year), and corporate or marketing objectives. The decision-making process for marketing tools will be discussed later in this chapter.

The principal communications tools used by contractors are brochures, newsletters, specially targeted mailing pieces, public relations, and advertising.

BROCHURES

A printed corporate brochure is the most fundamental and useful marketing tool for the contractor. More and more owners and design firms request the contractor's brochure as an initial step in the sales process (Figure 14-1).

The corporate brochure's primary mission is to allow the contractor to hurdle that crucial initial sales step, the first impression. If the brochure is an attractive, high-quality piece, containing a well-written account of the contractor's experience and the benefits it offers to clients, the company's salespeople will have an advantage over their competitors. The message that should be carried in a first-class brochure is that the contractor is a well-managed, capable organization deserving consideration.

Here are some characteristics of corporate brochures.

- *Use.* Before deciding to produce a corporate brochure, the contractor should consider the target audiences and how they can be reached. A brochure can be distributed by mass mailing to target markets, select mailing to prior contacts, and limited distribution to others, or it can be hand-carried to sales interviews. It can be used to introduce the company to new sources of business, reinforce relationships with existing clients, and communicate a new image.

  One contractor received more than 100 responses when 1400 of the company's new corporate brochures were mailed to a carefully selected list of major corporations. With follow-up, the company was able to secure places on a number of select-bidders' lists. That is an extraordinary response, however, and should not be expected. A response rate of 0.5 to 2.0 percent is considered good in direct mail.

- *Purpose.* The primary objectives of a corporate brochure are to command the attention of owners, communicate information about the company, establish credibility, and begin to gain confidence. A brochure that accomplishes those objectives will assist the contractor in the prequalification phase of the sales process.

- *Format.* Brochures come in a variety of formats, sizes, and shapes, including full-color or black-and-white, with flexible or fixed binding, large or small photographs and light or heavy text, textured or high-gloss paper, and other variables.

  Generally, color has greater impact if it is high quality. The length of the brochure—anywhere from four to 40 or more pages—should be the minimum required to tell the contractor's story effectively to the target audiences. Standard size, 8½ x 11 inches, is safe and useful, but brochures that are slightly oversize or undersize vertically or horizontally can be distinctive. Fixed binding makes the best presentation and is easiest to use. Large, dramatic photographs work well to make an important visual impact. Paper stock is a matter of personal taste. Overall, a well-designed appearance gets good results.

- *Content.* The corporate brochure should be a complete document with a beginning (who the company is, what it does, why it is better), a middle section presenting services offered (markets served by project type, or capabilities provided), and an end (miscellaneous services, a conclusion to sum up and invite inquiries, and a client list). Text should cover about 15 to 25 percent of the page area, be oriented to client benefits, and provide brief case histories. Photographs should dominate, since visual impact is of prime importance.

- *Cost Range.* Full-color brochures of 8 to 24 pages, for 2000 to 3000 copies, can cost from $10,000 to $70,000, varying with printing quality, amount of outside assistance, amount of photography, and special features. The same number of copies of a black-and-white brochure of similar length can range from $5,000 to $45,000.

- *Frequency.* A corporate brochure should be updated every two to three years and replaced every four to five years. The preparation process forces management into a healthy marketing review, which can be beneficial and profitable.

Once the contractor has produced an effective corporate brochure, the company may find the need to show greater depth of experience in one or more areas to penetrate a new market or expand in an existing one. This can be accomplished with special-market brochures, such as one on the power field, health care field, foundations, or CM.

One important by-product of a corporate brochure is its impact on morale within the contractor's own organization. One contractor found that a new brochure generated an enthusiastic response from employees and their families, who had not realized the size and scope of the company.

Sundt Corp.   Our People Make the Difference

FIG. 14-1 Corporate brochures.

CONTINUING COMMUNICATIONS: NEWSLETTERS, MAGAZINES

Construction buying is a lengthy process, with many interim steps between the earliest contact and the signing of the contract. Therefore, it is important for the contractor to be at the forefront of the buyer's mind when the buyer is ready to make

FIG. 14-1 (*continued*)

the purchase. An impressive corporate brochure is an excellent introduction, but if it reaches an owner in the very early stages of a buying decision, the end of which is months or years away, the owner will probably place the brochure on file. The contractor needs to remind the owner continually of the company's existence, activities, and name. A periodically published newsletter permits the contractor to reach target audiences, in a soft-sell manner, one to twelve times a year.

Meeting the Challenges of Our Next Century in Construction

The growth of our company has been based on meeting challenges: public works, defense facilities, nuclear development, mining, and history's most extensive highway and bridge building program, the interstate highway system. Today, we see new construction challenges for our determined force of veteran personnel and our fleet of modern equipment. The Kiewit organization is solidly positioned to help both industrial and commercial clients capitalize on opportunity and remain competitive.

We are working with owners, architects, engineering firms, development organizations, and joint-venture partners to

■ Develop and deliver new energy resources.
■ Complete more cost-effective power producing facilities.
■ Install efficient materials processing and handling systems.
■ Build or modernize dependable land-based and marine transportation systems.
■ Produce processed or manufactured goods faster at less expense with highly automated and computerized plants.
■ Create successful commercial complexes and productive office environments.
■ Construct outstanding centers for health care and recreational purposes.

Through our decentralized network of regional Kiewit operations, we maintain a firm grasp of local conditions. Local management exercises full authority to commit corporate assets, while our active headquarters executives assure ample support for your project regardless of size. This multidimensional approach

coupled with a record of competitive prices, enables Kiewit to meet your needs for projects ranging in value from $10,000 to $1 billion or more.

Our assurances are backed by the sincere commitment of **an organization wholly owned by the employees.** Kiewit people continue to satisfy and keep clients by assuming personal responsibility for results. We find that we build faster with our own people and our own equipment in an environment of safety and quality.

We invite you to put Kiewit integrity and performance to work on your next project. You can expect the same outstanding results that hundreds of owners have realized throughout Kiewit's past century of achievement.

Walter Scott, Jr.
Chairman of the Board and President

(Left) Interior of a facility for processing and storing radioactive waste for Westinghouse.

FIG. 14-1   (*continued*)

Solid Wood Products

recent, plywood plants in the South. For Temple-Eastex, we designed and constructed the Pineland plywood plant in only 18 months, delivering savings from lower interest costs and early production income. By using all facets of our organization – engineering, general construction, fabrication, and electrical and mechanical construction – we achieved the short schedule.

For Willamette Industries, we assisted in converting major portions of a sawmill in Zwolle, La., into a plywood plant using fast-track techniques to complete it on a tight schedule and within budget.

Higher Quality at Lower Life-Cycle Cost

Our design for an automated hot water plywood soak vat operation at Champion Building Products Co.'s Corrigan, Tex. facility was one of the first to use prestressed concrete and an indirect heat system for the process. It produced a higher quality veneer with more production reliability – while eliminating pollution problems and greatly reducing life cycle maintenance costs. We also constructed major portions of Champion's plywood plant in Camden, Tex.

Projects designed and/or built for Owens-Illinois plants include dryers, presses, a log deck, an 8-ft lathe line, process machinery, foundations, structures, and pollution control systems – all on or ahead of schedule. Much of the work required maintaining production during construction – a requirement we can meet on your project.

Energy-Saving Pollution Controls

Temple Associates engineered the pollution control installation for Champion's wood-fired boiler in Corrigan, Tex. By performing research and specifying a precipitator installation that works as well or better than wet scrubbers, we eliminated water pollution problems and cut maintenance costs while saving energy.

Dryer Design Increases Productivity

International Paper selected Temple Associates to solve their plywood veneer dryer problems in Nacogdoches, Tex. Increasing veneer capacity and cutting energy consumption substantially, Temple Associates' design achieved much more than solving the condensate problems we were initially retained to study.

Temple Associates was also selected by International Paper to construct major portions of a stud mill and plywood complex in Wiggins, Miss., and complete new sawmills in Georgetown, S.C., and New Boston, Tex.

Stud, Planer, & Sawmills

In only nine months, Temple Associates designed and constructed a sawmill producing 60 million board feet per year for Temple-Eastex Incorporated.

For Weyerhaeuser Co., we designed a hardwood sawmill in Wright City, Okla. We also designed lumber-handling systems for the first facility in the South using a computerized chipping edger for Weyerhaeuser's Dierks, Ark., plant. For Owens-Illinois, we constructed stud and planer mills in Jasper, Tex. And for Conwall, Inc., we designed and constructed two planer mill/dry kiln facilities in Washington, and Augusta, Ga.

Value Engineered Savings

Temple Associates can save substantial sums by recommending alternatives in plant design and construction methods. For example, we reduced excavation and concrete forming costs on Boise Southern's stud mill in De Quincy, La., enabling a completion well below our guaranteed maximum and cutting related construction time 20%.

We look for ways to reduce costs on every project and have saved significant sums on many

FIG. 14-1   (*continued*)

The marketing newsletter is a well-designed, professional publication that is aimed at people outside the company and is different from a house-organ type of newsletter. News of bowling or softball teams or employee marriages is of no value to an owner and could even be detrimental in terms of image. For a local contractor whose company and employees are known to clients, however, such news could be of interest and add a human quality. Many contractors have found newsletters an excellent means of communicating regularly with clients and prospects.

- *Use.* A client-directed newsletter or minimagazine, published on a regular basis, keeps "suspects," prospects, clients, past clients, and other buying influences informed of the contractor's activities. Each issue can highlight a different market or introduce a new service. The newsletter provides salespeople and executives with a reason to recontact prospects and clients. It extends the life of the corporate brochure and is a repeat marketing tool, whereas the brochure has one-time use only on any individual.

- *Purpose.* The newsletter's purpose is to provide a vehicle for the contractor to keep its name, capabilities, projects, services, and management before the company's sources of business. It maintains the contractor's image and, through its repetition, helps to build confidence.

- *Format.* Newsletter and minimagazine formats run the gamut from one- to two-page sheets with typewritten text and offset photographs to elaborate four-color magazines, such as those published by Dravo Corporation, Fluor Corp., and other major construction corporations. It is advisable for the newsletter to be well designed and printed on high-quality paper.

- *Content.* Articles should present projects and services in a way that interests owners. A news style similar to that found in a business or trade magazine is appropriate. Any unusual or difficult aspect of a project, or any achievements that benefited the owner, always attracts attention. Photographs, as in brochures, should be large and dramatic.

- *Cost Range.* Costs for newsletters vary greatly from under $1000 to as much as $20,000, $25,000, or more per issue, with lower costs for simple one- or two-page issues in black and white and higher costs for eight or more pages in full color.

- *Frequency.* One of the keys to an effective newsletter is its regular publication. For most contractors, quarterlies or semiannual newsletters are adequate. More frequent publication of a less elaborate, one- to two-page newsletter is favored by some firms. The major considerations are the amount of newsworthy information the contractor can generate over a certain period, how many issues of a newsletter that translates into, and whether the budget can support that number of issues. If a semiannual or quarterly publication or newsletter is not feasible because of budgetary constraints or lack of newsworthy material, an annual report or update is recommended. Publicly held construction companies not only comply with the law by producing an annual report, but they gain the advantage of a major new marketing communications tool each year. The private contractor can produce a less extensive annual review without the financial data.

Figure 14-2 shows examples of regularly published newsletters. Note that the headlines are designed to show achievements that benefited the owner.

SPECIALLY TARGETED MAILING PIECES

Another marketing communications method that the contractor can employ to recontact prospects and clients is the special mailing piece. This brief flyer-type brochure, usually four to six pages or less, covers a single subject and is directed to inform certain audiences. Special mailing pieces can be effective in some situations, but they should be a part of a marketing communications program, not its only component.

- *Use and Purpose.* When the company has developed a new service—such as CM, design/build, materials supply, or maintenance—or when it has completed a significant project, a special mailing piece may be called for to tell significant potential prospects about the news event. The advantage of the special mailing piece is that it calls the reader's attention to one specific aspect of the contractor's capabilities where increased sales are desired.
- *Format and Content.* Special mailing pieces range from single-sheet folded self-mailers to six-page minibrochures. The mailing pieces shown in Figure 14-3 illustrate two types. The Econobase piece announces a new product: sub-base material composed of crushed concrete rubble, produced at a plant purchased by a large heavy contractor. The mailing piece was aimed at other contractors seeking an economical alternate to crushed stone. The speak-the-same-language mailing piece, aimed at domestic and foreign corporations, describes the successful relationship with a major Japanese design/construction firm and the completion of a plant for a well-known Japanese manufacturer. In some instances contractors have included response cards as a means of generating inquiries, and they do work.
- *Cost Range and Frequency.* A realistic cost range for specially targeted mailing pieces can run from under $1000 to several thousand dollars, plus postage. The frequency will be irregular, since the mailing piece is timed to coincide with the development of a new service or completion of a noteworthy project.

PUBLIC RELATIONS

Public relations is a broad and often misused and misunderstood term. It is frequently used interchangeably with marketing and improperly used to refer to all marketing activities. On a narrower scale, public relations, or PR as it is commonly called, means press coverage. *Webster's Eighth New Collegiate Dictionary* defines public relations as "the business of inducing the public to have understanding for and goodwill toward

Published by Bor-Son Construction Companies, Minneapolis, MN

Summer 1981

Bor-Son achieved below-budget savings and on-time occupancy for Capp Industries' Hotel Seville.

Value Engineering Keeps Hotel Construction Costs Under Budget

The Hotel Seville project came in $90,000 under budget, due to Bor-Son's value engineering.

As general contractor for the 17-story hotel, Bor-Son consulted with the architect, James M. Cooperman & Associates, during the design phase and recommended changes in the concrete structure. That recommendation proved to be a major savings for Bor-Son's client, Capp Industries.

The 143,000-sq-ft hotel contains a bar, restaurant, gift shop, pool, and a Spanish-style lobby with Mexican quarry tiles, wood-beamed ceiling, and wrought-iron fixtures. The Seville offers above-code security to all patrons. Every room has a smoke detector, all guest rooms and public areas are protected by sprinkler systems, all exposed surfaces are completely fireproofed, and a computerized floor monitoring system was installed to assist rescue efforts in the event of an emergency. In addition, the Seville has a built-in control system to conserve energy. Connected to all 250 guest rooms, the regulating system turns down the heat and turns off the air conditioning in unoccupied rooms.

According to Project Manager, Jim Mortenson, Bor-Son started excavation on December 13, 1979. The Hotel Seville opened its doors to guests on March 9, 1981.

To Our Clients and Friends: a Record-Breaking Year at Bor-Son

The Bor-Son Companies achieved a record-breaking year in 1980. We were selected by clients for contracts totaling more than $102.5 million in new work—up from $66 million in 1979. In our total project mix, we signed and/or completed major commercial, (Continued on page 2)

FIG. 14-2 Newsletters.

a person, firm, or institution."[1] This definition would have public relations encompass all the activities a contractor engages in to foster goodwill, including:

- The appearance of its offices and equipment
- The conduct of people on the job site
- The cleanliness of its equipment

Bor-Son West   Northern Federal   Decathlon Athletic Club

Preconstruction Services for Residential Projects

When Cedar-Riverside Associates and the Housing and Urban Development (HUD) agency joined forces in the early 1970s to develop Cedar Square West, a unique, cooperatively funded housing complex, they invited Bor-Son Construction to join the planning team.

As a major high-rise housing specialist, Bor-Son's role involved plan review, cost analysis, scheduling, construction methods, and general project consultation, as well as construction of the entire complex.

Don Jacobson, now director of development for Bor-Son, was formerly director for the Cedar Square West planning team. Don's years of experience as a prominent local planner enabled him to expedite this ambitious housing program.

Completed On Schedule and Within Budget

In order to meet the accelerated 21-month completion schedule, Bor-Son mobilized a 500-person work force. Costs had to be carefully controlled within the various federal and private budgets established for each phase of the project. Bor-Son's specialty, the post-tensioned concrete system, was used exclusively for the project to reduce costs and construction time.

Another project requirement was the coordination of construction so that initial occupancy could be accomplished while construction continued, thereby generating earlier rental income for the owner. Despite these challenges, Bor-Son completed the entire project ahead of schedule and within budget.

Cedar Square West features high-density, heterogeneous housing arranged around a commercial centrum. The 1,303 housing units, ranging from subsidized to luxury housing, are integrated within nine interconnected major buildings up to 43 stories high. Some 48,000 sq ft of commercial space, an underground parking garage containing 839 parking spaces, and extensive open space are included within the Cedar Square West complex.

Innovative Funding

A pilot project of HUD's New Communities Program, Cedar Square West was one of the first core urban renewal projects to be cooperatively funded by federal, private, and institutional sources.

One hundred different options for housing types, with four different rent levels and mortgage programs and seven sources of funding, were included in the financial packaging. Extensive coordination and resourcefulness were required on the part of the entire planning team, due to the complex nature of the program.

The Cedar Square West complex contains 1,650,000 sq ft of housing, commercial space, and parking.

FIG. 14-2 *(continued)*

- The dress and appearance of office personnel
- The manner in which the company's phone is answered
- The look of its job signs and stationery
- The extent of community involvement
- Articles appearing in newspapers and magazines

FIG. 14-3 Special mailing pieces.

- Coverage on radio and television
- Overall image

While all those aspects of the contractor's interaction with its public are important and should be properly addressed, this section will focus on one aspect of public relations—publicity.

Plaza Materials Company   Quality Sub-base for Less!!

These Times Demand

ECONOBASE

**Save With
ECONOBASE
on a Range of
Applications**

If you are a contractor, subcontractor, municipality official, commercial or industrial purchasing agent, or private individual, you can benefit from Plaza Materials Company's economical new product —ECONOBASE.

Our materials serve a wide variety of construction applications:

Backfill	Wearing Surfaces	Sub-Base	
■ Pipelines	■ Parking Lots	■ Parking Lots	■ Driveways
■ Trenches	■ Walkways	■ Sidewalks and	■ Concrete Slabs
■ Foundations	■ Construction Sites	Walkways	■ Athletic
		■ Roadways	Facilities

**Dependable
Delivery
to Your Site**

Our convenient location in the Greater New York Area makes us accessible to you — as well as economical. If you are from the Metro Area, you can pick up ECONOBASE directly from our Yonkers plant. Or you can request delivery — by barge, rail, or truck — to your construction site.

Regardless of where you are located, or whether your project is private, commercial, industrial, or municipal, ECONOBASE can meet your needs for economy, dependability, and quality.

FIG. 14-3   *(continued)*

Publicity is the process of obtaining editorial coverage of the contractor's company and projects in media read, heard, or seen by the company's prospects and clients. Such editorial coverage (time or space) is provided free. The cost to the contractor is in the preparation of publicity materials, such as press releases, photography, and staged events. The main disadvantage of publicity is that the contractor has no control over whether media will provide coverage or, if they do, how it will be written. In the first instance, the contractor can lose the money spent to prepare material. In the second, something erroneous, embarrassing, or damaging could be said. Unlike all other marketing communications tools, in which the contractor controls what is said, when it appears, and who it reaches, publicity is outside the contractor's control. Nevertheless, a well-planned program offers many benefits.

Implementing a successful publicity program requires the use of many of the same principles employed in selling to owners. In the media, editors are analogous to owners. The contractor, through staff or an outside agency, needs to establish credibility, capture the editor's attention, build personal relationships with editors, and sell them on writing or broadcasting a story about the company or one of its projects.

- *Use and Purpose.* Publicity, as a marketing communications tool, helps the company achieve its marketing objectives by reaching prospects and clients through an additional information channel, adding credibility to the company's name through appearance in respected media, creating greater awareness of and interest in the contractor's name and activities, and fostering a desired positive and successful image for the company. Publicity also helps launch new services or capabilities, gain the confidence of the contractor's audience and counteract or reduce the impact of negative publicity, if it should ever occur.

- *Format and Content.* Sparking the interest of a busy editor is not an easy matter. Generally, a simple phone call or letter does not suffice unless the story has great intrinsic drama. If one or a few media are targeted for coverage, editors should be approached individually in a lengthy letter providing significant background information. When the contractor seeks broader coverage in a number of media, the tool of the trade is the press release, which can be about a company event such as a management change, anniversary, expansion, acquisition, or major new contract, or it can cover a project-related event. Whenever possible, the letter or press release should be accompanied by high-quality or dramatic photographs.

- *Events.* Another way to gain an editor's interest is to stage events. A planned publicity campaign is built around newsworthy corporate and project milestones. Nearly every project has several story possibilities: contract signing, ground breaking, construction progress, topping out, and dedications. At company events, it is important to have press releases, a photographer, and company literature—anything that might be useful to an editor.

- *Cost Range and Frequency.* To be effective, publicity must be planned as a program or campaign. A press release now and then or a call to an editor every once in a while will not accomplish much. The contractor needs to review marketing objectives and determine where publicity will help achieve them. Publicity objectives for six months or one year should be established. The program can then be translated into numbers of press releases to be prepared, media to be targeted, or events to be staged.

    No press releases or events should be considered unless they have real news value. The cost of a publicity program can range from several thousand dollars a year to many tens of thousands for a larger company.

Press information for any of those items should highlight the project's size (if significant), the importance to the community or a link with a major issue in the news (such as the environment, energy savings, defense, or high technology), new or unusual design or construction features, historic value, and employment possibilities.

Company milestones can include major anniversaries such as ten or fifty years in business; promotions of top executives; reorganization or start-up of a new division; acquisitions, joint ventures, or new branch offices; new contract awards; executives being named to important business, government, charity, or community boards or positions; and receipt of significant awards.

The ideal frequency of press contacts, either personally or through a press release, is a matter that requires judgment. The objective is to give media personnel newsworthy material as often as possible. Giving editors information that is old or of little interest outside the company will diminish the contractor's credibility with the press.

Judgment must also be applied in selecting which media to contact with which stories. Some milestones are of local interest only, and a major press release disseminated nationally to business and consumer publications and broadcast networks would be a futile exercise. The reverse situation—a story that has broad appeal and a chance to secure regional or national coverage—requires insight and creativity to be dealt with effectively.

- *Negative Publicity.* Construction, being a high-risk, high-stakes business conducted in full view of the public, is inevitably prone to unsavory occurences, ranging from petty dealings to major crises or disasters. Any of these seems to seize the attention of the media. Even when the contractor is ultimately found to be innocent, the public associates the company with something not right for a long time.

  Publicity, like marketing, should not be reactive. One good-sized building contractor with no publicity program was cited in the city's press as the contractor for a major civic auditorium where cracks had developed. Not only was this the only time the company's name was mentioned in the media, but the firm was linked with an embarrassing and possibly serious problem. However, the contractor had no mechanism for dealing with the press. Had the company sponsored an active public relations program, its name would have appeared in the media regularly in connection with many positive and civic-minded activities. It would have developed relationships with journalists and could have received more favorable editorial treatment.

In his article, "How to Meet the Press," author Chester Burger provides specific guidelines for successfully communicating with the press. He offers rules of the game, including two general criteria and ten guidelines:

> *General Criteria.* First, it is necessary to have a sound attitude . . . not one of either arrogance or false humility. . . . The business executive respects his own competence and greater knowledge of his own subject, but realistically recognizes that the reporter or critic is skilled in the art of asking provocative questions. . . .

Second, it is always wise to prepare carefully for a press interview. Never should an executive walk into a meeting with the press, planning to "play it by ear." . . . The best preparation consists of anticipating the most likely questions, attempting to research the facts, and structuring effective answers to be held ready for use. Probably it is unwise to carry such notes into the interview.[2]

Specific Guidelines

1. *Talk from the viewpoint of the public's interest, not the company's.*
2. *Speak in personal terms whenever possible.* [Try to use "I" or "my" rather than an impersonal corporate "we."]
3. *If you do not want some statement quoted, do not make it.* [Avoid off-the-record statements.]
4. *State the most important fact at the beginning.* [Begin with the conclusion, not a lengthy explanation.]
5. *Do not argue with the reporter or lose your cool.* [Present the story fairly and adequately, respond directly to questions, and never ask questions of the reporter out of anger or frustration.]
6. *If a question contains offensive language or words you do not like, do not repeat them, even to deny them.* [Reporters often use the gambit of putting words into the subject's mouth.]
7. *If the reporter asks a direct question, he is entitled to an equally direct answer.* [Don't give abbreviated or even yes or no answers.]
8. *If an executive does not know the answer to a question he should simply say, "I don't know, but I'll find out for you."* . . . Never "play dumb," deny knowledge, or give anything other than a forthright refusal.
9. *Tell the truth, even if it hurts.* . . . Thoughtful people understand that no one is perfect. . . . What the public will not understand or tolerate, however, is dishonesty.
10. *Do not exaggerate the facts.*

CORPORATE IDENTITY AND IMAGE

Here again are two often-misused terms. The difference between them is that the first is internally controlled and the other is an external perception.

Corporate identity is the sameness, in character and appearance, of the company's name and logo on printed matter and forms. It is the consistent application by company policy of a design to be used on everything from business cards and letterheads to equipment and job signs. This visual consistency results in immediate recognition of the company, both by its own employees and by the public and the business community. It is the company's "uniform" that unites its people and presents a single identity to the outside world.

The corporate image exists externally. It is the mental picture held in the minds of the people the contractor comes in contact with. The contractor has much less control over its image than over its identity, which can be changed overnight. Esso instantly became Exxon by changing its name and logo and altering everything carrying the company imprint throughout the world. The image of the company remained intact as that of one of the world's leading multinational petrochemical corporations—a huge, reliable provider of high-quality petroleum and chemical products.

So, too, with the contractor. The company cannot change its image through a name change or a communications effort alone. Image is made up of a number of factors:

- Size of company and size of projects built
- Reputation
- Capabilities
- Type of projects built (one type, or diversified)
- Quality of work
- Cost of work
- Adherence to schedule
- Reliability
- Services
- Professionalism
- Site appearance
- Name recognition
- Community activity and participation

These factors are real. Often the company's image lags behind reality. A contractor may be thought of as a school builder long after it has become a diversified regional company. Another contractor may be seen as first-class for a while after it has started to decline. People continue to see what they expect to see. However, a marketing communications program that tells a true story of change within the company can begin to change its image.

One midwestern contractor, Bor-Son in Minneapolis, reported that a change in the perception of the company on the part of architects and owners occurred through regular publication of a dramatic client-directed newsletter. Comments received by the company indicating its change in image included, "We had no idea how many projects you had built in the Twin Cities area," and "We didn't know you were that big and diversified" (refer back to Figure 14-2).

Here are some characteristics of a corporate identity program.

- *Use and Purpose.* A well-designed contemporary corporate identity program subtly communicates a number of messages to a contractor's employees, prospects, clients, and business and community associates (Figure 14-4). It signifies a single, unified, and solid corporation; modern management; up-to-date technology; and a company with purpose and direction.
- *Format and Content.* A corporate identity program can be based around a logo (a symbol, like crossed H-beams or a star) a logotype (a stylized version of the company name, written out, such as Dravo Corporation uses), or a combination of both. A logotype, which uses the full name or a combination of logo and company name, is the best, since the contractor is primarily selling its

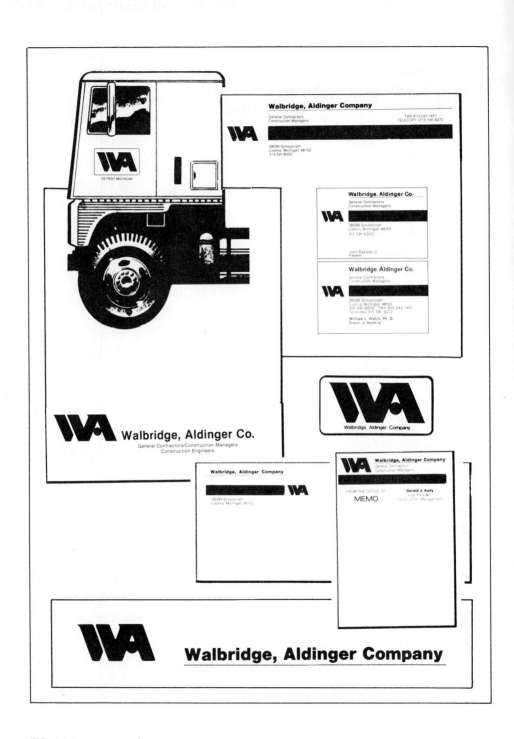

FIG. 14-4 Corporate identity program.

name. The design should be applied consistently on stationery (letterheads, envelopes, business cards, mailing labels, press releases), forms (purchase orders, estimating forms), literature (brochures, proposal covers, advertisements), job signs, and equipment (trucks, cranes, bulldozers).

- *Cost and Frequency.* Applying a new logo and design wherever the company name appears will be the largest cost factor. The contractor with one office, relatively few pieces of equipment, several job signs, and modest stationery needs will require an investment in the range of $1000 to $2000. The far-reaching, complex construction giant with hundreds or thousands of pieces of equipment, 20 branch offices, hundreds of employees needing business cards, hundreds of thousands of pieces of stationery, forms, and decals, and a couple of hundred job signs makes a substantial investment when it presents a new corporate face to the world. That cost could be around the low hundred-thousand-dollar mark. The cost of designing a new corporate identity program can range from several hundred to tens of thousands of dollars, depending upon the size of the contractor and the contractor's needs.

ADVERTISING

Advertising is another marketing communications tool aimed at informing, persuading, preselling, and motivating one or more of the company's markets. Through various media, advertising reaches an audience ranging in size from thousands to millions.

Advertising comes in many forms: magazines and newspapers, radio and television, outdoor displays, signs, and novelties (matches, calendars, lighters). Because advertising is a public medium, it conveys a certain authenticity. Advertising cannot substitute for personal selling, but as part of an overall marketing mix, advertising can gain a presence in a market for the contractor.

Successful Contractor Advertising.   One medium-sized building contractor in Pennsylvania that wanted to change its image as a hospital contractor in order to penetrate the burgeoning office building market took a full-page advertisement in a city business magazine. Combining the advertising with a personal selling effort to developers and designers, a new corporate brochure, a publicity campaign, and high-quality proposal packaging, the company was able to secure contracts for new office buildings (Figure 14-5).

On a larger scale, Morrison-Knudsen Co., Inc. (M-K) began a national corporate advertising campaign in 1977 with the objective of increasing awareness of M-K and gaining greater recognition of the company's name and capabilities (Figure 14-6). Occasionally, each of M-K's divisions (heavy and marine, power, buildings, industrial, and mining groups and manufacturing specialties group) advertises its services. The divisions fund their own campaigns, but all advertising is coordinated and approved by M-K's vice president of marketing and planning. Since 1979 all advertisements have been prepared by an outside agency. For its corporate campaign, M-K advertises in *Business Week, Forbes, Fortune,* and *Engineering News-Record.* Divisional

FIG. 14-5   Successful contractor advertising: local campaign.

advertising runs in such publications as *Power, Railway Age, Coal Age, Oil and Gas Journal,* and *Architectural Record.* At times M-K conducts specialized advertising, such as a one-year campaign for locomotive rebuilding in *Progressive Railroading, Modern Railroads,* and *Railway Age.*

In the five-year period from 1978 through 1982, M-K's advertising generated about 6500 inquiries. Most of them were requests for further information. To test the effectiveness of the advertising in relation to the company's original objectives of increasing awareness and gaining greater recognition, M-K has conducted several telephone surveys of corporate executives. They believe that identification of the M-K name has increased and that attitudes toward the company's services have improved.

- *Use and Purpose.* Advertising is a special marketing communications tool that requires full understanding, planning, setting of specific objectives, testing, and most of all a substantial financial commitment. Advertising can be an effective means of putting across the company's message to a broad or narrowly defined target audience on a repeat basis.

  Even effective advertising only triggers the initial phases of the selling process, however. What must follow are other marketing tools and personal selling, so that prospects become clients. Through repeated exposure in respected media, the contractor's advertising can enhance recognition of the company's name and capabilities and improve attitudes toward it—thus smoothing the way for salespeople to start the selling process on a positive note.

- *Format and Content.* Whatever form the contractor's advertising takes, it should be dramatic, never boring. Boring advertising does not sell or command attention, so it will reach a low percentage of its intended audience.

  Print advertising in newspapers and magazines is the most effective for contractors, because it enables them to reach specific markets. It may reach as few as a hundred or so key prospects, but they are the ones contractors need to reach. David Ogilvy, founder of Ogilvy & Mather, one of the world's largest advertising agencies, suggests, "The most important decision [is how] you position your product." Positioning is determining the company's niche in the marketplace. The second most important decision, Ogilvy states, is:

  What should you promise the customer? A promise is not a claim, or a theme, or a slogan. It is a benefit for the consumer. It pays to promise a benefit which is unique and competitive. And the product must deliver the benefit you promise.
  Most advertising promises nothing. It is doomed to fail in the marketplace. . . . Unless your advertising is built on a Big Idea it will pass like a ship in the night. It takes a Big Idea to jolt the consumer out of his indifference—to make him notice your advertising, remember it and take action. Big ideas are usually simple ideas . . . a first-class ticket. It pays to give most products an image of quality—a first-class ticket. . . . If your advertising looks ugly, consumers will conclude that your product is shoddy, and they will be less likely to buy it. . . . Innovate. Start trends— instead of following them. Advertising which follows a fashionable fad, or is imitative, is seldom successful. It pays to innovate, to blaze new trails.[3]

- *Cost.* Two variables govern the cost of advertising: the amount of space taken (full page, half-page, quarter-page) and the size of the audience the medium reaches. Savings can be achieved for multiple advertisements (ads run three, six, 12, or more times in a given period): special positions (back cover or page 2) or issues (annual directory or special advertising section) may affect cost.

Robert O., your oil field's ready.

Three months ahead of schedule!
Morrison-Knudsen people have tackled some pretty rugged projects in the giant engineering and construction company's 70-year history, but few were more unforgiving than ARCO's Kuparuk River, Alaska, oil field.

Kuparuk's in polar bear country, 250 miles north of the Arctic Circle, 27 miles west of Prudhoe Bay, an expanse of frozen nothingness with a lot of oil underneath it. Dark, windy and cold (chill factors of −70° F are common).

There 700 people—from M-K and ARCO—spent two years and nearly $100 million building a city of pre-fabricated modules (some weighing in at 1,700 tons and rising six-stories), installing 70 miles of above-ground pipe-line, and erecting a steel bridge across a river that had a nasty habit of flooding every Spring.

What's noteworthy is that they managed to do all this in three months less time than they planned. When you consider that ARCO will pump

Kuparuk in the time it takes you to read this ad, that three-month time saving becomes very significant.

How did they manage it? The project team leaders were all old Alaska hands—M-K has completed many projects in Alaska and its staff includes a collection of people who like working in its challenging environment.

These people knew from experience how to maintain total control, and how to communicate. Their computers, satellites and exquisitely detailed systems kept everybody everywhere up-to-date.

We at Morrison-Knudsen are especially proud of what our people and their ARCO partners accomplished at Kuparuk. It demonstrates fully what we offer our clients: on-time, on-budget performance anywhere.

If you have a big, tough project on your drawing board, let's talk about it. Call our CEO, Bill McMurren, at (208) 386-6700. M-K asks only one thing of its clients: A good shot at a fair profit.

FIG. 14-6 Successful contractor advertisement: national campaign.

A measure of advertising efficiency is cost per thousand, or the cost to the advertiser of reaching 1000 readers. It is calculated by the cost of an ad divided by the number of thousands of readers or subscribers. An ad costing $2000 reaching a magazine's readership of 100,000 carries a cost per thousand of $20.

To reach 1000 people in a target audience by direct mail costs $200 in postage alone. Thus, advertising is an efficient medium, even though all 1000 readers may not see the company's ad. Another consideration is the number of readers that fall within the contractor's target audience. The contractor may want to reach presidents and vice presidents of facilities, which may be only 4000 out of a total circulation of 100,000—that substantially increases the cost per thousand.

Today, many publications have "demographic issues" to allow an advertiser to select the exact audience it wants to reach and to obtain space at a reduced cost. Demographic issues can cover certain geographic areas (a city, a state, a region), certain businesses (if it is a newspaper or consumer publication), segments of an industry (if it is a trade magazine), and key figures (chairpersons and presidents, vice presidents of engineering).

- *Frequency.* Just as important as cost is the frequency of the ad. One of the major advantages of advertising is that it permits the contractor to repeat a message many times. Building awareness, recognition, and preference is a long-term process. Good advertising can help achieve that, but the contractor must reach its audience periodically, at least once a month. Given a limited advertising budget, frequent ads in a smaller space can be more influential than larger ads appearing once or twice.

A midwestern contractor tried placing one full page in his city's demographic issues of *Time, Newsweek, Business Week, Sports Illustrated,* and *U.S. News & World Report,* a special package developed by a syndicator. The cost was more than $10,000. The contractor received no response to the one-time ad and decided that advertising did not work.

Another contractor of similar size in the Northeast ran a small one-column ad, 6 inches long, every other week for years in the business section of his city's top newspaper. The result, according to the company's president, was a sizeable increase in recognition of the company's name, which has helped sales.

Any advertising campaign, in one or more publications, should be given the commitment and resources to run once a month or more for three to six months before its effectiveness is evaluated. The cost may range from several thousand dollars for a fraction of a page in lower-circulation publications to hundreds of thousands of dollars for multiple full-page advertisements in national business magazines.

PHOTOGRAPHS AND AUDIOVISUAL MATERIALS

High-quality dramatic photographs are essential for the contractor. The company should develop a library of color slides and prints of construction in progress and completed projects, taken by talented, creative commercial or industrial photographers.

The cost for top photographers may be as high as $500 to $1500 per day, plus expenses, for the biggest names in the field, but the resulting photography library will be an invaluable aid in assembling impressive slide presentations, sales books, or proposals that will help win contracts. High-quality photographs, taken regularly on important projects, can be used for brochures, newsletters, special mailing pieces, and advertising.

The contractor considering audiovisual marketing tools, such as slide presentations linked to a soundtrack, films, or videocassette tapes should plan carefully. A number of contractors have invested the $1000 to $2000 per minute needed for such materials only to find they are of limited use in marketing and sales. Usually they are shown to only a few people at a time and cannot be distributed to hundreds or thousands of prospects the way printed material can, although videocassettes can be sent to people with the equipment to view them. In most sales interviews it is awkward to lug heavy equipment around and set it up in someone's office, darken the room and show a film or videotape that takes ten to twenty minutes or more. Good print material can accomplish the same thing in a few minutes, and valuable sales time can be spent discussing the prospect's needs.

Videotapes or films are useful when they zero in on a specific intriguing project or on one particularly fascinating aspect of the company's operations. An educational film that explains the design/build or CM approach can be well worth an investment. Barton-Malow Company's film and videocassettes on the construction of the Pontiac Silverdome near Detroit became a bestseller, helped the company to become widely known, and boosted sales. Had the company produced a film entitled "Who Barton-Malow Is and What It Does," it would have met with far less success. Similarly, Kenny Construction Co., Inc. has had several films and videotapes professionally produced on the unusual tunnelling techniques it used on massive underground projects in Chicago. Kenny distributes the films and tapes as widely as possible and has received good comments on them.

Some subcontractors or suppliers share the production expense of producing films or videotapes on a specific project in return for their use.

MARKETING COMMUNICATIONS OBJECTIVES

One of the basic purposes of marketing is to search out prospects and convert as many as possible into clients. If the contractor has but a few potential prospects, the task can be managed with personal selling on the part of a company executive. As the contractor grows and its markets expand to the point where there are hundreds or thousands of prospects, the task, though more difficult, still focuses on two areas:

1. *Exposure.* Physically appearing before the prospect to make him or her aware of the company's existence.
2. *Persuasive education.* Conditioning the prospect to have a favorable attitude toward the company.

Essentially the objectives of marketing are to expose a large number of people to the company's name and capabilities, and to deliver a convincing and motivating message. To achieve exposure, the contractor uses one marketing tool or a combination of them in an effort to capture the attention of the audience. The tools, combined with personal selling, are intended to search out the "suspects" and move them through successive stages to action. The stages form a communications spectrum (Figure 14-7).

Unawareness, the lowest level in the communications spectrum, is the stage at

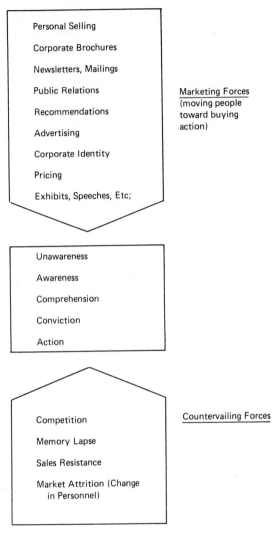

FIG. 14-7   Marketing communications spectrum.

which people have never heard of the company. At the next level, awareness, people will be able to recall the company's name. At a bare minimum, marketing tools should achieve prospect awareness. At the comprehension stage, the prospect is not only aware of the company name but may recognize the logo and have some understanding of the contractor's capabilities.

In the construction selling process, marketing tools can achieve only comprehension. The next stages, conviction and action, are attained through personal selling. Conviction is the point at which the prospect believes the contractor can perform as well as he or she claims and has the capabilities needed for the project. In the action stage, the prospect signs a contract and becomes a client.

In the consumer products field, marketing tools, particularly advertising, carry the entire marketing workload from unawareness right through to action. The consumer buys the product seen in a magazine or on television. But with industrial or construction services, marketing tools must increase the productivity of the salespeople by relieving them of a substantial part of their communication workload.[4]

PLANNING THE COMMUNICATIONS PROGRAM

The communications program is vital to the contractor's overall marketing effort and helps determine success or failure. The program is the contractor's offensive in winning the battle for the prospect's mind. It represents a substantial initial and ongoing investment, an outlay made to achieve benefits in the future.

The program's various marketing communications tools should be developed only after the contractor has completed its strategic analysis. Management must know which markets and prospects it wants to reach, what its corporate and marketing objectives are, what its strengths and weaknesses are, and what resources it will commit to the marketing effort.

The tools the contractor employs to reach its target audiences form the basis of its communications program. Decisions are based on answers to four marketing questions:

1. What are the company's marketing objectives?
2. What are the company's communications needs to achieve those objectives?
3. What should the total communications budget be to achieve the objectives?
4. How should the budget be allocated among various marketing tools?

Marketing Objectives.   The contractor should establish its marketing objectives based on analysis of:

1. Business volume required to meet corporate objectives
2. Present and potential markets
3. Present and potential clients
4. Current and future salable services
5. Current and anticipated competition
6. Past and anticipated successful strategies
7. Ability to satisfy potential client needs
8. Economic and other external factors
9. Company strengths and image

Communications Needs.   As we have seen, prospects need to be taken through a communications spectrum, from unawareness to action. An analysis of the contrac-

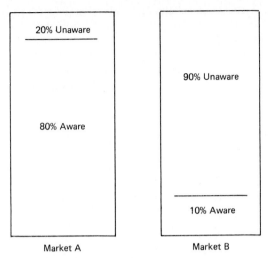

FIG. 14-8   Prospect awareness.

tor's present and potential markets to determine prospects' levels of awareness and comprehension is helpful in determining areas of need.

In Figure 14-8, the degree of prospect awareness can be gauged through an image survey (discussed later in this chapter) or by an informed guess. Markets can be defined as business arenas that have a set of customers with common requirements and a set of identifiable competitors. Markets A and B can represent project markets (health care, power, industry) in a given area (city, state, region, nation) or targeted geographic area. Where awareness is high, as in Market A (the contractor's home state, say), marketing tools are less helpful and more personal selling is needed. Market B could be a new project type (such as office buildings for developers and corporations) or a new territory (Georgia, Texas, Arizona) that the contractor wants to penetrate. The low awareness level in Market B calls for extensive use of marketing tools to build awareness, then personal selling.

A graph comparing the effectiveness of various marketing tools at different levels of prospect readiness to buy is shown in Figure 14-9. The graph shows that brochures, advertising, publicity, and newsletters are more cost-effective in building awareness than cold calls from salespeople. Prospect conviction and action are achieved largely through personal selling.

Marketing tools in no way substitute for personal selling, which is required if the prospect is to move through conviction to action. Marketing tools serve only to augment the effectiveness of salespeople. An image survey, discussed later in this chapter, is another method of determining marketing needs, as is analyzing marketplace feedback from the company's salespeople.

Budget Decisions.   The budget for marketing communications tools is integrally related to the overall marketing budget. The contractor's marketing budget should

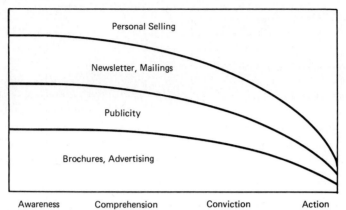

FIG. 14-9   Communications mix as a function of prospect readiness to buy. *(Adapted from Philip Kotler, Marketing Management: Analysis, Planning, and Control, 4th ed., Prentice-Hall, Inc., Englewood Cliffs, N.J., 1980, p. 491.)*

include sales and marketing personnel, as well as the proper tools to support them and perform various communications functions.

Many contractors who do not develop a marketing budget set expenditures too low, so that only personnel needs are satisfied or, at the other extreme, only marketing tool needs are met. In the first instance, sales personnel are given the extremely difficult task of doing the work of marketing tools plus the personal selling tasks. The result is to greatly reduce the salesperson's effectiveness.

Every year, the contractor must decide how much to spend on marketing and marketing tools. Personnel expenses should predominate, at a ratio of, say, 70:30. Some of the following considerations can alter that ratio:

1. **Needs and Objectives Analysis.** Did the company's analysis show a high requirement for marketing tools? If so, the percentage for marketing tools should be increased.

2. **Return on Capital.** Will the capital tied up in marketing tools yield enough in profits to pay its way? If it is an investment in higher future earnings, when will those earnings be increased?

3. **Affordability.** How much can be invested in marketing tools? What other opportunities are there to be invested in?

4. **Competitor Comparison.** How do the company's marketing tools compare with those of key competitors? Are they getting more exposure to prospects? Is their visual image better than that of competitors? Is the company's story being communicated to prospects as well as or better than competitors'?

5. **Zero-Base Consequences.** If nothing was spent on marketing tools, how would that affect the business-getting abilities of the company?

A sample budget for marketing tools can be calculated in the following manner:

Annual volume	$30,000,000
Marketing budget @ 0.5 percent	150,000
Less: Personnel @ 70 percent	−105,000
Marketing communications tools	$ 45,000

The marketing tools budget is an annualized figure. In this example, for this size of marketing budget, if a new corporate brochure is required, it will consume a substantial portion of the marketing tools budget in one year. If the brochure costs $40,000 and has an anticipated life of four years, it can be amortized at $10,000 per year, leaving $35,000 per year for other marketing tools. This approach can be used to develop guideline figures.

Selection of the Marketing Tools Mix.   Once the contractor has set its total marketing communications budget, the next step is to make allocations to various tools.

The company's communications needs must be analyzed, based on current and targeted markets, image, and competitive situation, to point up areas of weakness and needs. It is important for the contractor to keep in mind that different marketing tools serve different functions during the sales and communications processes. The objective should be to develop a well-rounded communications program that supports the sales effort by reaching prospects repeatedly through a variety of media.

Figure 14-10 shows that various marketing tools play different roles in the sales process at various stages. Repetition through the follow-up stage is important for communication because people are bombarded with commercial messages every day. To avoid overload, people filter out most messages and selectively pay attention to a few. People in the market for an automobile or a camera notice automobile or camera advertising. Owners planning a new facility notice a contractor's marketing tools.

A marketing communications program can start with a corporate brochure and proceed through other marketing tools over time, depending on the contractor's needs and objectives. For the contractor starting a program in a limited geographic market,

Communications Level	Unawareness	Awareness	Comprehension	Conviction	Action
Sales Stage		Introduction	Follow-up		Contract Signing
Marketing Tools		Corporate Brochure	Newsletters		
		Publicity	Mailings		
		Advertising			
Personal Selling		Initial Sales Call	Periodic Contacts		
					Proposals
					Presentations
					Negotiation

FIG. 14-10   Marketing tool functions.

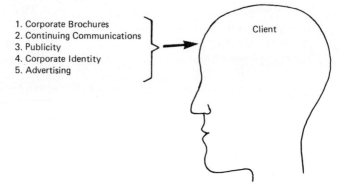

1. Corporate Brochures
2. Continuing Communications
3. Publicity
4. Corporate Identity
5. Advertising

FIG. 14-11   Marketing tool priorities. Marketing tools are employed to implant the contractor's name and marketing message in the mind of the client. The figure shows the priority of those tools used in communicating with owners, the contractor's primary audience.

a brochure and newsletter can be developed in the first year and then an evaluation can be made. If the newsletter is meeting the company's objectives, its publication can continue and its frequency can be increased without the addition of other marketing tools. As the company expands, it can add tools to penetrate new markets and reach broader audiences.

Figure 14-11 shows the progression of use of marketing tools the contractor can follow to reach prospects and clients. Combined, the tools represent a comprehensive marketing communications program. The more channels the contractor uses, the greater the chance that its message will be received by its audience.

Almost all large contractors marketing in the private sector have a complete communications program. Smaller companies can maintain a lower-scale program. Brochures may not be as numerous or as elaborate, newsletters will be briefer and less frequent, publicity irregular, and advertising modest. But for the smaller organization's limited audiences, markets, and services, the marketing impact and success can be significant.

IMAGE SURVEYS

In the selection of a contractor, much depends on the attitudes and perceptions the owner and his or her advisers have toward the companies they review. Through marketing communications and personal selling, the contractor attempts to alter those attitudes and perceptions in its favor.

The construction company that has a clear grasp of how the marketplace views its company (versus competitors) will be on firm ground in developing marketing strategies, sales tactics, marketing tools, and messages that will improve its competitive edge. The best way to obtain this type of information is through an image survey of the contractor's business community. Seek opinions from past, present, and potential clients, architects, engineers, subcontractors, bonding agents, and bankers.

The image survey is similar to the market research that large corporations perform continuously to monitor consumer preferences for products and services. Another task of market research for the large corporation and the contractor is to gather data on the overall size, trends, potential, competitive environment, influencing factors, and buying practices of a particular market.

By gathering information, the contractor can determine:

- How it is viewed versus competitors in areas of performance (cost, schedule, quality) and attitude.
- What the marketplace views as its strengths and weaknesses.
- The sizes and types of projects it is considered for.
- Which markets it is strongest or weakest in.
- What the company's marketing strategy should be.
- What its overall image is and what to change, if anything.
- Why the company wins certain jobs and loses others.
- What it will need to do to expand in some markets or to enter others.
- What the owner's selection criteria are.

The image survey and its results are only a beginning. What matters is what management does with the information to change its own perceptions of the company, its operations, its attitudes, and its approaches to the marketplace.

Sometimes contractors are reluctant to embark on an image survey because they feel it will reflect negatively on the company. They think owners won't provide information or will perceive them as being weak or in trouble, or that the survey will stir up bad feelings over petty matters. Experience with numerous contractors' image surveys does not bear out those concerns.

If the survey is presented positively, because of the company's desire to improve its services to clients, and if it is properly designed and implemented, only beneficial results will be obtained. Most respondents are willing to speak openly and candidly, particularly to a third party such as an independent research firm. If they feel generally positive about the contractor, they are quite willing to share those views and be helpful. If they hold mainly negative views, they usually are glad to complain to someone who will listen. And that information, if echoed elsewhere, is helpful to know.

Occasionally, respondents in government agencies or with large corporations will not offer opinions because organization policy forbids it. But that is the exception more than the rule. Certain steps are involved in developing an image survey:

Step 1. Decide on Desired Results.   What type of information do we want? Or, what are the key factors in our winning or losing jobs? Or, what is our image in the marketplace? How are we viewed in comparison with our competitors?

Step 2. Identify the People To Be Surveyed.   These should include current and past clients, prospects and potential clients, lost clients, architects, engineers, subcontractors, bonding agents, business executives, bankers, and other influential people. For most contractors, interviews with 15 to 25 people are enough to begin to see trends. That will require starting with 20 to 40 names, since it is difficult to reach everyone. Larger contractors with broader markets may require 50 to 100 or more interviews.

Step 3. Decide Who Will Conduct the Survey.   The best results are obtained by an independent person or firm. People are more willing to speak openly to a third party than to the company involved. A public relations or market research or management consulting firm (or person) familiar with the construction industry is best, because they can speak knowledgeably with respondents.

Step 4. Develop the Questionnaire.   To yield good information and in such a way that it can be compiled, the survey must be conducted in a consistent manner. Designing research questionnaires is the art of developing a logical series of easily answered questions that elicit the desired information. It is literally writing a script. In the questionnaire format:

1. An introductory statement should identify the caller and give the purpose of the call. Promise anonymity.
2. The interviewer can reveal the name of the contractor/sponsor or not. If not, ask the names of contractors that the respondent is familiar with.
3. Ask for ratings, on a scale of 1–5, of contractors in various performance areas—costs, schedule, quality, responsiveness, management, attitude.
4. Ask for selection criteria.
5. Probe for types of services sought from contractors.
6. If sponsor's name is revealed at the end, question for perceptions of the contractor's capabilities in various types and sizes of projects.
7. End with thanks for help and a question as to whether the respondent wants to add anything.

Step 5. Determine the Survey Method.   Telephone surveys of fifteen to twenty minutes work well. Mail surveys draw too low a response. In-person surveys are costly.

Step 6. Fix a Survey Timetable.   Allow three to four weeks for undertaking about 15 to 25 interviews and evaluating the results. For larger surveys with numerous respondents, allow six to twelve weeks.

Step 7. Evaluate Results.   The survey's numerical results can be tabulated manually and significant quotes extracted for their flavor. Numerical results can be presented in chart form for visual impact. Larger surveys can be computer coded and analyzed. Areas of strength and weakness should be apparent.

Once the survey has been completed, management should use the results to effect marketing and sales changes to capitalize on strengths and correct areas of weakness.

Often contractors are surprised by an image survey's results. For example, the company may believe its strong suit is on-time schedule performance when that may not be perceived in the marketplace. Or the company may feel it couldn't compete effectively with some larger contractors, when the survey might show it is being rated ahead in several areas. With some contractors a hard-to-deal-with reputation emerges; with others excellent or poor subcontractor relationships are found.

The company may find that the marketplace perceived a lack of depth in organization (a one-person-show), or an image of being "expensive," or of being "unprofessional" or possibly "very professional" in presentations. All results are valuable information for the contractor to act on and become more competitive and successful in the marketplace.

DEVELOPING MARKETING COMMUNICATIONS TOOLS

It is important in developing effective marketing tools to understand the communications process. "Communication" comes from the Latin *communis,* meaning common. Through the process of communication, a sender transmits a message through media to a receiver to establish a "commonness"—that is, to share an idea or information. The process is shown graphically in Figure 14-12.

The sender could be an individual or an organization. The encoded message is the form that the thought is reduced to—written words, visual image, spoken language. Media are the channels of communications used: magazine, television, brochure, newspaper. Decoded message is the meaning that the receiver gives to the message. Response is the receiver's set of reactions to the message, and feedback is what the receiver communicates back to the sender.

The development of marketing tools requires that the sender, the contractor, must first know which audiences it wants to reach and what responses and feedback it desires from them. Second, the contractor should understand the conditions that must be fulfilled to arouse those responses.

Let us review these requirements and see how they translate into practical terms for marketing tool development.[5]

First, *the message must be so designed and delivered as to gain the attention*

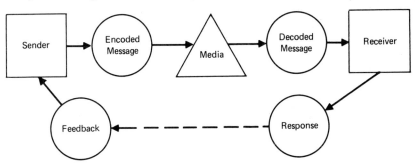

FIG. 14-12 The communications process.

of the intended [*receiver*]. Everyone receives far more communication than he or she can possibly accept. What most people do is scan their environment and selectively receive and decode messages that fit their needs and interests, based on a quick impression.

That first, attention-grabbing impression comes from a color, a word, a sound, an image. If the receiver's attention is not gained, he or she may never be open to the message.

A contractor's marketing tools must seize the attention of its various audiences through:

- Visually bold, dramatic, yet dignified corporate design, which is achieved by a talented graphic designer.

- Dramatic photography, taken by a creative, experienced professional.

- High-quality printing that produces rich, bright colors, or high-contrast black and white.

- Benefit-oriented or intriguing headlines (five times as many people read headlines as body text).

Second, *the message must employ signs that refer to experience common to both the sender and the receiver so as to get the meaning across.* This is where the sender seeks to achieve "commonness" with the receiver. Messages must speak the language of the receiver and not conflict with his or her experience.

The contractor's marketing tools must carry messages that:

- Speak to the intended receiver in his or her language, not in construction jargon or in technical terms.

- Distinguish between audiences by carrying a different style or approach for top management, engineers or architects, media editors, smaller businesses, and major corporations.

- Are written by professionals who understand the contractor and the audience.

Third, *the message must arouse personality needs in the receiver and suggest some way to meet those needs.* People take action to fill needs and to meet goals, and they choose the action that comes closest to meeting those needs and goals. Personality need, as related to construction decisions, might include the needs for security, freedom from anxiety, status, understanding, and so forth.

The contractor's marketing tools must:

- Show solutions to problems or significant achievements for owners.

- Present an image of a sound, experienced, well-established company that can listen to owner concerns, answering the needs for security and understanding.

- Show that the contractor understands the owner's concern that the facility be constructed well, on time and within budget—and with the fewest headaches.

- Explain the contractor's services and the ways the contractor helps to achieve the owner's goals.

- Show staff—executives, office staff, field people—to impart a message of understanding and meet personality needs on a person-to-person basis.
- Use words in letters and text headlines that refer to "you" and "yours," rather than "we" and "ours."

Fourth, *the message must suggest a way to meet those needs that is appropriate to the group situation the receiver is in at the time he or she is moved to make the desired response*. People live in groups. Groups have their own social structure and culture. The contractor's message is much more likely to succeed if it fits the patterns of understanding, attitudes, values, and goals of the receiver.

The contractor's marketing tools should:

- Speak to the various needs of different target audiences—whether hospital administrators, utility executives, manufacturing company facility managers, real estate developers, chemical company engineers, or purchasing agents.
- In public relations or publicity materials, meet the editor's needs for newsworthy information of interest to readers.
- Meet the group's needs for organization by appearing organized, through a consistent design of corporate identity (stationery, equipment markings, job signs) and a singular "look" to brochures and other literature and an overall professional appearance.

MORE METHODS OF MARKETING COMMUNICATION

The creative construction marketing person continually searches for additional ways to reach prospects. Any gathering of prospective sources of business is where the construction company should have a representative. He or she can be attending, speaking, or stationed at an exhibit booth. All these activities provide further means of exposure for the company name and opportunities for direct contact with prospects.

Sometimes meetings can be created by the contractor who hosts a seminar for architects, engineers, and owners on a topic of interest. Articles written by or for people in the company can be placed in publications likely to be read by prospects and will give credit to the author or the contractor.

Whichever additional marketing communications means are chosen, the contractor should use them regularly, so that they become part of an ongoing program. As with other marketing tools, one-shot attempts are not very effective. The company can experiment with different methods and select the best ones for inclusion in a program.

Speeches.   Speaking before local groups, such as Rotary or other business luncheons or architects' associations, can give the contractor many opportunities for new business. The company name receives wide exposure through announcements and promotional mailings for the meeting, at the meeting, and afterward in the group's newsletter. If the company has a particularly good speaker who can talk on a subject of wide interest, the contractor can aim to appear before regional or national meetings of designer or owner associations.

The contractor, by virtue of being at the podium, is considered an expert and is elevated in stature. However, it is important that the contractor's representative have good speaking skills and be able to prepare and deliver a talk on a topic of interest to the audience. On the local level, the topics could include a noteworthy project the company is working on or has just completed, a new technique or approach to construction that saves time or money, or changes in the construction industry that affect owners or designers. For regional and national meetings, the topics need to have broader appeal. A project discussed would have to be large in scope or significant in technology or have wide geographic application.

If the contractor's talk is newsworthy, a press release can be developed and distributed, and the company can receive still further exposure.

Seminars.   If the contractor can develop a series of construction-related topics of interest to design firms or owners in the area, it can consider hosting in-office seminars periodically, such as monthly or quarterly. They could be held at lunch hours or after five. Some design firms and contractors have done this successfully.

Exhibits.   Exhibit booths at relevant trade and association meetings place the contractor in a position to meet a number of prospects face to face. For the company to obtain results from the meeting, marketing and other executives have to plan the approach, have a professional well-designed booth stocked with company literature, decide who will attend, and select a space on the exhibit floor that promises heavy traffic. It is a good idea to have someone from the company attend the meeting the year before planning an exhibit, to gauge the attendees, the level of exhibitors, and the size of the meeting. Conventions of owner associations, such as the American Hospital Association, have been effective for contractors, particularly those offering construction management services.

Article Writing.   Publications that accept articles with by-lines can be good sources of additional publicity and exposure. The publication should be reviewed for its readership and the style of the articles it accepts. High-quality photographs, if the publication uses them, can help ensure acceptance of the article.

Entertaining.   Some people consider entertaining to be a direct sales function, and it is. However, it *is* a part of the marketing program. In fact, before organized marketing was widely accepted, entertaining was the chief means of getting business for many contractors. Entertaining can range from a lunch or some sports tickets to free vacations in the Caribbean or at hunting or ski lodges. Many contractors still utilize this method effectively in their business development efforts. Others stay away from anything more than a lunch or dinner. One contractor in the Midwest takes clients to the Kentucky Derby and the Masters golf tournament each year, in addition to using marketing tools and personal selling.

Major entertaining has to be done prudently with people who seem to be receptive, or when it appears to be an acceptable way of doing business in a certain indus-try. In general, though, entertaining seems to be playing a diminishing role in marketing.

PRODUCTIVE USE OF MARKETING TOOLS

Once the contractor has prepared effective marketing tools, the company faces its next major task: using them productively. The most productive use of brochures, newsletters, and mailing pieces occurs when they are gotten into the hands of as many of the right people as possible. As one contractor said, "They do no good in a closet."

Yet it is surprising how many contractors will invest tens of thousands of dollars preparing thousands of copies of an attractive brochure and then hand them out one at a time because they cost $20 each. Unit cost analysis may be important for esti-mating job costs, but economizing can work against a contractor in a marketing effort.

Before we describe the best use of marketing tools, it is important to discuss a fact of marketing life that goes against the grain of most construction executives. It is the concept of waste. Contractors are accustomed to buying a yard of concrete, or a ton of steel, or paying someone for an hour's work, and they make certain the com-pany is getting its money's worth. In marketing, the contractor might mail out 1000 brochures and 600 people might throw them out without giving them more than a glance; 200 people might review them, and 100 or fewer might respond. That means that 90 percent of the brochures—the ones costing $20 each—may be "wasted." Or the contractor might advertise in a magazine with a circulation of 100,000 and only 2000 readers may remember the ad. That amounts to 98 percent "waste."

The problem in marketing is that one does not know beforehand who will respond to a marketing tool and who will not. One industrialist put it this way: "I know I'm wasting half of my advertising dollars. I wish I could figure out which half."

On the brighter side, the contractor whose brochures cost $20 each can look at the gains this way:

Cost of mailing	
1000 brochures @ $20	$20,000
Postage, stationery, misc. @ $1.00	1,000
	$21,000
Potential new work	
Number of responses	50
Number with real projects within next two years (estimated)	25
With ratio of serious prospects to clients at 5 to 1, number of new clients	5
Company's average size of job	$5 million
Total potential work from mailing	$25 million

Besides the immediate response to a cold mailing of brochures, there are a num-ber of receivers who will file them and may respond at a later date. Or they may be receptive to a future personal sales call because they feel somewhat familiar with the company through its brochure.

One heavy contractor in the Southeast that had mailed out several thousand copies of a new brochure was, as a result of the brochure or additional correspondence, immediately placed on a number of preferred-bidders lists. It eventually obtained $15 to $20 million in new work and eight months later received a call from a large pulp and paper company that had the brochure on file. The paper company wanted to discuss a $3 million site development job, which the contractor later won.

Contractors have found that a broad mailing of an effective brochure to target audiences can change the image of the company almost overnight. If the brochure and thus the company seem impressive enough, owners and designers will use the brochure to start a file on the company. That helps the contractor to build awareness in its markets. But waste there will be, and each company has to weigh the pros and cons.

Mailing Lists.   It is true that, by a percentage-of-effectiveness measure, handing a brochure or newsletter to a prospect in person ranks highest. The percentage of effectiveness drops when the brochure is mailed to people familiar with the sender or the company, and it drops even lower when the brochure is mailed cold. However, a few percent of thousands can represent a desirable number of new prospects that would not otherwise have been discovered.

There are four categories of mailing lists:

- Lists of past clients and prospects—those who have been responsive to the company in the past
- House lists—lists built from personal contacts of company employees
- Business lists—those compiled by mailing-list houses, such as Dunhill, Dun & Bradstreet, and National Business Lists, or by trade publications
- Compiled lists—names drawn from association and business directories and telephone books

Contractors with large lists place them in computers. Others use manual systems, fulfillment houses, or a mechanical list system. Lists should be segmented according to geography, ZIP Code, and client type. A good mailing list is an important asset. It should be kept up to date and new names added for continued expansion.

For publicity, a media mailing list is essential. Two good sources of names are:

- *IMS/Ayer Directory of Publications.* IMS Press, 426 Pennsylvania Avenue, Fort Washington, PA 19034
- *Bacon's Publicity Checker.* Bacon's Publishing Company, 332 S. Michigan Avenue, Chicago, IL 60604

Covering Letters.   Important mailings of major tools, such as a new corporate brochure or annual report or update, or an anniversary issue of a newsletter, receive more attention if accompanied by a personal letter. The mailing list can be segmented by client type and a separate letter targeted to each group. The letters should summarize the benefits the contractor offers to each owner or design category. They can be prepared on a word processor so they appear to be individually typed, which increases readership.

Article Reprints.   When articles about significant projects or about the company are published, the contractor should obtain reprints. Reprints can be sent to target segments or to everyone on the company's mailing list, and they can be useful in maintaining contact with prospects. An article on the company can go to an entire list; an article on an office building can be sent to corporate owners and developers.

　　To sum up, marketing tools are meant to be disseminated. When placing printing orders, always overorder so that there will be more than enough copies on hand. A larger supply can spur distribution of the tools. The more of the right people who receive the contractor's marketing communications, the greater the opportunities for new business.

NOTES

[1]*Webster's Eighth New Collegiate Dictionary*, G. & C. Merriam Company, Springfield, MA, 1980, p. 925.

[2]Chester Burger, "How to Meet the Press," *Harvard Business Review*, July–August 1975, pp. 62–70.

[3]David Ogilvy, "How to Create Advertising That Sells," an advertisement appearing in *The New York Times*, April 7, 1971, p. 56.

[4]See Russell H. Colley, "Defining Advertising Goals," in Steaurt Henderson Britt and Harper W. Boyd, Jr., *Marketing Management and Administrative Action*, McGraw-Hill Book Company, New York, 1968, pp. 662–663.

[5]Wilbur Schramm, "How Communication Works," *Marketing Management and Administrative Action*, McGraw-Hill Book Company, New York, 1963, 1968, p. 646.

15

Controlling and Evaluating
the Marketing Program

Like any investment or any segment of the contractor's business, the company's marketing program must be continually monitored and its performance periodically appraised to judge its value.

Assessment is the final link in the never-ending circle that is the planning and marketing process. Planning and assessment are thus interdependent. Overall business and marketing plans furnish the objectives that performance is measured by. In turn, information gathered during monitoring and assessment is used as valuable input to adjust plans. The contractor must know exactly what it hopes to accomplish as a business so that it will have something concrete to monitor, measure, and evaluate.

Controlling and assessing construction marketing pose difficult problems because they require so many activities, and because there are so many variables that contribute to winning a job or to improving the company's growth and profitability. It is more difficult still to break out and appraise a single marketing variable such as a brochure or publicity. However, measuring marketing performance serves several useful purposes in:

- Gauging the return on the company's marketing investment.
- Indicating to top management the overall effectiveness of the program.
- Furnishing information for decision making and adjusting strategic plans.
- Motivating employees involved in marketing by providing them with feedback on performance.

- Allowing the company to move quickly to remedy marketing problems or take advantage of new opportunities.

METHODS OF APPRAISAL

Marketing controls and performance evaluation need to be both quantitative and qualitative. Top management must review the facts and figures of financial investment, return, and expenses, as well as judge the efficiency of sales efforts, certain marketing tools, strategies, and tactics. Appraisal is an ongoing process. Monthly reviews of such items as expenses, quarterly review of others such as sales, and annual strategies are necessary.

On an annual basis, top management should review the overall marketing plan to measure performance against objectives. If there are any serious gaps, management should determine why they occurred and what can be done about them. As part of the annual review, management can assess how well the company is doing in relation to its competitors.

FINANCIAL CONTROLS AND REVIEW

There are several facets to the financial control and analysis of the marketing program:

Profit Increment. Once a year, the company's overall profits are compared with those of the previous period, the increment in marketing expenditures, and the company's objectives, as in Table 15-1.

Certainly, there can be many nonmarketing factors resulting in increased volume. Increases can come from a major job obtained from an existing client, or from a greater volume of work in the marketplace, or from more jobs won through competitive bidding. If the company's work is from the private and the public sectors, the private-sector (marketing-related) portion can be separated and its profit/marketing analysis performed independently.

TABLE 15-1 Profit Analysis of Marketing Expenditure (in millions)

	Previous year	This year	Differential
Volume	40	50	10
Profit (before taxes)	1.2	1.5	0.3
Marketing	0.15	0.2	0.05
Net worth	4.0	4.6	0.6
Return (after taxes)	15%	16%	1%

$$\text{Return on marketing increment} = \frac{0.3}{0.05} = 6$$

Another profit analysis to be made is that of individual projects or market sectors. The question to be answered is, "Are our marketing resources properly allocated to generate the most profitable types of work?"

Return on Investment.   As can be seen in Table 15-1, the company's return on investment increased from 15 percent ($600,000 in retained earnings, divided by $4.0 million net worth) to 16 percent ($750,000 divided by $4.6 million). This increase should be compared with the company's objectives in its strategic marketing plan.

Growth.   If growth is a company goal, a comparison should be made between increase in volume and marketing expenses. In the case shown in Table 15-1, an increase of $50,000 in marketing expenses—depending on other factors—may have resulted in the 25 percent rise in volume.

Sales.   The components of overall company growth are sales by various aspects of the company: a salesperson or sales force, a branch office, a division, or a profit center. Marketing expenses for each can be measured against results obtained.

Budgets.   Each month, sales and marketing expenses should be compared, line item by line item, with budget amounts. For the larger contractor this should be done on a market or divisional or territorial basis.

EFFICIENCY AND EFFECTIVENESS: A QUALITATIVE REVIEW

There are many elements in a marketing program that cannot be measured in numbers but require a qualitative evaluation. Management makes observations and comparative analyses and applies a judgment.

In part, the qualitative analysis of marketing will be numerical, such as determining the number of inquiries generated by an advertising campaign, or the number of sales calls per week made by business development people. But more of the qualitative review involves informed, objective opinions and answers to tough questions, such as, "Have we increased the level of awareness of our company in the pharmaceutical industry?"

The qualitative analysis is a review of the efficiency and effectiveness of marketing functions and tools. The areas to be examined include:

- Strategic planning
- Client orientation, attitudes, feedback
- Sales and marketing organization
- Marketing information and research
- Marketing communications tools
- Marketing resources
- Competitor comparison

1. Strategic Planning. Because of the possibility of rapid changes in the marketing environment, the contractor must periodically assess its overall business and marketing strategies. At an annual or semiannual review, management can evaluate its strategic planning by answering questions such as these:

- Do we have a formal detailed strategic marketing plan? Do we update it annually, adjusting short- and long-term objectives?
- Is our current strategy clear, reasonable, and based on hard data? Have we communicated our strategy to employees?
- Are our growth, profit, return on investment, market expansion, and diversification objectives challenging but not impossible to achieve?
- Have we developed alternate or contingency plans?
- Have we assessed our current and potential markets in terms of size, structure, trends, client needs, competition, and likelihood of change over the next five to ten years?
- Do we have an adequate control and evaluation system?
- Have we analyzed our strengths, weaknesses, threats, and opportunities, and are we exploiting or avoiding them?
- Is marketing's role in profit achievement clearly defined and realistic?

2. Client Orientation. Clients are not just the focal point of marketing; they are the reason businesses exist.

- Does management think in terms of serving the needs of specific client groups or markets?
- Does the company have the services to meet those needs that represent long-term potential for growth and profit?
- Does the company classify potential clients into manageable groups and know where it stands with them?
- Does management know how current and potential clients are changing, what their attitudes are, what their buying practices are, and who influences them?
- Does management know what the economics of clients' businesses are, and what benefits clients seek from a contractor?

3. Sales/Marketing Organization. The contractor should periodically review its organizational structure, individual performance, positions, relationships internally and with clients, and personal selling approaches. Marketing builds client awareness and comprehension; sales persuades and motivates clients to act in closing contracts.

- Is the style of our sales/marketing organization well suited for our company and clients?
- Are the major sales and marketing functions well integrated, and do the people work well with other company departments such as estimating, project management, and data processing?

- Is staff size consistent with our company's needs and objectives?
- Is the sales/marketing organization efficient and economical, with clearly defined roles and responsibilities?
- Is there good morale and communication?
- Are our marketing people adept at planning and implementing a strong sales support program?
- Do our salespeople understand and sell the benefits of our company?
- Are their presentations well planned, organized, and rehearsed?
- Do our salespeople spend a high percentage of their time in personal sales calls on prospects?
- Are our salespeople calling on influential people and decision makers?
- Do our salespeople receive proper support from other departments and top management?
- Are our salespeople acting as market researchers by gathering important information about prospects and clients and communicating it to management?
- Are we selling a high percentage of negotiated projects?
- Are our salespeople trained in modern selling techniques?
- Are our salespeople effective in penetrating new prospects, persuading them, and helping the company win projects?

4. Marketing Information and Research.   A key function in the success of the marketing program is the gathering and centralizing of information about potential clients, market trends and segments, competitors, and the economic environment. The contractor with an effective information system has a competitive advantage.

- Have we recently performed studies of prospects and potential markets?
- Does management receive adequate and timely information for decision making, adjusting plans, avoiding threats, and exploiting opportunities?
- Do we know the sales and profit potential of different project types in different geographical areas?
- Do we know what our image is among clients and prospects and how it compares with competitors'?
- Do we have an adequate system for gathering and using a broad base of data on market trends, prospects, future markets, and the economic environment?
- Do we have an analysis of lost and won jobs to provide information for sales and marketing decisions?

5. Marketing Communications Tools.   An annual appraisal of the contribution and results of the company's marketing communications program is important. Management needs to know whether its resources are being expended efficiently, and whether target markets are being covered adequately and are receiving the right messages.

- Are our marketing communications tools geared to the company's marketing objectives and strategies?

- Have we clearly defined target market segments, and do we reach them through appropriate tools and media on a timely and periodic basis?

- Are the messages in our marketing tools oriented toward the benefits clients seek in a contractor?

- Are our marketing tools consistent in design appearance, quality level, and professionalism? Are we projecting our desired image?

- Do we differentiate ourselves from our competitors with a USP (unique selling proposition)?

- Are we properly positioning our company in the marketplace?

- Are our proposals impressive, responsive, and effective in helping us to win jobs?

- Do we have a consistent corporate identity that is easily recognizable in the marketplace?

- Do we know whether our marketing tools are reaching our target audiences, and what their reaction is?

- Do we have the proper mix of brochures, newsletters, publicity, and advertising to build awareness in and gain the confidence of target market segments?

- How do our marketing communications tools compare with those of our competitors?

6. Marketing Resources.   The company's marketing investment in dollars and personnel must be reviewed at least once a year.

- Are our marketing resources adequate for the size of our company, the extent of the markets to be covered, our growth and profit goals, and diversification and other needs?

- Do we allocate our marketing resources in proportion to marketing need? Do we allocate the current and desired market area contribution in proportion to volume and profit? (Are we spending 80 percent of marketing efforts on markets that constitute 80 percent of our volume and/or profit?)

- Do we do a good job of identifying, evaluating, selecting, and acting on new business opportunities?

7. Competitor Comparison.   As contractors become more proficient and aggressive in their marketing efforts, it becomes increasingly important for the individual company to monitor its standing in relation to that of its competitors.

- Are we remaining even, losing, or gaining market share in various business segments?

- Is our success rate on negotiated projects, particularly those requiring formal presentations, increasing or decreasing?

- Are we learning about potential projects as early as competitors?
- Are we expanding in markets in which we are as well qualified as or better qualified than competitors?
- Are we being outsold by, or do we outsell, competitors in any way that indicates a trend?
- Are there new competitors in our traditional markets? Are they gaining a share of the market? If so, what techniques are they employing to obtain contracts?

The rapidly changing marketplace, coupled with the contractor's dependence on marketing and the company's considerable sales/marketing investment, require continuous control and appraisal of the program. Information gained through the annual or more frequent assessment of the marketing program supplies management with further data for making decisions and planning.

16

Strategies for Tomorrow: Making the Future Happen

It is much less what we do than what we think, which fits us for the future.

— *Philip James Bailey*

The one certain thing about the future is that it will be different from what exists today.

While no one can predict future events, much less control them, the contractor can develop strategies for tomorrow that anticipate the likeliest areas of change and have a process for taking advantage of them. No contractor can totally eliminate risks and uncertainty, but good management can make the future less risky. The biggest risk of all is to do nothing and see what happens. The contractor rooted in tradition and in existing conditions may be an early victim of change. To maintain the status quo is to leave survival to chance.

Events occurring within and outside the construction industry in the 1960s and 1970s and into the 1980s have had a profound effect on almost every contractor. Some contractors have grown and prospered during these times of rapid change, many have maintained marginal operations, and many have gone out of business. Construction is "the most vulnerable kind of business in hard times," Dun & Bradstreet tells us.

Studies of business show that any major or structural changes in an industry places the greatest demands on small and medium-sized firms—the vast majority of construction companies. And with construction being a high-volume, high–break-even business, it is particularly hazardous.

Major forces continue to act on the industry, causing accelerating change. Some of these forces are listed here.

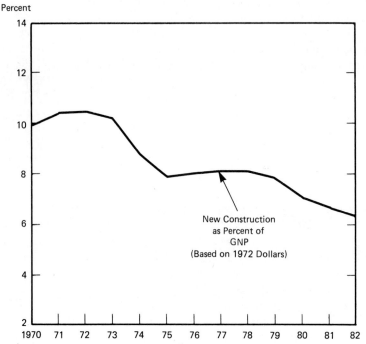

FIG. 16-1   Construction's share of total economic activity declines. *(Bureau of the Census and Bureau of Economic Analysis.)*

- Construction is not a growth industry; by 1982 it had declined to 6.3 percent of the gross national product, from over 10 percent ten years earlier (Figure 16-1).
- Inflation and high interest rates take their toll.
- Business cycles are shorter.
- Markets shift rapidly.
- Technology in office and field operations continues to advance.
- The trend is toward open-shop labor in the private sector, particularly in growing portions of the nation.
- The trend is toward negotiated contracts, with formal contractor selection procedures.

The individual contractor faces increased competition in its traditional markets, which are themselves changing. New strategies and capabilities are needed to compete, even in markets the contractor has served in the past.

The successful contractor of tomorrow is the one who views change as providing new and different opportunities. This contractor examines his or her company and the external environment and develops plans and strategies for exploiting business opportunities. Marketing provides the implementation for well-conceived plans.

In the depth of the recession in 1982, most of the members of a statewide midwestern paving contractors association had all but given up hope for new work. In the past they had depended on municipalities and, to some extent, on developers for work. The managers of one company sat around the office reading novels and watching television out of despair. Other association members who were more enterprising widened their range of business contacts, both in and out of state, sought out the developers with projects, diversified into related construction fields, and began a sales campaign to commercial and industrial companies. Through a combination of planning, aggressive sales, and marketing, and a thorough willingness to change entrenched methods, they continued to prosper during hard times.

In the Northeast, a heavy constructor that started as a foundation contractor in 1944 added highway and bridge construction over the years and had a volume of $12 million by 1970. During the 1970s, while several of its competitors—sizable heavy contractors in the New York City area—shrank in size or went out of business, this contractor continued to diversify. It added capabilities in building construction, materials supply, pipelines, transmission lines, electrical construction, real estate development, site development, and tunneling. And it purchased an open-shop contractor in Florida. By 1982 the company's volume topped $150 million, with more than $350 million in projects in progress and an equipment fleet worth $40 million.

But searching for new opportunities so that a construction business can realize its potential is often psychologically difficult. Change is often opposed by the very entrepreneurs and executives who developed the company. They do not want to change their well-established methods and style of management. Frequently they view formal planning, organized marketing, and new directions as a personal attack on their pride, authority, and success. Yet a failure to adapt to change can threaten the growth and survival of the construction enterprise they skillfully and diligently built.

To make the future happen by developing strategies for tomorrow, the construction executive must be willing to do something different and to commit resources to new opportunities. Decisions must be made and tasks performed in an organized, systematic way. The job begins by allocating the resources that the contractor has control over: knowledge, concentration, and time. The contractor has to ask, "What should our business be like in the future, and how will it be different from today?" and make the commitment to the answer by saying, "These are the things we will have to do to make sure of our success in the future. We will make them happen."

Not every contractor needs to develop new strategies for tomorrow. Some will be able to coast for a long time on their own momentum by working for clients and markets that are slower to change and by relying on the efforts of previous executives. But even the leadership companies nationally and in various markets will, at some point, have to face a future that is different. If they do not work on making the future happen, they will neither be in control nor understand what occurs.

BASIC DECISIONS

Today's business decisions, backed by the resources to carry them through, inevitably shape the construction company's future. Certainly, every construction executive makes decisions every day relating to present business. The decisions that must be made to make the future happen relate to fundamental strategic questions:

1. What is our concept of the business?
2. What kinds of opportunities will we need to seek in the future?
3. Should we specialize, diversify, or develop a fully integrated organization?
4. What is the right size for our business?
5. If we are to grow, should we build from within or buy a company?
6. Should we be acquired or acquire? Should we form joint ventures? Or should we retrench and become a smaller company?

To provide itself with an understanding of the business and data on which to base strategic decisions, management must analyze:

- Past and present revenues, profits, resources
- Overhead and other costs
- Present and potential clients and markets
- Strengths and areas of special expertise
- External environment and competition

Management can use these analyses to develop a program for action that builds on strength, seeks opportunities, establishes priorities, and sets objectives. It is a program for positioning the contractor's business for the challenges of tomorrow.

In developing its program, management might consider the following ideas:

- Finding or developing a whole new enterprise related to the company's core business.
- Developing a new capability or service.
- Entering a new project or geographic market.
- Creating a marketing strategy new to the market segment.
- Positioning the company in a unique way.
- Developing a dramatic communications program.

Morrison-Knudsen Co., Inc.'s continuing strategic planning and marketing program have maximized the company's opportunities in many new areas. The company's 1981 annual report states:

> In recent years, the long-established construction and engineering activities of the company have been expanded to include not only the building of ships and the development of real estate, but also operation of major coal and lignite mines under long-term contracts, ownership of equity interest in a large Montana coal mine, coating of steel pipe for offshore petroleum lines, remanufacturing of railroad cars and locomotives, maintenance of private and business aircraft, and fabrication of specialty products for industry.

Certainly the purchase of a major coal mine or entry into the shipbuilding business are not the kind of opportunities for diversification available to most contractors, but the M-K example illustrates a planned and systematic approach to making the future happen that other contractors can apply to smaller and more local enterprises.

TOMORROW'S MARKETS AND TRENDS TO WATCH

Construction markets are a constantly changing mosaic, responding to economic, social, environmental, and demographic forces. A good market research or business intelligence-gathering system will provide the contractor with early warning signals for dangers to avoid or opportunities to capitalize on.

Washington, D.C.-based futurist John Naisbitt cites ten "megatrends" that are shaping our future:

1. *We are in a "megashift" from an industrial to an information-based society* . . . only 13% of the U.S. work force is employed in manufacturing, while 60% either produces or processes information. . . . Manufacturing, the production of industrial hardware, is irretrievably moving out of the country.

2. *For every high-technology action, there is a "high-touch" reaction, or the technology will be rejected.* . . . Today's computers would permit many of us to work at home. Most of us still go to the office. People need to be with people.

3. *Our economy is becoming part of a global structure, moving away from isolation and national self-sufficiency. As a result, we will no longer be the world's dominant force.* . . . All the industrial countries, including Japan and Germany, are beginning a phase of deindustrialization. By the year 2000, the Third World will be manufacturing as much as 30% of the world's goods.

4. *U.S. corporate managers are beginning to think about the long term rather than the next quarter.* . . . Entrepreneurs, by nature, are building for the future.

5. *Our centralized structures are crumbling. We are decentralizing and growing stronger from the bottom up.* . . . Decentralization parallels the decline of industry. We no longer need to cluster at railheads, ports, or raw-material sources. . . . You can live and work almost any place. Power is shifting from Washington to states, cities, and neighborhoods. . . . Members of Congress spend increasing amounts of time acting on behalf of well-organized and focused special interest groups. . . . Regional coalitions are growing. . . . [there is a] coming East–West battle over energy. . . . Our national media will change shape . . . as specialized cable TV and local programming proliferate.

6. *We are reclaiming our traditional sense of self-reliance, after four decades of looking to institutions for help.* . . . An estimated 1 million families now educate their children at home. Increasingly, we are also looking after our own health. . . . There has been an entrepreneurial explosion.

7. *Citizens, workers, and consumers are demanding and getting a greater voice in government, business, and the marketplace* . . . companies are increasingly welcoming worker participation in decision making because it is now in their economic interest to do so.

8. *We are moving from hierarchies to networking; the computer is smashing the pyramid.* . . . A network is not a thing; it is a process, a three-dimensional com-

munication structure in which the constantly changing participants treat one another as peers because information has nothing to do with status in a hierarchy. Information is power. . . . The computer is smashing the Soviet pyramid, and the same thing is happening in the U.S. corporation. As a result, the way people are managed in organizations will never be the same.

9. *The North–South shift in the United States is real and irreversible for the foreseeable future.* . . . The shift is to the West, Southwest, and Florida—not to the South. . . . The shift has already created three megastates: Florida, Texas, and California, which will act increasingly like separate nations.

10. *We no longer live in an either/or, chocolate-or-vanilla world; people have demanded and are getting a multitude of choices.* Former consumers of mass-produced goods now must be offered variety, because the consumers themselves are not all the same.[1]

The West, Southwest, and Florida population shift is creating ten cities "of great opportunity," according to Naisbitt:

- Albuquerque—keeps lowering its taxes; it has plenty of water and its population is the country's second youngest.
- Austin—might become a miniature Silicon Valley.
- Denver—rivals Houston as the energy capital of the country.
- Phoenix—has low business taxes that attract high-tech, information-age industries.
- Salt Lake City—has a young, well-educated population and a low crime rate.
- San Antonio—is a city that people favor.
- San Diego—is a city that continues to grow.
- San Jose—is the capital of Silicon Valley.
- Tampa—keeps growing; it wants "clean industry."
- Tucson—is not just a retirement town; the average age is 28.2, or two years younger than the national average.[2]

INDUSTRIES OF THE FUTURE

Investment expert Frank Cappiello, who appears regularly on the national TV program "Wall Street Week," views these areas as ones that "hold promise for exciting new growth companies:"

Technology

- Business and office equipment
- Communications, including CATV, satellites, and video and data transmission
- Computer software
- Defense electronics

- Home entertainment and home business systems
- Materials substitution
- Microcomputers
- Robots
- Specialty chemicals
- Telecommunications

Health and Medical

- Drugs and drug administering
- Health care facilities and services
- Medical devices
- Medical equipment and supplies

Consumer and Business Services

- Business employment services
- Computer-related services
- Rental services of all kinds
- Specialty retailing

Energy

- Conservation technologies
- Energy alternatives, including solar and synthetic fuels
- Extraction equipment
- Services
- Transportation

Other

- New concepts for manufacturing and production
- New leisure-time products and activities
- New retailing and marketing methods and services
- Unique or specialty consumer products for the home or business[3]

CONSTRUCTION MARKET PERSPECTIVE

From 1972 to 1982, the United States construction market fell from $194.0 billion to $144.8 billion (in 1977 dollars), a decline of more than 25 percent.[4] But many major market segments fluctuated during the decade. Multifamily housing was off by almost two-thirds, office building nearly doubled, highways dropped by half, industrial building grew by 50 percent, and religious and educational building slackened, while electric power construction remained flat and hospitals and institutions slipped by 25 percent.

Public construction was off by $14.2 billion, from $46.4 billion to $32.2 billion, but in terms of percentages the decline was almost the same as for the total construction marketplace, about 23 percent. The private residential market produced the most dramatic change by plummeting $39.4 billion and slipping in market share from 44.7 percent to 32.7 percent.

Still another part of the construction picture are the disproportional shifts, where areas such as the Northeast and the Midwest accounted for large parts of declining market segments and smaller portions of rising ones.

While construction activity is expected to expand, its growth will depend on the strength of the economy and on long-term interest rates dropping for a sustained period to foster a strong construction market. However, projected large federal budget deficits may prevent the interest rates from remaining at sufficiently low levels to stimulate real construction growth.

MARKET SEGMENT OUTLOOK

Whatever the eventual size of the overall construction industry—and it may not recover to 1972 levels until 1990 or after—market segments will vary widely in the future, shaped by such forces as Naisbitt's megatrends. Other trends that will affect construction markets are our increasingly elderly population, high crime rates, inflation, business cycles, energy, and scarce resources. Discussed below are outlooks for some construction markets.[5]

Regions.   The northern industrial states face a long period of depressed construction because of declining population (Table 16-1) and the long-term adjustment problems

TABLE 16-1 Population Statistics for Major United States Cities

	1980 Metro area population	Population change 1970–80, %
Houston	2,905,353	+45.3
Denver	1,620,902	+30.8
Miami	1,625,781	+28.2
Atlanta	2,029,710	+27.2
Dallas	2,974,805	+25.1
Los Angeles	7,477,503	+6.2
Washington, D.C.	3,060,922	+5.2
San Francisco	3,250,630	+4.5
Chicago	7,103,624	+1.8
Philadelphia	4,716,818	−2.2
Boston	2,763,367	−4.7
New York	9,120,346	−8.6

Source: U.S. Department of Commerce

of the region's basic industries. Construction activity in the South is expected to remain strong as the region continues to attract people and businesses. With oil and gas exploration and earnings growth slowing down, the energy-producing states of the Southwest will not experience construction growth comparable to that of the 1970s.

It should be noted, however, that certain metropolitan areas and some market segments will provide exceptions to these regional forecasts. The Northeast, for example—the Boston area particularly, with its high-technology industry—and portions of New Jersey and Connecticut, with their corporate headquarters and research activities, will continue to generate construction work. The Dallas–Fort Worth market is expected to remain strong, despite slower growth for the region as a whole. In the growing South, though, certain commercial segments of Atlanta's economy are, as of this writing, overbuilt, and the market could remain soft for several years.

Multifamily Housing.   Multifamily construction historically accounts for about one-third of total housing starts. If interest rates remain high due to large federal budget deficits and business demand for credit, housing construction will not expand greatly. From a low of 375,000 units in 1982 (compared with a peak of 1,000,000 units in 1972), multifamily construction should reach 600,000 units by 1987. A weak spot will be subsidized construction. Strength will be seen in construction of condominium and cooperative units and of rental projects, where rents are rising.

Hotels and Motels.   Because it depends heavily on discretionary rather than essential spending, the hotel and motel business parallels the health of the economy. Rapid growth of this market in the late 1970s and early 1980s, coupled with rising room charges and reduced business travel, have left many cities with overbuilt hotel conditions. The demand for budget motels and luxury hotels continues to expand, however, creating a split market.

Office Buildings.   Although office construction set an all-time record in 1982, that ended a six-year upswing and has left most United States cities overbuilt. Over the long term, the outlook depends on white-collar employment, interest rates, inflation rates, and office rents. With white-collar employment growing at 2 percent annually, half the rate of addition to office space inventory, office construction starts will decline through the mid to late 1980s before beginning another upturn.

Other Commercial Buildings.   This category, which has been declining since 1979, includes a variety of facilities such as shopping centers, warehouses, banks, parking garages, grain elevators, fast-food restaurants, and gas stations. Shopping-center construction had fallen off dramatically by the early 1980s as a result of high interest rates, high vacancy rates, recessions, low housing starts, and increased transportation costs. Investors turned to purchase and renovation of existing centers. Long-term gains in housing starts should spur construction of new shopping centers. Specialty centers and up-scale, high-end retailers remain strong.

Warehouse construction had been one of the hardest-hit areas, largely because computerized controls encourage inventory reduction, causing surplus space. Eventually, by the mid-1980s, warehouse construction will increase.

Industrial Construction.   Declines in private industrial building activity by the early 1980s had been slight, even though interest rates were high, corporate profits depressed, and capacity utilization rates at their lowest point in several decades. The megatrend shift away from heavy manufacturing and toward information and information-processing industries accounted for substantial reductions in investment in certain segments and increased spending in others. According to the U.S. Department of Commerce 1980 Annual Survey of Manufacturers, six of the 20 manufacturing industry groups accounted for 63 percent of the investment in new industrial structures:

Nonelectrical machinery	12.8%
Chemicals	12.3%
Electrical machinery	10.9%
Transportation equipment	9.8%
Food processing	9.3%
Petroleum refining	7.8%

In terms of structures, construction of research and development facilities has increased substantially. Thus, more and more industrial space is occupied by quasi-office workers—highly paid assembly, laboratory, and computer personnel—who require office-type amenities. Industrial-sale leasebacks gain in popularity as companies seek to obtain capacity while conserving cash.

There will be a considerable amount of construction of plants to produce liquid fuels from coal, tar sands, and oil shale. As of 1982, the U.S. Synfuels Corporation had $14 billion in remaining authority for loans, loan guarantees, price guarantees, and direct construction of synfuel plants.

As for mining structures, 95 percent of the total in the late 1970s and early 1980s has been for oil and gas wells, with the remainder for coal and nonfuel minerals structures. The outlook depends upon developments in world energy markets. Although increasing amounts of capital will be required for drilling for oil and gas as wells become depleted, a major outside source is likely to be oil and gas partnerships.

Overall, the long-term outlook for industrial construction is bullish. Investment tax credits, expanded economic growth, increased profits, and higher capacity utilization rates will encourage an upswing in industrial construction.

Electric Utilities.   Energy conservation, slow industrial growth, and increased availability of natural gas have slowed the demand for new power plants. In the early 1980s construction declined, with most activity being the result of a backlog of projects started before 1980. High construction costs and high interest rates, as well as changing regulations, have further discouraged the building of new power plants. Due to high costs and regulatory risks, no new nuclear plants may be started before 1990. However, increases in industrial production and home building in the mid-

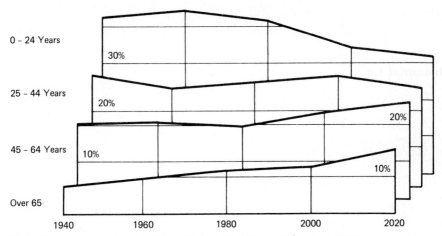

FIG. 16-2   America is getting older. *(The New York Times, February 4, 1983.)*

1980s should expand the demand for electricity and prompt the construction of new power plants, as well as new pipelines for gas transmission.

Health Care.   Hospital construction should remain strong through the 1980s. The increasing age of the United States population is an important factor contributing to an increasing demand for hospitals. People over sixty-five require an average of five times as much hospitalization per capita as people under sixty-five (Figure 16-2). Hospital construction is largely dependent on government health policies and the need to meet accreditation standards. An enormous amount of capital expenditures will be required to renovate and replace worn-out physical plants. A study conducted by the U.S. Department of Health and Human Services concluded that $130 billion (in 1980 dollars) in capital expenditures would be required between 1980 and 1990 to replace obsolete facilities. That is about 50 percent more, on an annual basis, than was spent in 1982.

The primary source of capital to finance hospital construction is the tax-exempt bond market. Despite high interest rates on municipal bonds, the use of tax-exempt bonds intensified in 1982. Other sources included retained earnings, philanthropy, and government contributions. Hospital construction is unaffected by most economic factors, because payment for services is made primarily through government programs and private health insurance.

Renovation, Rehabilitation, and Restoration.   McGraw-Hill's F. W. Dodge Division forecasts that $30 billion will be spent annually on rehabilitation projects through the 1980s. The Economic Recovery Tax Act of 1981 provides incentives for rehabilitation of buildings thirty years old and over. Buildings thirty years old are eligible for a 15 percent annual depreciation, those forty years old for 20 percent, and those certified historic landmarks for 25 percent. Often older buildings can be recycled and compete effectively against new properties, which require substantially higher rents.

Public Construction.   With the near-completion of the interstate highway system, the diminishing need for school construction, the deferred replacement of aging structures, and the poor financial condition of state and local governments, public construction continues to decline. The only increases expected are in the construction of military facilities and, with passage of the 1983 five-cent-a-gallon gasoline tax, in repair and renovation of highways and bridges.

The estimated cost for restoring the nation's deteriorating infrastructure through the year 2002 is $3.03 trillion (in 1982 dollars) for repair or replacement of aging roads and bridges, leaking water supply lines, unsafe dams, and energy-wasting buildings.[6] If Congress ever embarks on a large-scale public works reconstruction program to prevent further deterioration, public construction could become one of the faster-growing sectors of the economy.

In 1982 spending for maintenance and repair of the nation's aging network of *highways and streets* exceeded spending for new construction for the first time since 1957, when data was first collected. And the trend should continue.

Since 1978 the EPA construction grants program for *sewage treatment plant* construction has declined and is expected to continue to diminish. Conversely, the outlook for *waterworks* construction is bright and may become one of the more rapidly growing categories of public construction. Increases in housing starts will spur construction of new waterworks and water distribution lines, financed largely through sale of municipal bonds for water and sewers. With the aqueduct systems of most older cities being ancient and requiring extensive replacement work, and with waterworks able to raise user fees to generate revenues, a steady increase in replacement construction is likely to continue through the 1980s.

Water resources construction is expected to increase in the 1980s as existing federal dams and canals begin to need substantial reconstruction.

Construction of *military facilities* includes military housing, airfields, incinerators, warehouses, docks, radar installations, and roads. Spending for such facilities will fluctuate with overall defense expenditures, which are expected to increase substantially in the mid-1980s.

Other categories of public construction that are anticipated to increase are federally owned *manufacturing, assembling, and processing buildings, airports,* and *prisons,* the last in response to high crime rates and public demand for longer periods of convict incarceration.

With the number of births increasing since 1976, student enrollment will increase in the 1980s, holding the possibility for construction of new *schools*.

International Construction.   Most of the foreign contracts signed by United States firms in 1981 were for refineries, synthetic fuel plants, marine projects, and power generation facilities. United States contractors were found to be least competitive overseas in forestry projects and in manufacturing plants. International construction activity is affected by worldwide economic conditions, and by a variety of export subsidies and import barriers. Capital expenditures by United States firms for facilities outside the United States represent a good market for construction contractors.

IMPLICATIONS: MERGERS, NEW MARKETS, OPEN SHOP, DESIGN

The ever-changing construction marketplace poses endless challenges. Competition tightens, old markets shrivel or disappear, new markets emerge, growth demands continued expansion, population shifts, and business conditions fluctuate. Coping with external and internal threats and taking advantage of new opportunities call for the contractor to approach the business in new ways.

For some construction companies, facing the future will mean entering new and growing geographic markets; establishing an open-shop capability; developing new skills in design, hospital renovation, or construction; or moving from the public sector to private bids or negotiated construction. Successful entry into new markets often requires more than marketing ability. The contractor may need to augment its capabilities. To facilitate change, contractors are turning to one or more of the following methods.

Merger or Acquisition.   Developing a business or a segment of a business to enter a new project market or geographic area requires time. Acquisition of another contractor can reduce the time needed to operate successfully in the new market. A contractor should consider acquisition for one or more of the following reasons:

- To offset declining traditional markets.
- To grow or expand faster.
- To save time required to develop local knowledge and contacts in new area.
- To save time required to develop knowledge and experience in new project markets.
- To afford opportunities for people in the parent company.
- To reduce effects of construction cycles in a single area.

The purchase of a successful contractor is not cheap. The management of the acquired company wants to be paid for its knowledge, resources, and markets. Even if the contractor has the financial resources to acquire another company, it must still develop people and a new organization to provide direction and possibly marketing assistance, and it must measure the subsidiary's performance.

Merger experts conclude that successful acquisitions result from:

- The *acquiring* company's bringing something to the *acquired* contractor (financial or management assistance, marketing or technical expertise, improved or computerized controls or systems)
- An acquisition's being part of the parent company's long-range plan
- Compatibility or "fit" in management style, capabilities, and philosophy
- Incentives for the management team and key employees to remain after acquisition

- The parent company's providing a top executive to oversee the acquired company and having it report to him or her
- Sound business relationships between the two companies, which means timely solutions to problems and flexibility on both sides

A contractor can consider being acquired if:

- The company cannot grow to the right size to serve its markets.
- The company has outgrown the philosophy, practices, and business approach of the founder and is no longer able to realize its potential.
- The company lacks sufficient funds to redeem the stock of major retiring shareholders.
- The company lacks a strong cadre of middle management and top executives are concerned about succession.
- Changes in the marketplace require new capabilities that would require too long a period to develop.

Branch Offices.   One alternative to acquisition for gaining access to a new geographic area is opening a branch office. One northeastern-based contractor, after starting a branch office, concluded that "construction is a very provincial industry. It takes years to develop credibility and relationships with subs, suppliers, and union business agents." The company closed the branch office and acquired a contractor in the West. Other contractors have been successful, however. One approach is beginning with a small operation and bidding public work.

Kitchell Contractors of Phoenix took a slightly different approach to expanding to Dallas. According to Vernie Lindstrom, chairman and CEO, Kitchell representatives spent six months introducing the company to architects, owners, subcontractors, suppliers, lawyers, and the media. "Within our strategy, we only wanted to pinpoint those areas [where] we had the strongest chance for success . . . hospitals, office buildings, industrial plants, and commercial buildings." At the end of six months Kitchell held an open house for the community and in the next thirty days got two jobs—one for $10 million and another for $15 million.[7]

Points to consider in starting a branch operation are:

- Reaction of bankers and bonding agents
- Resources available for long-term staying power
- Strains on current management and key personnel
- Willingness of key personnel to travel or relocate
- Results of research on the area
- Qualities the company will bring to the new marketplace (competitive edge, niche in the market, or exportable unique skills)
- Labor situation in new area (union or open shop and availability of good personnel or subcontractors)

Joint Ventures.   A joint venture has the advantage of being a relatively short-term commitment for the purpose of obtaining or performing on a single project. Some people joke that a joint venture is where one company has the financial strength and the other the experience, and at the end of the project these change hands. Many successful joint ventures are formed between a local contractor and a larger out-of-state contractor in order to win a major project. Typically the local contractor knows the area—its officials, subs, suppliers, and labor market—and possibly the owner, and the larger contractor has the large-project experience, control systems, financial or bonding ability, and sometimes the image to secure and execute the project.

In forming joint ventures, it is vital that there be early agreement on the division of responsibility—how the work will be done, by whom, and for what portion of the fee or contract amount.

"Double-Breasted" Operations.   To compete in open-shop areas, many contractors have either purchased nonunion contractors or created nonunion subsidiaries. So that union agreements are complied with, management of the two companies must be kept separate. To accomplish that, some contractors form a holding company that is parent to both firms. The holding company will have considerable resources, because it will own the assets of the original construction company. Thus the new nonunion subsidiary can provide a substantial financial statement to owners.

Open-shop construction is prevalent in many areas of the South and Southwest and is a growing factor in other regions outside the downtown areas of major cities. Even in some cities, open-shop construction has captured certain project-type markets, such as residential and renovation work. Some contractors have started nonunion subsidiaries to serve these particular market segments, while continuing to operate on a union basis in other markets. Labor attorneys and advisers should be consulted before the contractor embarks on such double-breasted operations.

CONCLUSION: A DIFFERENT KIND OF CONSTRUCTION EXECUTIVE?

In the past the job of a construction executive was relatively uncomplicated. The executive bid on jobs and performed successfully. True, construction has never been an easy business, but in the 1950s and 1960s, a smart contractor who knew the construction business could—and did—prosper.

In the 1970s changes took place at an accelerating rate that permanently altered the way business was done. To cope with the myriad competitive, economic, governmental, labor, societal, and market factors, the industry began to require a broader-gauged construction executive—not a person who lacks understanding of the construction process, but one who does understand *and* has in addition the knowledge and ability to function as a sophisticated business person.

While profit remains the primary goal, tomorrow's construction executive must become involved in a variety of business problems and challenges, some that once faced only executives in the largest of construction companies and major corporations and some that are new to managers everywhere. The winds of change affect all sizes and types of construction firms. Tomorrow's successful contractor must be as aware of concrete-forming techniques as he or she is of strategic planning and marketing. The contractor can no longer afford to be an observer but must make the future happen, if the company is to have one.

In the years ahead, the construction executive will need to focus on the company as a modern business enterprise; on the mission of the business; its objectives, direction, and strategies; its competitors, markets, sales volume, return on investment, and special areas of competence. The executive will need to consider issues such as growth, diversification, threats and opportunities, personnel and organizational development, and economic trends. Through strategic planning, the construction executive will chart the company's course. Through effective marketing and sales, the company will reach its destination.

This is not to imply that the contractor's product—the delivery of high-quality construction services—will diminish in importance. Quite the contrary. The contractor must remain vigilant to ensure that his or her company's services are the best and must continually search for new methods to gain better control over costs and time and to employ the latest field and office technologies. For, in the final analysis, it is the client who will determine the ultimate success of the contractor's business.

The challenges to the construction executive of tomorrow are to apply the same systematic, planned, organized, and professional approach to business management and marketing as the contractor in the past did to some of our most challenging works. The successful future of the business depends on it.

NOTES

[1]Tom Richman, "Peering into Tomorrow," *Inc.*, October 1982, pp. 45–48.

[2]Ibid, p. 48.

[3]Frank A. Cappiello, *Finding the Next Super Stock*, Liberty Publishing Company, Inc., Cockeysville, MD, 1982, p. 14.

[4]U.S. Department of Commerce, Bureau of Industrial Economics, *Construction Review*, November–December 1982, p. 3.

[5]Ibid.

[6]"Infrastructure," *Constructor*, May 1983, p. 34.

[7]Christopher S. Monek, "Markets and Marketing for Today's Building Contractor," *Constructor*, September 1982, pp. 20–21.

Index